African Parrots

by Rick Jordan & Jean Pattison

Toby, Bill, and ...
May your lives be full of ... always

Jean Pattison

Adrian Queen

hancock

house

ISBN 0-88839-444-6
Copyright © 1999 Rick Jordan

Cataloging in Publication Data
Jordan, Rick, 1958-
 African parrots

 Includes bibliographical references and index.
 ISBN 0-88839-444-6

 1. Parrots. I. Pattison, Jean. II. Title.
 SF473.P3J67 1999   636.6'865   C99-910146-3

Editor: Nancy Miller
Production: Nancy Miller and Ingrid Luters
Cover photos: Front cover (clockwise from top left)—Lee Horton, Lyrae Perry,
Jan Beatrous, Jan Beatrous, Jean Pattison. Back cover—Steve Garvin.

Published simultaneously in Canada and the United States by

HANCOCK HOUSE PUBLISHERS LTD.
19313 Zero Avenue, Surrey, B.C. V4P 1M7
(604) 538-1114 Fax (604) 538 2262

HANCOCK HOUSE PUBLISHERS
1431 Harrison Avenue, Blaine, WA 98230-5005
(604) 538-1114 Fax (604) 538-2262
Web Site: www.hancockhouse.com *email:* sales@hancockhouse.com

Contents

Dedication

This book is dedicated to the American Federation of Aviculture, Inc. Since its inception in 1974, the AFA has sought to educate governmental agencies, breeders, pet owners and avian enthusiasts alike on the importance of, and methods for, maintaining birds in a captive environment. Disease prevention, husbandry, conservation, captive preservation, legislative education, field biological studies, and avian medical research have been the primary focuses of the AFA. Successful efforts in these areas have made the AFA a household word in the U.S. and, now, in other countries as well. The AFA also monitors and provides input to the participants of the Convention on the International Trade in Endangered Species (CITES), taking the AFA resources and educational materials worldwide.

The unity of captive breeders and keepers of birds has never been more important than today. Due to many different pressures on wild habitats, and on the birds that reside within those habitats, the world is changing its focus on conservation and the concept of worldwide biodiversity. This new focus occurs along with many changes developed by aviculturists in husbandry and captive breeding principles, and has increased the importance of the role of the AFA. These responsibilities bring with them new financial demands on the organization. Unlike many nonprofit organizations, the AFA doesn't receive governmental funding and grants. Funding is realized only through book and magazine sales (*The AFA Watchbird*), an annual convention, and donations from friends and members. For this reason, Jean Pattison and Rick Jordan have decided to donate their royalties from this book to the AFA. For more information about the AFA, write to PO Box 56218, Phoenix, Arizona, 85017.

Preface

The biggest threat to most avian species is deforestation and the destruction of their native habitats. For this reason, both the authors, Jean Pattison and Rick Jordan, believe that a stronghold of every species of parrot must be established in captivity if their kinds are to survive into the future. As well, the authors believe that not only must each species be represented in captivity, but also they must be well managed; and these populations must become capable of sustaining themselves in captivity, indefinitely. This objective can only be reached through sound educational materials that reinforce the concepts of professional captive genetic management for every species now kept in aviculture. The concept of a managed captive population, and good record keeping, prompted the authors to write this book and donate the proceeds to the American Federation of Aviculture, Inc. For more than twenty years now the AFA has been there to support bird breeders and enthusiasts with information about breeding and legislative matters.

Jean and Rick have spent many years studying and breeding parrots in captivity. Their combined experience covers more than thirty years of hands-on avicultural practice, and most of the information in this text has been derived from the actual knowledge and data collected by these two seasoned breeders. Throughout the text there are some very valuable hints and suggestions from Jean Pattison, affectionately known as the "African Queen," and chapter eleven, Basic Husbandry and Breeding Tips, was written by her exclusively. Additionally, the two authors were able to tap into very valuable information from many of their friends and fellow aviculturists. The late Tom Ireland of Lake Worth, Florida, has had a profound influence on the authors, and many of the tips found within the text were suggested to the authors during their time together. This book would not have been possible without the cooperation and contributions from many other people as well. Jean and Rick would like to thank each and every one of them for their assistance on this project.

Many thanks to:

Jan Beatrous, Robert J. Berry, Dr. Marge Wissman, Laurella Desborough, Dr. Darrel K. Styles, Mark Moore, Scott Stringer, Scott and Linda Lewis of Old World Aviaries, Roland Debuc and the African Lovebird Society, Lyrae Perry, Steve Garvin, David Hancock, Torben Rafn for the Scandinavian aviary information, Cindy Garvin, Lee Horton, Rosemary Low, Dr. George Smith of Peterborough, England, Gary Blankenbiller, Janis Clark, Sheldon Dingle, Wanda Elder, Trevor and Fay Ashington of South Africa and Cherane Pefley.

Bird theft is an increasing problem in the United States and elsewhere. The Florida Federation of Aviculture, with the assistance of Jan Beatrous, has developed an internet website where information on thefts can be collected. This site contains theft information from around the world and it may assist persons or law enforcement agencies in the recovery of stolen birds. For further information visit the website at:

httpı//www.hirdtheft.orq

1 Introduction to African Parrots

1.1 The Different Genera of Parrots in Africa

Taxonomy is the classification of animals and plants with respect to their natural relationships to each other. The way in which taxonomic groups are defined can be confusing, and can even be a bit intimidating to some people. It is, however, important that breeders learn the basics of taxonomic assignment in order for them to better understand the relationships between the types of birds they keep. Furthermore, in the captive environment, where a parrot cannot always choose its own mate, the aviculturist must be aware they may be forcing a mating that would not normally occur in the wild.

The term genus (genera for plural) is a category that usually includes a group of species and subspecies. Species categorized under a genus listing generally have things in common, such as skeletal structures or natural habits. Despite these similarities, these two separate species often exhibit some type(s) of obvious difference from each other, and from other species within their genus. Birds of two different species are classified as "separate species" if they are both included in the same genus, yet they do not interbreed in the wild. In other words, these two populations of birds are very closely related and may even frequent the same food sources, but they do not breed with each other, thus maintaining their individuality as two distinguishable groups or species.

A good example would be that of the Senegal parrot (*Poicephalus senegalus*) and the Meyer's parrot (*Poicephalus meyeri*). These two species are considered to be separate species, even though they are both included in the genus *Poicephalus* and their natural ranges do overlap in central Africa. Despite the fact that there is opportunity for them to interbreed, these two populations (species) have maintained their individuality from each other. This crossbreeding concept is often extended theoretically when defining species that do not have overlaping ranges in the wild. Of course there are exceptions to every rule, and occasionally a bird is sighted in the wild that is a cross between two defined species! Since this is not the rule, and the species involved maintain their distinct populations, the taxonomic assignments are maintained.

A lower (further) classification known as subspecies is often used to delineate between a race or "geographical difference" of populations of the same species. The interbreeding concept tends to break down at this level as many subspecific populations will naturally interbreed in the wild. Yet, somehow, a distinct difference between the groups of birds is maintained with only an occasional "intermediate" form (subspecies #1 bred to subspecies #2) being found.

There are several parrot genera found in Africa and they are the genus *Agapornis* (the lovebirds), *Psittacus* (the African greys), *Coracopsis* (the Vasa or black parrots), *Psittacula* (the rose-ringed or ring-necked parakeets) and *Poicephalus* (the small grey- and brown-headed parrots). As well, there are several genera of parrots now extinct that are described from fossil remains found on the African continent.

Sample Taxonomic Assignment of a Senegal Parrot
(*Poicephalus senegalus versteri*)
  Class: Aves
  Order: Psittaciformes

Family: Psittacidae
Genus: *Poicephalus*
Species: *senegalus*
Subspecies: *versteri*

As an avicultural note, keep in mind that many parrots will breed in captivity in a simple setup that may not be custom designed specifically for their species. For example, a simple cube or rectangular-shaped wire cage with a wooden "grandfather-clock" style nestbox is often used as the universal setup. Certain species customizations, such as an L-shaped nestbox for nervous species like the Meyer's parrot, have proven themselves over the years and can make the difference between reliable breeders and untrustworthy parent birds. A good breeding setup takes into consideration the entire breeding environment, not just the cage size and shape of the nesting box. Breeding results have proven to be more consistent when mate selection, neighboring species considerations, rainfall, light, diet and temperature have all been figured into the equation.

1.2 Why Are Some Species Considered Rare?

Trapping and exportation of parrots from their native habitats have taken place for centuries. In the past, trapping and exporting were often carried out by small-scale, local trappers, who were just trying to make a living. During the 1970s and 1980s, the keeping of parrots as pets became very popular; large, commercial operations were established to harvest birds from the wild and ship them to consumers around the world. During this time much of today's wild-caught breeding stock was acquired and some of that stock now forms the basis of many avicultural collections in zoos and in the private sector.

Some parrot-producing countries (countries of "wild" origin) did not allow the trapping, collecting or exporting of native birds. The species exclusive to these countries were, for the most part, rare in captivity outside the country of origin. In addition to export restrictions, aviculture or captive breeders had not established maintenance standards and diets for all species that were being traded in large numbers. The huge supply of wild-caught parrots seemed never-ending; therefore, close study and scientific husbandry practices were not a priority. These problems and high mortality rates during transport of birds contributed to the rarity of some species in aviculture today.

Availability is another factor that influences how common a species is. Imported birds that were commonly available were often ignored by breeders because their price was low and the supply was abundant. What eventually resulted was a reduction in the importation of such birds and, subsequently, a reduction in supply to breeders and hobbyists. Not all species that are now rare in our aviaries are considered rare in the wild. As a matter of fact, many rare aviary birds are "agricultural pest species" in the wild and are present in the native habitat in huge numbers.

Of the African parrots, there are several members of the genera *Poicephalus* and *Agapornis* that have never been exported from their countries of origin. This means that they remain rare in captivity and are not established in aviculture. The yellow-faced parrot (*Poicephalus flavifrons*) is a prime example of a bird that was and still is not available through international trade. This is due to the prohibition on trapping and exporting this species from Ethiopia, its only range country. This is despite the fact that hundreds of thousands of their cousins (other *Poicephalus* parrots) were being transported out of Africa. The yellow-faced parrot inhabits the mountainous regions of Ethiopia and is not common in captivity anywhere in the world. We can only hope that the native habitat of the yellow-faced parrot will be preserved, so it does not join the growing list of extinct species.

1.3 National and International Restrictions

The parrot keeper of today is well aware of the many rules, regulations, import and export laws and pending legislation in the United States and other countries. The U.S. no longer allows the importation of any parrot species now listed in the appendices to the CITES convention. There are very few exceptions to this law, and any importation of a parrot species is now scrutinized under special conditions. In 1992, the U.S. passed the Wild Bird Conservation Act of 1992 into law—a law that now appears to be virtually a U.S. import ban on all CITES listed birds. Although most of the parrots included in the genus *Poicephalus*, *Agapornis* or *Psittacus*, are not rare in the wild, they are listed on CITES Appendix II as a precautionary measure and to assist in the monitoring of international trade. This has resulted in few, if any, imports of these birds to breeders in the United States. Exceptions for captive-bred offspring originating from foreign breeders have not been worked out at the time of this writing (1999). This has resulted in no importation of African parrots since the passing of the law. However, in Europe importation of wild-caught Jardines, Senegal parrots and African grey parrots is still legal and taking place.

International trade in most African parrots continues in other parts of the world with Senegal and Tanzania now being two of the largest exporters of their native wildlife. Many other nations in Africa do limit the trapping of parrots within their countries, initiating permitting systems where a wildlife dealer must get a permit to trap wild birds. In addition, quotas are placed on certain species limiting the numbers that can be taken from the wild in one season. Unfortunately, the position of the latest international laws seems to imply the trapping and exporting of wild-caught birds of any species will eventually be prohibited. This may result in the establishment of large breeding facilities in the countries of origin of some parrot species. Once established and registered with their respective governmental agencies, these *in situ* facilities should be permitted to export their offspring into the international live-bird trade. The replacement of wild birds in trade with those of captive-bred origin will have a monumental impact on conservation efforts in the natural habitat for many species. Flocks that had previously been overtrapped will, once again, be able to recover without the pressures of trapping and continued trade.

Pet owners and breeders around the world can contribute to this conservation effort by encouraging local lawmakers to restrict trade in wild-caught birds and encourage continued trade in captive-bred specimens. Of course, this concept also has its problems. An accepted form of marking and identifying captive-bred birds must be established on an international basis. Rules must be formulated to preclude the laundering of wild birds under the guise of having been bred in captivity. Once a worldwide marking system and breeder registration system is in place, trade in captive-bred birds of any registered species will dominate the world market. This should allow conservation biologists to concentrate on habitat preservation, a focus that will undoubtedly benefit both aviculture and wild populations of birds.

1.4 African Parrots as Companion Birds

Parrots, as a whole, possess some very endearing qualities such as the ability to mimic human voice, their devotion and intelligence, and a willingness to adapt to life among human companions. These qualities make most parrot species an ideal pet or companion animal. If nurtured properly when young, many become dedicated and affectionate pets. To take a wild-caught bird and try to make a pet out of it often results in disaster because wild birds often exhibit innate behavior associated with survival, and they have not learned to accept human beings as their companions. Wild-taken African parrots are well known to be "growlers" and avoid human contact at all costs.

During the decade of the 1980s, thousands of wild African parrots were trapped and taken into captivity. It was during this decade that the keeping and breeding of these birds became very popular. More and more, aviculturists were successfully breeding African grey parrots and the smaller *Poicephalus* parrots. Captive-reared, hand-fed baby parrots changed the pet industry with regard to companion birds. A tamer, more stable bird was being produced in captivity, and due to the overwhelming success of these breeding endeavors, the prices of domestic African parrots began to fall.

Today in the United States, it is nearly impossible to find a wild-caught African parrot for sale as a pet. The captive-reared birds of today are more suited to a life of human companionship and are in demand because of their friendly qualities and talking or mimicking ability. The African parrots have become very popular among pet bird owners not only for their ability to mimic human voice, but also because they are, generally, quiet birds that do not demand as much attention as do the larger parrots. The combination of their ability to talk, their smaller size and caging requirements and their quiet nature, have made the African grey and several *Poicephalus* species, the most sought after pet birds in the U.S. and the rest of the world. Like their relatives the lovebirds and cockatiels, many species of African parrots will soon be breeding to multiple generations in the captive environment. Eventually any and all species of parrots that respond well to captive breeding efforts will be considered a domesticated pet species. In other words, the main source of these birds will be from breeders, and the need to take more from the wild will diminish as each species becomes established through avicultural pursuits.

15

1.5 Behavioral Problems—Consult the Experts

Despite the amount of attention given a pet bird, patterns of bad behavior can evolve between the owner and the pet. In some cases, the behavior problem is actually that of the owner and not the bird. Bad habits are hard to break once they have been reinforced and permitted to exist for any period of time.

Fortunately, a few people in this country, and hopefully others, are interested and experienced in the training and behavior of pet birds. They have spent many hours developing different training regimen methods to deal with birds that have established undesirable behavioral patterns. Pet bird behaviorists can often turn a bad bird into a good bird in short order. In addition to this, they can teach the new owner of a pet parrot what they should and should not do when handling their birds. It is highly suggested that the owner and pet consult a pet bird behaviorist at the first sign of trouble in the relationship. Many of the consultants deal with biting, feather chewing, aggressive behavior, destructiveness and other common undesirable habits.

When seeking any professional assistance for your birds, ask for references. It is vital you make sure your behaviorist is a respected member of the avicultural community.

2 Captive Management Programs

2.1 Why Is Captive Management Important?

Captive management usually refers to a regional, national or global effort to conserve or preserve a species. Although most species of African parrots are still abundant in the wild, there is a need for aviculturists (captive breeders) to manage the genetic materials they now hold in the aviary. Natural resources, such as parrots and the habitats in which they live, are vanishing due to pressures from human encroachment and commercial development. International interest has spawned treaties such as the Convention on International Trade in Endangered Species (CITES). This treaty, now boasting more than 140 member countries, has set out to conserve wild populations of animals, birds and plants, through controlled international trade. All species of parrots now found on the African continent are listed in the appendices of the treaty, and the trade in these birds is closely monitored by the Convention.

True conservation of a species can only take place through cooperation between captive breeders and field biologists performing studies in the natural habitat. Over the past three decades, hundreds of thousands of African parrots have been trapped and shipped out of their countries of origin. These parrots now make up the breeding stock base of the world's aviculture. If not properly managed, captive populations can break down genetically (become unbreedable) and the need to supplement captive breeding populations with more wild birds could result.

Responsible breeders have begun to keep records on the birds they rear. These records assist in the captive management of African parrots all over the world. Through proper management, inbreeding and other deleterious genetic dysfunctions can be avoided in the captive flock. The demand for parrots as pets is high. If CITES and other concerned organizations are to succeed in preserving wild populations and their habitats, this demand must be filled by birds that have been bred in a captive environment. Sound captive management will ensure the worldwide trade in parrots can someday be completely supported by birds that have been bred in captivity.

2.2 What Is a Studbook?

One of the most important tools of captive management of a species is the studbook. This book holds information about the origin of founder stocks and aids in identifying and tracking the offspring of breeding pairs in a given breeding or species survival program. Leg band numbers or identification numbers help to keep track of offspring and additional breeding stock added to the species' gene pool. Smaller captive populations, as might occur with a rare species, may rely on the studbook holder to assist in the proper management of the remaining gene pool. The studbook information can be very useful in determining how offspring should be paired to effect a healthy captive population of that species for generations to come.

Local bird clubs and avian interest groups should be encouraged to form studbooks and breeding consortiums for their members. Smaller groups of birds are more easily managed; the paperwork for a national or international breeding consortium can become extremely voluminous and burdensome. In many countries, breeders who now hold captive rarities are beginning to work together and are forming unofficial programs to manage their available gene pool. As these local efforts and other studbook programs grow in popularity, consolidation of some data will become inevitable, and a truly cooperative effort will begin to form between the participants. These are the kinds of efforts that will eventually allow CITES and our own governments to ease the restrictions now placed on international trade in captive-bred parrots and other animals.

2.3 Inbreeding—How Can We Avoid It?

With movement toward a better-managed captive flock, there is much concern about the potential problems caused by inbreeding. Sometimes referred to as line breeding (because the family tree suddenly becomes a straight line), inbreeding is the practice (purposeful or accidental) of breeding closely related birds or animals. People who breed show dogs have line bred dogs for centuries. This was often an attempt to produce the perfect specimen of a specific breed. If a certain family of dogs had excellent qualities, such as body conformation, the breeder may have bred two siblings together to produce puppies with the same qualities. Unfortunately, inbreeding can cause such problems as weak, sickly, sexually dysfunctional or genetically impaired animals. This can occur when two recessive genes that produce negative qualities come together in one animal. In birds, these recessive genes can result in offspring that will not thrive or eggs that will not hatch.

The biggest threat of inbreeding is that many qualities, such as sexual reproductive capability, longevity or heart or other organ dysfunction, may not be visually obvious and could be bred into the next generation of offspring. These offspring then go on to pass the characteristics into further generations of offspring. It does not take long before that particular line of animals becomes undesirable or is totally dysfunctional and can no longer breed.

19

Through the use of studbooks and cooperation in captive breeding management programs, inbreeding can be minimized. Meticulous notes should be kept as to the weaknesses or strengths of particular specimens. Close supervision of breeding can be used to perpetuate the strongest and longest-lived parrots. It should be noted that the selection of the best qualities for a caged environment may not parallel those needed by the same species in the wild. Therefore, through selective breeding, captive parrots will undoubtedly change and may no longer be exactly like representatives of the same species that remain in the natural habitat. After as few as three generations, parrots in the captive environment will become domesticated and should no longer be candidates for release programs or other conservation efforts to return birds to the wild.

2.4 Record Keeping—Simplicity Is the Key

This is one subject that horrifies most breeders—not because it is a difficult task, but because standards for keeping genetic and breeding records have not yet been accepted by everyone. Therefore, every breeder has their own way of keeping records on the birds they produce.

Record keeping need not be frustrating and time consuming. The basic information needed is as follows.

- Where did the founder stock come from?
- How old are the birds?
- What are their identification numbers (leg bands, etc.)?
- What are the identification numbers of all of their offspring? What year?
- What is the final disposition of these offspring? (Where were they placed?)

Simple enough! With this basic information kept on all birds in captivity, we could construct an international studbook on a species if the need arose. Of course, things often go wrong, like the loss of one mate or another and the creation

20

of a new pair, but the records must go on, reflecting the new data exactly as it happened. Using a simple numbering or leg band system ensures records can be compiled and organized in the future. For computer users, there is an excellent Windows-based record-keeping program called Avimate.

2.5 Leg Banding—The AFA Way!

There are several manufacturers of bird leg bands in the United States. The AFA and several other national avian organizations, have developed a system of keeping track of leg bands used on captive-bred birds. A numbering system can be devised by the breeder that will provide valuable information about the banded bird. This is, of course, assuming the breeder kept records.

Depending on the size of your breeding population, the numbering system you choose can mean the difference between success and failure in record keeping. It is important not to duplicate leg band numbers that will be used on the same species of bird. If you breed large quantities of one species or another, you may find it difficult not to duplicate numbers over time. Use the year of production to assist in keeping these numbers from becoming useless. For example, Senegal parrot number AFA 788-95, may have been produced from pair #4 in 1995, whereas Senegal parrot number AFA 788-96 came from pair #23 in 1996. As long as one can differentiate between the parent stock, the numbering system will suit the purpose.

The benefit of ordering your leg bands through the AFA is that you will not be issued the exact same number and breeder code as that used by another breeder. Some may be frustrated not being able to use the initials they want, but in the future this differentiation will be vital to good captive management. The support of national and international avicultural groups is vital to the survival of captive breeding around the world.

3 The Senegal, Meyer's and Red-bellied Parrots

3.1 The Senegal Parrot: Range, Distribution and Regional Variations

The Senegal parrot can be found throughout central and western North Africa from western Senegal and Mauritania eastward through southwestern Chad. In his book *Parrots of the World*, Joseph Forshaw claims "they are common inhabitants of savanna woodlands but they tend to prefer open areas."

Senegal parrots are considered "very common" and widespread throughout the humid regions of central Africa. In many countries, they are considered crop pests and are well known in agricultural regions. Their habits seem to be somewhat migratory during the dry season. Flocks disappear with the arrival of the springtime rains and reappear after the rains have gone in summer and trees are in fruit or seed. They are fond of figs and the seeds of the locust bean tree, as well as mahogany and shea butter trees (Forshaw).

There are three recognized subspecies of the Senegal parrot. All three are approximately the same average size. The color of the chest and abdominal areas is used as the differentiating factor between the subspecies. The nominate or first subspecific form, from which the species has been named, *Poicephalus senegalus senegalus*, is distributed in the westernmost part of the range. This subspecies is described as having a "lower abdominal area of yellow"

22

(Forshaw). This particular subspecies is common in aviculture due to the large export shipments that took place from Senegal and Mali during the 1980s.

The second subspecies, *Poicephalus s. versteri*, is described as being the same as the nominate form except that the lower abdominal area is deeper orange-red and the green of teh back is darker. This particular form of the bird would not be considered common in captivity due to its limited range through the Ivory Coast, Ghana, Togo and into western Nigeria because these countries have not been major players in the parrot export business and few representatives of this subspecies were exported from these areas. The few that do exist in aviculture have probably been paired with mates of other subspecies, producing a bird that may have a yellow lower abdomen marked with dark reddish orange.

The last subspecies, *Poicephalus s. mesotypus*, is described as having "the green of the chest extending further down through the abdominal area of orange." Past export records from the Cameroon region indicate this subspecies should be fairly well represented in captivity.

Aviculturists have often tried to ensure captive pairs consist of two birds of the same subspecific assignment or are both of the same regional variation. This was not always possible and some crossbreeding did occur. This made identification of the young difficult or impossible to differentiate from pure, wild-caught bloodlines. What has occurred, at least in aviculture, is that we now have a Senegal parrot, not three different subspecies. There are those who seek wild-caught stock of one subspecies or another, often concentrating on the yellow or red abdominal area as a point of differentiation. Due to the scarcity of one subspecies or another in captivity, the mixing of bloodlines is inevitable and one captive species of the Senegal parrot will emerge.

3.2 Range, Distribution and Subspeciation of the Meyer's Parrot

The Meyer's parrot can be found throughout central and eastern Africa. Six different subspecies are described by Joseph Forshaw in *Parrots of the World*, but due to the difficulty in differentiation of the types, in captivity within the United States few aviculturists maintain subspecific pairs.

In the old days of wild-caught bird importation, many Meyer's parrots were imported into the U.S. As previously stated, a vast majority of the imported birds originated from either Senegal or Tanzania, the countries that most often dealt with American importers. The Meyer's parrot does not exist in Senegal, but is quite common in western Tanzania, this alludes to the fact that the subspecies most often kept in the United States would be *Poicephalus meyeri saturatus*. A few shipments of birds were imported from Cameroon and therefore, the nominate race *P. m. meyeri* is also represented. Of course, differentiation between the subspecies is very difficult and has led to "inter-specific crosses" of the available birds. We can be reasonably sure the three subspecies from the southernmost portion of the continent are not common in aviculture due to export and import records from that region.

The nominate race *P. m. meyeri* and the most commonly available subspecies, *P. m. saturatus*, are extremely similar. The only noticeable difference is the color of the rump; the nominate race has a blue rump and *saturatus* has a green rump washed with some lighter blue. This is not much to go on when you are trying to make a differentiation in order to keep with the practices of good breeding management.

Noted author and expert on African parrots Terry Irvin of Eshowe, KwaZulu-Natal, prepared a description chart in the book title *African Birds in Field and Aviary* that described the differences in the subspecies of the Meyer's parrots. Synopses of his explanations are as follows:

Poicephalus meyeri meyeri—light ash brown, breast and abdomen pale green with bluish sheen, head has yellow band across crown, rump is light blue and thighs are light green paling to yellow.

Poicephalus m. saturatus—dark ash brown, breast and abdomen green, head has yellow band on forehead, rump is mixed green and pale blue and thighs are green paling to yellow.

Poicephalus m. matschiei—dark ash brown, breast and abdomen light to bright blue, head has extensive yellow from forehead to crown, rump is bright blue and thighs are light blue paling to yellow.

Poicephalus m. reichenowi—dark ash brown, breast and abdomen green, head has no yellow at all, rump is bright blue and thighs are light green paling to yellow.

Poicephalus m. transvaalensis—pale ash brown, breast and abdomen bright blue, head has yellow band across top, rump is bright blue and thighs are light blue paling to yellow.

Poicephalus m. damarensis—pale ash brown, breast and abdomen bright blue flecked with grey, head has no yellow, rump is bright blue and thighs are bluish green paling to yellow.

3.3 Range and Distribution of the Red-bellied Parrot

The red-bellied parrot was not a common bird in aviculture until the mid-1980s. During this time period, limited shipments of this bird were brought in by U.S. and European importers and the species began to grow in popularity.

Only two forms of this bird are recognized by ornithologists and a debate as to whether there is any difference between the two still exists. One thing for sure, the nominate form, *Poicephalus rufiventris rufiventris*, is the only form common in aviculture.

Red-bellied parrots inhabit arid lowlands and woodlands in Ethiopia, Tanzania and Somalia. Exporters claim the only red-bellied parrots to come into the United States came out of Tanzania and are, therefore, the nominate race as claimed above.

A dramatic dimorphism is present in the African red-bellied parrot. Mature males sport a beautiful orange-red lower abdominal area where the female is green.

3.4 Sexual Dimorphism

To a certain extent, all parrots exhibit some sort of physical sexual dimorphism. The most prominent example of sexual dimorphism in the *Poicephalus* parrots is the red-bellied parrot. Males of this species acquire a beautiful orange-red lower abdomen, thus the name, while females remain green in the abdominal area. Breeders of red-bellied parrots cannot seem to make up their minds about the juvenile plumage of this species. Some say juveniles resemble females, and others say they resemble males. One thing is certain, young birds that are splashed with red color on the lower abdomen are not necessarily young males. The only sure way to know is to have the bird DNA or surgically sexed by a competent avian veterinarian, or wait six to none months for them to mature.

In the Senegal parrot, subtle dimorphism can be difficult to recognize if there is only one or two subjects available for study. Female Senegal parrots often sport a smaller beak with a sharper, more rounded curve toward the chest. In males, the beak tends to be longer and wider and it juts out from the face at less of an arc. In addition, females often tend to have a larger area of green on the upper chest. This green extends deep into the abdominal area, giving the impression of a very sharp V shape at the termination point. In males this green is often a blunt V shape and it only extends about halfway between the chest and the vent area.

The Meyer's parrot is the most difficult of all to sex visually. The color scheme of the Meyer's parrot is virtually the same for males or females. Females, for the most part, have a much smaller head, facial area and beak, than do males. The body weight of a female Meyer's parrot is usually fifteen to twenty grams less than most average-sized males as well. These weight comparisons are based on observations of wild-caught birds. Although these examples of sexual dimorphism may seem subtle and difficult to rely on, when inspecting a large group of birds they become more obvious. If breeding is the objective, it is always best to rely on veterinary determination of sex.

3.5 Simple Breeding Setups

All three of these species of the *Poicephalus* parrots require limited cage space for successful breeding. They often prefer smaller cages measuring a meter or so in length, perhaps because they provide a more limited area to defend and thus give the birds a more secure feeling. Small parrots placed in huge cages of several meters long tend to be nervous, active flyers that rarely settle and begin breeding. For humane and health reasons, it is recommended that birds be given larger flight cages at the first attempt to breed them. Nervous pairs can then be singled out and moved to smaller, more secure cages, if needed.

Choose welded wire mesh that is substantial enough to withstand the chewing habits of parrots (14-gauge wire would be a minimum). The size of the mesh should be no larger than 1 x 1 in. to prevent predators from getting into the cages. Some smaller snakes or even mice may still be able to squeeze through this size wire. The biggest risk is disease if rodents are allowed to run through the birds' food and water bowls. Some predators and rodents will eat eggs and attack and kill chicks too, but these predators rarely pose a threat to the adult parrots.

Cages can be constructed as wire cubes or rectangular cubes. Cages should be as large as possible and should never cramp the birds or limit their ability to fly. The average size cage for a breeding pair of small *Poicephalus* parrots would be three-foot square; but longer flights of six feet-plus are recommended. Perches should be about an inch in diameter and they should be placed so as to provide easy access to the nesting and feeding areas. A minimum of two perches in the cage is recommended.

Nest boxes used for most *Poicephalus* parrots should be constructed from wood or plywood sheets that are no thinner than half an inch (12 mm). If the birds are to be housed out of doors, thicker wood should be used or a thin metal liner can be installed to prevent the birds from chewing an escape route through the box. All-metal boxes are also useable, but some type of wooden inserts or floor should be placed inside to prevent the eggs from lying against the metal. Metal boxes transmit heat and cold and, if unlined, may be a problem during nesting.

The grandfather clock nesting boxes work fine. However, many wild-caught African parrots are shy and do not breed well if any light can shine in the entrance hole and down into the nesting chamber. For this reason, some people prefer a boot-shaped box or L-shaped nest box. These two styles allow the birds to climb down into the chamber and then to one side or another to get away from the light of the entrance hole. Nest box dimensions should be a minimum of 12 x 12 x 14 in. deep and should be constructed of heavier materials in areas of cold or hot weather. A two-inch entrance hole and a ladder extending down the entire inside panel should be used to provide easy access for the parrots.

The placement of the nest box is a matter of choice. Some aviculturists prefer to have the nest on the same side of the cage as the food and water. This makes servicing the cage easier as it can be done from one side. Others believe that the birds prefer to nest as far from a food source as possible because of the disruption when food bowls are changed and so place the box at the opposite end of the cage. Both arrangements have proven to work for Senegal, Meyer's and red-bellied parrots. Because these birds (if wild-caught) tend to be shy and nervous, nest boxes should be placed in the cage at a point that would be least traveled by the caretaker or other humans and animals. If you must walk by the front of the cage frequently, then the best place for the nest would be at the back of the cage.

Diet and nutritional information for these parrots can be found in section 7.7.

3.6 Egg Laying and Incubation Statistics

It is often easy to tell when a female parrot is getting ready to lay eggs. Ovulation brings about certain changes in a bird's body and an astute aviculturist will usually spot the signs. In many parrots, the uterus of the female becomes engorged just before egg laying and a slight bulge is often noticeable just above the vent area. Some females exhibit a noticeable bulge as much as two weeks prior to egg laying and may also maintain this look for weeks afterward. It is usually a good sign that egg laying is inevitable. In addition to this physical sign, females preparing to lay will often take a new interest in the nest box and may spend more time inside than ever before.

The usual clutch size for these *Poicephalus* parrots is from three to five eggs. Younger hens will often lay only two or three eggs in the clutch; birds in their prime breeding age, three to fifteen years of age, may lay four or even five.

If incubation does not begin with the laying of the first egg, but instead commences after the second egg is laid, the time period from the laying of the first egg to the hatch

29

of the first chick may be twenty-six or twenty-seven days. In actuality, the incubation period of the Senegal parrot, Meyer's parrot and the red-bellied parrot is about twenty-four or twenty-five days under optimal conditions.

The chick should break through the internal membrane approximately two days before expected hatch, and should make a pip mark on the external shell within twenty-four hours of that internal pip. Hatching usually goes better under high humidity conditions of 70 percent relative humidity or higher and may take as long as forty-eight hours from the time the external pip mark appeared on the shell.

3.7 Companion *Poicephalus* Parrots

As far as a pet bird goes, the Meyer's and red-bellied parrots are extremely sweet birds, but they are shy and often do not respond well to a household with loud children, dogs or other pets. There are exceptions to every rule and many people with children and/or pets also cherish their tame companion Meyer's or red-bellied parrots. After a period of adjustment, these two species, if bonded to a human, become loving and devoted to that person.

Unlike the tame Meyer's or red-bellied parrot, the Senegal parrot is more outgoing if hand-fed from a young age. Domestically produced, hand-fed Senegal parrots can be very entertaining and affectionate companion birds. They enjoy riding around on one's hands or arms and are constantly on the look out for something to jump onto (trouble is what they are usually looking for).

The voice and mimic abilities of these three *Poicephalus* parrots seem to be limited. Many do learn a few words and sounds but will not establish a large vocabulary. This may be due to the high-pitched natural call of these species and their ability, or lack of it, to hear, and subsequently mimic, the lower tones in the human voice. It has been noticed that parrots kept by women, that is, a woman who speaks to the bird in high-pitched tones, are often better talkers and will pick up words and expressions with greater ease.

Because of their compact size, *Poicephalus* parrots do not require huge cages. However, do not use cages designed for cockatiels or finches as the bars of these cages are small enough that parrot-sized beaks can break them and the bird may injure itself or escape. Choose a cage in which the bars are approximately one inch apart and are constructed of heavy gauge wire.

Today's retail pet store is usually a great help in choosing a cage. They know what precautions must be taken to assure a bird is safe within its home. Ask your local professional for assistance before you choose a cage. Companion birds should not be locked in a cage all day long. They need to have some free time outside the cage when they can stretch and play. Cages with play areas on top are ideal for most pet parrots. On the other hand, never allow your pet bird liberty twenty-four hours a day. A cage is a must for safety and psychological reasons, even if it is only used at night. Pet birds allowed to live on a T-stand or at liberty most often meet with disaster at some stage of their life.

4 The Jardine's Parrot

4.1 Range, Distribution and Taxonomy

The Jardine's parrot is common throughout its central African range. There appear to be three distinct areas inhabited by this bird and three separate forms have seemingly evolved out of this distribution. An eastern population occurs in Tanzania, northward through Kenya while the central population is found in Angola and extends northward to southern Cameroon and eastward to where it meets the population in Tanzania. A third, more western population occurs on the Ivory Coast from Ghana to Liberia.

Examination of the three different subspecies of the Jardine's parrot also reveals that intermediate forms exist in areas where the different populations overlap in the wild. This is understandable as the three forms, although different, still resemble each other very much; they are capable of interbreeding and producing viable offspring. This may explain the existence of a fourth subspecies named in Joseph Forshaw's *Parrots of the World*, where he lists *Poicephalus gulielmi permistus* as being a possible cross between the nominate form and that of *massaicus*. Of course, in captivity the three subspecies are most often maintained separately and breeding programs for all three forms have been established.

In the west, along the Ivory Coast, the subspecies *Poicephalus gulielmi fantiensis* exists. This is the smallest of the three subspecies and is the most commonly kept form in captivity in the United States. Among American breeders, due mainly to its smaller size, this form is referred to as the lesser Jardine's parrot. It can be described as a bright green bird with black edges along almost every feather on the body. The back is marked with more black than the frontal areas often giving this bird the same general appearance as the nominate form. Some representatives of this subspecies are so heavily marked with black on the back and wings that they are mistakenly called the lesser black-winged Jardine's parrot.

Once mature, *fantiensis* has a forecrown that is most often orange, and some orange speckling is also found under the wings. It is not true that male birds have more color than females. In fact, in most cases extremely colorful birds have turned out to be female. The orange color can be present on the legs and on the carpal edges of the wings. However, this coloring is not always the case and there are some examples of this subspecies that do not have any orange on them at all, even on the forecrown. These uncolored birds are rare and an exception to the rule. Immature birds usually have a chestnut brown color rather than orange on the forecrown. This brown color remains until after the first or second molt, when it is replaced by orange. This particular subspecies is not much bigger than a large Senegal parrot in size.

Poicephalus gulielmi fantiensis also has a rather recognizable beak. Beginning at the growing edge, near the nares, the beak is horn colored (tan). This color extends to approximately half the length of the beak where it is then covered by plates (layers) of dark grey or black. These plates usually do not extend to the tip of the beak, and so the tip is often the horn color of the uppermost edge of the mandible. This gives the entire beak a mottled look of horn, grey and black.

The eastern population, *Poicephalus gulielmi massaicus*, is often referred to as the greater or Congo Jardine's parrot. *Massaicus* is the most easily distinguished from the other two forms due to a different shape and body color than the other two forms. It is larger in size than *fantiensis* and only slightly smaller than the nominate form from central Africa. This subspecies appears smaller than it really is due to its natural posture, usually leaning forward and almost perpendicular to the perch. The body color is a brighter green and it only has about half the amount of black markings found in the other two forms. The forecrown on mature birds is orange, but it is a deeper orange than found in *fantiensis* and it is usually very restricted and does not extend back past the eye. Immature birds usually lack all orange color except for a fleck here and there. Once mature, the beak is totally horn colored, unlike the varying degrees of darker color found in the other two forms.

The third population from central Africa is the most dramatic. Only slightly larger (in weight) than *massaicus*, *Poicephalus gulielmi gulielmi*, the nominate form of the Jardine's parrot has been unofficially named the true black-winged Jardine's. This is due to the large amount of black pigments found in the wings of the mature birds, and some birds appear to have solid black wings when viewed from behind. This subspecies has a different posture and shape than massaicus and it resembles a large version of the lesser Jardine, *P. g. fantiensis*.

This central form, *P. g. gulielmi*, has a more red-orange forecrown. In some birds it is almost maroon. This color is also present on the bends of the wings and on the legs just above the feet. Immature birds, like in the other two forms, have a chestnut color in place of the red forecrown. Young birds begin to acquire the red orange forecrown at about a year of age and grow dramatically more colorful with age. The beak of *gulielmi* juts outward from the face as in the Cape parrot and it is predominantly blackish rather than the horn color of *massaicus* or the mottled color of the *fantiensis*.

4.2 Breeding Setups for the Jardine's Parrot

Probably the most difficult part of breeding the Jardine's parrot is making sure you have two birds of the same subspecies. As well, it is important to have your birds sexed to determine they are a true pair. Once that is accomplished and the birds are mature, successful breeding should take place in short order.

Jardine's parrots are, in terms of husbandry, an intermediate bird between the smaller *Poicephalus* parrots and the Cape parrot. They do not require huge cages to acclimate to captivity and actually seem to prefer smaller setups and dark accommodations, similar to the grey parrot. Cages should be long enough to allow the birds to fly from front to back. The natural breeding season starts in October and extends into February or March. In captivity, this season is variable and some birds have bred throughout the entire year.

Nest boxes vary according to the breeder's particular taste. Some people use the standard grandfather-clock style, while others use the boot-shaped or L-shaped boxes. The birds do not seem to care. Probably the most important thing is to make certain the sunlight cannot shine into the nesting chamber at the bottom of the box. Unlike the smaller *Poicephalus* parrots, Jardine's parrots rarely bicker and fight. In this way they are similar to the Cape parrot. Perhaps out of boredom, proven or extremely bonded pairs may pluck each other, sometimes to the point of total baldness. This does not seem to hamper their ability or willingness to breed in a captive environment.

4.3 Egg Laying and Parental Habits

The usual clutch size for the lesser Jardine's parrot is three or four eggs. The two greater forms often only lay a clutch of two to three eggs. Fertility in mature pairs is high and all eggs in the clutch may hatch. Incubation usually commences with the first egg and the incubation period is about twenty-three to twenty-five days (depending on the weather and conditions within the box). Newly hatched Jardine's parrots are very small and resemble the chicks of the grey parrot except for a light-colored beak. Hand-rearing from day one is difficult and should not be taken on without total dedication.

As far as parental habits are concerned, Jardine's pairs are hit and miss. Some pairs are excellent and will feed and care for the young until they fledge, and others will mutilate and kill the young. Most pairs are good parents and can be trusted to raise the clutch. During the rearing process, parents must be offered good food in order to raise the young in a proper fashion. Fresh corn on the cob, vegetables, greens, fruits, pelleted foods and seed should all be supplied to the parent birds. Nervous parent birds that destroy eggs or chicks should be provided with a more secure, quiet environment. If all goes well, young Jardine's parrots usually fledge the nest at about six or seven weeks of age. Do not remove newly fledged babies from the parental cage until they are eating on their own.

4.4 Hand-rearing Jardine's Parrots

Feeding baby Jardine's parrots from day one is difficult. The first few days of life are critical and the chicks must be kept very warm while being fed high volumes of electrolyte or hydration formulas to give them a strong start. A high incidence of yolk sac retention, where an internal yolk sac is retained and becomes infected, has been noticed in these birds, causing death at around four or five days of age. This problem is compounded by feeding the babies formula that is too thick for the first few days in the nursery. Formulas for the first few days should not be much thicker than milk. Chicks with yolk sac retention usually turn a pale white and are cool to the touch. This condition lasts about twenty-four hours before the chick finally dies. In many cases, if the hand-feeder stops feeding when this condition is noticed and allows the chicks to empty their gut for about a day or so, the chick can be saved. During this time period keep the chicks warm but do not feed them any solids at all! Only limited amounts of liquid, in the form of electrolytes, should be ingested. Once the color returns to the chick and it feels warm, begin with the thin formula or electrolytes with limited solids again.

The easiest way to rear the young is to allow the parents to get them started. If this is possible, allow the parents to feed them and then pull chicks into the nursery at about eighteen to twenty-one days of age.

From here on in it's a breeze! Feed the normal consistency and treat the chick as you would any other. See the chapter on hand-rearing for more information about feeding and weaning the chicks.

4.5 Jardine's Parrots as Pets

The compact size and quiet nature of the Jardine's parrot make it an excellent apartment bird. Unlike some of the larger Psittacines, the Jardine's parrots are not screamers and do not demand attention. Pet Jardine's parrots notoriously use a soft whistle to get your attention rather than raucous calls and screams.

The mimicking ability of the Jardine's parrot has been described as average among birds of similar size and origin. Some people claim their Jardine's have picked up ten or twenty words, while others say their birds do not try to talk at all. Of course, this can also be said of many of the infamous grey parrots. The amount of time spent teaching a bird to talk and mimic will be the determining factor as to how well it responds.

Pet Jardine's parrots may be shy and prefer the company of only those they recognize. However, the overall personality of this species as a companion bird is very desirable and all three subspecies have been kept as pet birds and lauded as sweet, lovable roommates. Both males and females alike make good companion birds and most Jardine's owners do not have a preference.

5   The Cape Parrot

5.1 Range and Distribution

There are three races of the Cape parrot, *Poicephalus robustus*, described. In captive-bred birds, differentiation between the subspecies can be difficult if the origin of the founder stock is unknown. During the days of frequent importation into the U.S. and Europe, only small numbers of Capes were available from wild-bird import stations. This may have been due to its habit of traveling in small family groups in the wild and remaining in high tree tops to feed and roost resulting in trappers having difficulty procuring large numbers for sale to exporters.

The Cape parrot's range in the wild is throughout the central to southernmost extreme of the African continent. The nominate race, *robustus robustus*, is not well represented in aviculture because its natural range is the southernmost tip of southeastern Africa where exports have been prohibited for many decades. The majority of the specimens now found in U.S. aviculture are of the race *robustus fuscicollis*, originating from southern Senegal, into Ghana and Togo. Exporters in these countries were operating a thriving livestock business in the 1980s, during which time most representatives now in captivity were imported. Although a limited number of *robustus suahelicus* were imported from Tanzania into the U.S. during the very late 1980s and early 1990s a few can still be found in the hands of several dedicated aviculturists. However, in Europe, *suahelicus* is the most common species in aviculture.

5.2 Subspecific Differentiation

The nominate race of the Cape parrot, *Poicephalus robustus robustus*, is easily distinguishable from its two subspecies. When mature, this subspecies sports an almost butter-scotch-colored head instead of the silvery grey of the other two forms. Upon close examination, the head color includes yellow-brown, with dabbles of dark brown and some black at the vein of each feather. Since the ranges of the nominate form and the other subspecies do not cross in the wild, there is little chance that interspecific crosses exist in the wild. When dealing with captive-bred birds, however, crosses can take place and the resulting offspring may be offered for sale. In this form, adult females have a distinctive reddish forehead that males of the same species often lack.

Ranging into Tanzania, and exported on a fairly regular basis, specimens of *Poicephalus robustus suahelicus* are uncommon, but occasionally available in captivity. This subspecies is distinguished from the nominate form of *robustus* by its silver to grey head. In addition, the head is marked with other colors as well, being speckled with pink, tinges of light brown and rose or tan. Adult males rarely have the red frontal band on the forehead but females usually develop the deep pink-red band just above the nares in their first adult plumage.

Probably the most commonly kept subspecies of the Cape parrot is *Poicephalus robustus fuscicollis*, and most representatives of this race were originally imported from Senegal or Ghana. This race is difficult to distinguish from *suahelicus* having only a slightly bluer tinge to the rump and on the back under the wings. The subspecies from Senegal (*fuscicollis*) is also slightly smaller in size than *suahelicus*. Of course, dietary influences in captivity may make determinations, based solely on size, very difficult if not impossible. Responsible breeders should try to trace the import origin of their breeding stock to find out from which area their birds were imported. This could be the only definite way to keep the races pure in captive-breeding programs.

As a special note of interest, immature birds, both males and females, usually have the reddish pink frontal band above the nares. In most juveniles, this color disappears within the first year and then reappears on maturing females. Some males have been known to maintain a few red or pink feathers on the forecrown as well, but the male's band is very unorganized and splotchy at best. Females vary in color and will often develop a large area of pink on the front of the head, sometimes extending back beyond the eyes.

5.3 Breeding Setups in Aviculture

The Cape parrot has been bred in captivity in a number of ways. Some breeders in South Africa claim this species desires to fly and therefore must be housed in large flight cages in order to accommodate its breeding needs. This has been disproved by a breeder in Florida who has successfully bred them in suspended cages measuring only six feet long. So, the real key to success with the Cape parrot must be something other than cage size.

It should be stressed that cages should always be of an adequate size to give the birds freedom of natural movement and flight. To house any parrot in a cage that does not allow, at the very least, short flights from one perch to another, often results in unhealthy breeding stock. We must remember that captive diets are rich in fats and oils, and exercise is necessary to keep birds in breeding shape and good psychological order.

Breeding setups vary, as explained above. For the most part, cubical, suspended cages measuring at least five feet long and three feet wide are recommended. Larger flight cages are certainly welcomed where possible. Nesting boxes can also be of several different designs. Some breeders prefer to use the L-shape or boot box for Cape parrots, claiming that they are shy and like to hide in the bottom of the boot where no light can get to them. The traditional grandfather-clock style box has also been used successfully. When using this style of nest box, the deeper the better. It is true that captive wild-caught Cape parrots are a bit on the shy side, and often a deeper box will help them overcome their fears. Make sure there is an internal ladder of some sort so birds do not become trapped in the bottom of a deep, dark chasm! Several perches should be mounted inside the cage to encourage flight from one to the other. Perches should be of several different diameters and should be made of wood, as Cape parrots love to chew. For the purposes of sanitation, do not place perches directly above food and water bowls.

In the wild, upon inspection of the nests of the Cape parrot, we find that they often lack substrate or chewed wood in the bottom of the nest, giving rise to the theory that these birds are not elaborate nest builders. Breeders usually add something to the box so the hen does not lay the eggs on the bare wooden bottom. Clean pine shavings or clean mulch will work just fine. If the female does not desire this addition to the box, she will surely remove it before breeding commences.

The diet consists of the normal captive parrot fare. Seeds, nuts, fruits, vegetables and extruded pellets should be offered. Birds often have favorite foods, but this varies from pair to pair. Some claim that walnuts are favored, while others have noticed that their pairs relish peanuts in the shell but will only accept them during their breeding times. When chicks are present in the nest, a change in dietary habits may occur; therefore, it is wise to offer a wide variety of foods and slowly begin to tailor the diet to the pair's specific desires. See section 7.7 for more nutritional information.

Following are some other observations by successful breeders:

- Cape parrots love the rain.
- They prefer their privacy from other birds and human intervention.
- They usually begin breeding in October and will breed through February or later.
- Captive-bred birds can breed as young as two years of age but are more reliable after the age of four years. Some breeding pairs are now in their teens, but we do not know the upper age limit for breeding.
- Hand-fed chicks are affectionate and alert.
- Captive-bred chicks should be close banded with a size number 14 band (AFA leg band size) to prevent the band from falling off or getting snagged on something.

5.4 Egg Laying and Parental Habits

Breeders that have had success with Cape parrots claim the birds are very good parents. They seem attentive to the chicks but abhor interruptions from their human keepers. The few problems that have been recorded with parent-rearing seem to be the same as those for grey parrot breeders. Some parents may nip the toes or wing tips off of the young while they are very small, and others may only feed the two largest chicks in the nest if three or more are present. No one really knows why they do this. It does not seem to be related to food supply, but may be a way of population control. Remember that parental habits rarely change. If a pair of birds mutilates chicks, they should not be trusted to feed chicks in subsequent clutches. The exception to this rule would be if the pair is resituated into a different surrounding environment. In these cases, some pairs have been known to change their bad habits and become good parents once again.

As previously stated, the captive breeding season (in the Northern Hemisphere) begins in late fall and extends through spring and into early summer. The usual clutch size is three eggs, with four being laid by some older females in their teens. Incubation is twenty-eight days, as in grey parrots, and incubation often does not begin until the second egg is laid. Newly hatched chicks are covered with white down and have light-colored beaks and feet—strangely enough, they strongly resemble the young of Jardine's parrots, another indicator these two species may be closely related.

Cape parrots are not difficult to hand-rear. There are no special rules to the rearing or weaning process for this species. Young birds grow rapidly and are not sexually dimorphic until later in life. Both males and females develop the reddish or pink forehead as juveniles. This color then disappears in the first year, and reappears only in maturing females. The young wean at about eight to ten weeks of age and are usually playful and alert, some getting rather shy if ignored or not socialized with one another.

5.5 Personality and Companion Bird Qualities

Cape parrots are extremely intelligent birds, and if hand-fed, they are often devoted and amusing pet birds. Wild-caught specimens rarely settle into a companion situation or become totally tame and trusting. It is recommended that birds to be kept as pets be sought from a reputable breeder.

When choosing a companion animal of any sort, it is always best to buy one that has been bred in captivity. Wild-born animals never seem to abandon their survival techniques, which may be interpreted as aggression or failure to domesticate. In addition, keeping wild birds as pets may fuel the international market and result in a higher demand for more wild-caught birds—a situation that aviculture is trying to resolve through increased captive breeding. Captive-bred and hand-fed parrots are, by far, better adjusted to life in a captive environment. They interact better with their owners and do not require the taming and training that a wild bird would.

The Cape parrot's personality is a lot like that of the African grey parrot. Captive-reared specimens can become very affectionate, but they may have only one person that they totally trust and may shy away from other household members. The mimic capability of the Cape parrot is not truly known. This is partly because the species has been difficult to find in aviculture and most offspring end up going right back into breeding programs. A limited ability to talk has been noted by those who use domestically produced offspring for breeding stock. It is important to keep in mind that breeding birds are usually not exposed to much affection and coddling, so perhaps the Cape parrot's ability to mimic human voice is much greater than observed by these breeders.

In the near future, thanks to an ever-growing success in captive breeding, companion Cape parrots will be more readily available. Their inquisitive nature and affectionate demeanor make the African Cape parrot a prime candidate for the companion bird owner.

6　More *Poicephalus* Parrots

Note: The four species covered in this chapter are rare in captivity in the United States. Rare in captivity does not necessarily equate to a rare status in the wild. In most cases, a species is only rare in captivity due to limited take from the wild and the controlled international trade in the species. The brown-headed parrot and Rüppell's parrot are growing in numbers in Europe and are not considered captive rarities as they are in the U.S.

6.1 The Brown-headed Parrot

As its name implies, the brown-headed parrot (*Poicephalus cryptoxanthus*) is a rather dull bird compared to other members of the genus. Brown-headed parrots closely resemble the unknown Niam-Niam parrot supposedly from central-western Africa. In truth, this species so closely resembles Niam-Niam, aviculturists often confuse the two. One of the main differences is that Niam-Niam has green underwing coverts that are bright yellow in the brown-headed parrot. Another distinguishing characteristic is the golden yellow iris of the brown-headed parrot. This parrot's eye color is markedly different from Niam-Niam, Meyer's or Rüppell's parrots—in all three of these species the iris is bright red in mature birds. The species' brown head is often marked with yellow feathers, giving it a mottled appearance. As well, the undertail coverts and lower abdominal area may be green, marked with yellow flecking.

6.1.1 Range and distribution

The brown-headed parrot is found in the southeastern coastal regions of the African continent, extending as far north as Tanzania and as far south as northeastern South

Africa. In the wild, this species is described as "locally common" in most areas (Forshaw), and it is not considered endangered in any part of its known range.

6.1.2 Breeding observations

A private bird, the brown-headed parrot prefers smaller nest boxes and limited human intervention into the nesting process. A nest size of 10 x 10 x 14 in. deep is sufficient. Nest boxes should be placed in such a way that sunlight cannot shine into the bottom nesting chamber where the eggs are laid. The average clutch size is three eggs, although there have been reports of up to five in a single clutch. Incubating females can be shy and should not be disturbed once nesting begins. Incubation usually lasts about twenty-five days and young closely resemble those of Meyer's parrots. Nesting habits and behavior seem to be similar to the Meyer's parrot's habits and suggested setups and avicultural rules would be the same as described for most of the other *Poicephalus* parrots. It has been noted that the brown-headed parrot can be very prolific if mates are compatible and breeding setups acceptable.

Aviculturists in the United States have often ignored this species due to a lack of demand for the offspring. This has resulted in a diminished captive population from what used to be available during the years of heavy importation in the United States. A few dedicated breeders of the African parrots still keep the brown-headed parrot and are experiencing moderate success with captive reproduction. There is a definite need to establish studbooks and international cooperative breeding efforts to sustain the present U S population into the future. U.S. breeders should seek out studbook holders of this species in Europe and combine efforts to sustain this species in aviculture.

6.1.3 Companion qualities

Hand-reared brown-headed parrots, although a bit shy, can make very good pets. Like most of the smaller

Poicephalus parrots, they are not known for their ability to mimic or speak in human voice. Of course, due to the limited availability and the fact that most offspring being produced at this time are being sold back into the breeder trade, we may find that this bird can mimic as well as or better than its cousins the Meyer's or Senegal parrot.

Brown-headed parrots can be very sweet and affectionate. They often prefer the company of only one or two persons, but will usually "step-up" onto any outstretched finger once they are used to being held. The cage should offer plenty of toys to keep the pet parrot amused. This may help in keeping the bird from plucking its feathers or becoming too shy to be a good companion bird. There does not seem to be a preference for either males or females as pet birds. Both sexes offer equally acceptable qualities.

6.2 The Niam-Niam Parrot

The Niam-Niam parrot (*Poicephalus crassus*) is yet another member of the genus *Poicephalus* that is virtually unknown in captivity. Because it so closely resembles the brown-headed parrot (*Poicephalus cryptoxanthus*), reports of its existence in captivity do occur. In most, if not all, cases, inspection of the reported specimen results in the more common brown-headed parrot. The major difference between these two birds is that the brown-headed parrot has a bright lime green rump and yellow iris to the eye, while the Niam-Niam parrot lacks this colorful rump and has a red iris. As stated before, another difference is that Niam-Niam has green underwing coverts where the brown-headed has yellow. The differences between the two sound dramatic but are really very subtle.

Joseph Forshaw, in his book *Parrots of the World*, states that the Niam-Niam is still common near Cameroon, a segment of its range. Unfortunately, so little is known of this parrot that it remains almost a myth to captive breeders across the world. If, in fact, this parrot really exists and was not described from abherent specimens of the brown-headed or a natural hybrid, studies and captive breeding trials must be initiated with this species before it is lost to deforestation and habitat destruction in its native home. Since most other small *Poicephalus* parrots respond to similar breeding setups, we have to assume this species will also breed in the captive environment.

It is the opinion of the author that the Niam-Niam parrot was described from "unusual" specimens of the brown-headed parrot, or hybrids between Meyer's and brown-heads. This conclusion is based on the fact that virtually all of the birds examined have been males. If this was a true specie and was "still locally common" anywhere in its range, trappers or collectors would surely have found female birds of the species. I conclude that, like the intermediate parakeet (*Psittacula intermedia*) of India, this species is merely a naturally occurring hybrid and only the male birds are noticeably different than one of the two forms that bred to create this "myth." Immediate studies and field data should be collected about this species so it can be afforded the protection it deserves—if it should prove to be a valid species.

6.3 The Rüppell's Parrot

Rüppell's parrot (*Poicephalus rueppellii*) is a small- to medium-sized parrot only slightly smaller than the Meyer's parrot. The natural habitat of the Rüppell's parrot extends along the coastal region of South Western Africa just south of Angola. This parrot is not well established in captivity with the exception of, perhaps, in South Africa where several breeders have experienced successful nesting. In the United States, only a few pairs were ever imported. They did produce offspring, but bloodlines are so limited that a cooperative effort of some sort will have to be established with breeders abroad if this bird is to ever be commonly available in U.S. aviculture. This parrot is becoming very common in Europe, making captive-bred stock readily available.

The Rüppell's parrot resembles the Meyer's parrot in both color and size, excepting that the Rüppell's lacks the green color on the chest and lower abdomen. A marked dimorphism does exist between the sexes as the female sports a bright blue rump and lower back area. This vivid color is absent in the male Rüppell's and replaced by brown that can be slightly tinged with blue. Not much is known of the habits of this species in the wild. This is probably due to the difficulty in field studies because it travels in small flocks that tend to stay high overhead in tall trees (Forshaw). Given current restrictions in trade with the United States, it is doubtful that Rüppell's parrot will ever be common in aviculture.

6.4 The Yellow-faced Parrot

Yellow-faced parrots (*Poicephalus flavifrons*) are virtually unknown in captivity across the world. This may be due to the difficulty and legality of exporting it from its native habitat. Yellow-faced parrots are said to be fairly common within their restricted range in central Ethiopia. They inhabit upland forests where they feed on seeds, figs and the usual parrot fare. Nothing is recorded of this bird's habits, nesting behavior, eggs or husbandry. Due to the unpredictable climate in its native habitat, aviculturists must work something out with the CITES officials in Ethiopia to establish a few breeding pairs of this species in captivity. Several decades of drought in the nesting area of this species may bring about its demise in the wild. Rumors that a few pairs arrived in South Africa around 1992 have not yet been confirmed, and the outlook for establishing this species in captivity still looks rather dismal.

Examination of the skins of this species reveals that it looks very much like the Jardine's parrot in body size and shape. The red of the Jardine's is replaced by yellow in this species. In fact, there are so many similarities between this species and the Jardine's, it makes one wonder if the current population of this species was not established from an aberrant color mutation that occurred long ago. Of course this is merely speculation; hopefully someone will take the initiative to perform DNA studies on both of these species in the future.

7   African Grey Parrots

7.1 Grey Parrots in the Wild

The grey parrot is widely distributed throughout Central Africa. Shy birds, even in the wild, they prefer woodland forests and tend to stay away from towns and villages. The grey parrot is still quite common throughout most of its range, but is becoming less abundant in areas of increased human inhabitation as the forests and adequate nesting sites become agricutural land.

The wide range covered by this species includes many different types of habitat. They can be found in open savanna to lowland forests and coastal mangrove swamps. The African grey parrot has adjusted well to various ecosystems across Africa. Alternative vegetation and food availability in different regions have, over time, caused variations in the color and size of the grey parrot. These geographical differences in plumage may be to blame for some aviculturists claiming to have Congo greys or Cameroon greys, stating that one or the other is larger and lighter in color. Although not a valid scientific subspeciation, these regional differences are important and are discussed later in the text of this book.

7.2 Sexual Dimorphism and Sex Determination of African Grey Parrots

African grey parrots have been kept as pets and aviary subjects for centuries. Since all species of African grey parrots are basically monomorphic (males and females look alike) and determination of sex by a trustworthy physiological method was not perfected until as recent as 1970, breeding prior to that date was essentially luck. In the old days, keepers of African greys had no way of knowing the sex of their bird unless it laid eggs, indicating it was undoubtedly a hen. Behavior was not always a dependable method of determining sex as some birds played roles when housed with same-sex partners. However, aviculture has come a long way in the past twenty-five years and dependable methods of sexing have been nearly perfected giving today's breeder a head start on potential production.

In the old days, it was assumed that most parrot species exhibited no visual dimorphism between males and females, except of course the obvious ones like the Eclectus parrots. However, during the past few years, aviculturists have recorded subtle differences in the parrots they keep. These notes have resulted in a collection of knowledge that includes many subtle dimorphisms in species previously considered monomorphic. Some of these recorded differences are applicable to the African parrots as well.

These observations should never be used in place of surgical sexing procedures or DNA blood analysis—the two proven methods of sexing birds. Until we have perfected these visual observations, they should be used in conjunction with some other confirmation of sex. Even the sharpest eye cannot detect some of the subtle differences, and improper sexing could result in two birds of the same sex being put together as a breeding pair.

Surgical sexing is a procedure usually performed by an avian specialist or veterinarian. In this procedure, the bird is anesthetized while a small-caliber endoscope is inserted into the abdomen. The endoscope is used to view the sexual organs and is an almost foolproof way of sexing parrots. On occasion a mistake is made, but this is most often the result of sexing a bird that is young and does not have fully formed sexual organs.

DNA sexing eliminates the need to invade the bird surgically. Using this procedure, a small sample of blood is analyzed to determine the sex of the bird. This method is often preferred over surgical sexing because it is noninvasive. Using chromosome DNA sexing can be as simple as cutting a toe nail and collecting a small drop of blood to be analyzed by an experienced laboratory.

Over the years some breeders have learned a few tricks making it possible to visually determine the sex of African grey parrots and some of the others as well. In mature African grey parrots, *Psittacus erithicus erithicus* for example, there are a few subtle dimorphisms that are usually present. The use of these observations should be limited and used with other methods as confirmation only. First, it has been documented that the frontal portions, chest and abdominal area of female African grey parrots are lighter grey in color than on males of the same species. There is a lot of room for error in this assessment as there are many regional and nutritional influences that may make this determination difficult.

A second dimorphism is only present in mature African grey parrots. This difference is strongly marked in birds that have completed the first molt and cannot be used to determine sex in birds that are still in juvenile plumage. In this method, the underside of the red tail is examined. The exact examination point is near the vent of the bird where small scallop-shaped red feathers form a V on the underside of the tail. Examine each individual red feather that lines the inside of the tail. If these feathers have a faint grey line on the very edge of each feather and the quill itself appears to be grey, the bird is female. If these feathers are pure red with no grey edges, the bird is a male. This method proved to be 100 percent accurate in a trial that was performed at a wild bird importer's facility in Miami. Note that the vein of each of these feathers is often grey and this is not an indication of sex. It is the outermost edge of the feather that displays the difference.

7.3 Timneh or Congo Grey Parrot?—A Lesson in Taxonomy

The two species of the grey parrot most commonly available to the pet owner or breeder are the Congo African grey and the Timneh African grey. There is a marked difference in size between the two subspecies, but their general appearance is somewhat similar.

The Timneh grey parrot is a smaller, slightly less colorful version of the Congo grey parrot. The plumage of the Timneh is usually a darker grey in color and is often suffused with a brownish tinge. The most noticeable difference between the two subspecies is the color of the beak and the tail of the smaller Timneh grey. This subspecies has a lighter, horn-colored upper mandible (which is black in the Congo) and the tail is a dark maroon, marked with black or brown (which is bright red in the Congo). Furthermore, depending on the region from which the Congo grey may have come, the Timneh's chest and lower abdomen is usually not as light a grey as that of the Congo. There is a patch of light grey feathers on the abdomen of the Timneh, but it is very restricted and is often ill defined in Timneh males. To see these two birds side by side, one would almost immediately notice that the Congo grey is at least a head taller than the Timneh.

7.4 Breeding Setups for African Grey Parrots

For every rule in aviculture, there are at least ten exceptions. The same holds true with regard to the suggested caging and aviary setups used to breed African parrots. Something that works for one breeder may not work for another. Because each pair of birds is different and they may respond differently to certain methods, try to keep an open mind when designing a breeding setup. The key to breeding many of the species from Africa is patience. Changing the setup every year simply because a pair of birds did not breed will only result in constant disruption and will further lessen the breeding success.

There are essentially two types of cages used to breed parrots in captivity. They are often referred to as suspended cages or flight cages. Suspended cages, sometimes called California cages or Noegel cages after noted psittacine breeder Ramon Noegel from Florida, are simply wire cubes or rectangular cages. These cages are suspended above the ground by the use of pedestals or by hanging them from some overhead structure. Suspended caging is more common in the U.S., but is now used throughout the world because of its advantages with regard to the control of disease transmission, ease of cleaning and parasite and rodent control.

However, the use of suspended aviaries also has its disadvantages. It is more difficult to catch birds in a suspended cage than it is to walk into a full flight cage. In addition, large pieces of debris and food will often gather on the cage bottom as the wire may prevent it from falling to the ground. This creates a need for some type of tool or long handle to reach to the furthermost point of the cage bottom. Regardless of which type of cage is chosen, it must be kept clean in order to protect the birds from potentially harmful bacteria or fungi.

Flight cages have been used with success to house breeding pairs of greys. This style cage is usually constructed of wooden or metal poles with wire panels stretched between them and placed overhead as the ceiling. A walk-through door is used for access to the cage and the floor can be cement, dirt or gravel. Cement floors are preferable as they can be easily cleaned with a water hose. Dirt or gravel on the aviary floors is problematic in that the keeper must rake them clean, often disrupting the privacy and space of the birds inside. Additionally, dirt floors are a breeding ground for pathogens and parasites, both of which could prevent the pair from breeding. Whenever dirt floors are used, it is wise to have an avian veterinarian test, and if necessary treat the birds for parasites and worms on an annual basis. Tapeworms can be a recurring problem in many African species that are allowed access to the ground.

African grey parrots can be housed in rather small (humane) cages. This is due to their relatively compact size and a rather sedentary lifestyle. Even though they are strong flyers, most captive pairs do not prefer to fly, but are usually content to walk or crawl around the cage space. As a matter of fact, many established pairs will spend a majority of their time hiding in the nest box if one is provided.

On the average, cage sizes for the larger African species can be as small as 2 x 3 x 4 ft. long. These small cages are easy to maintain and give the birds a certain sense of security. The actual location of the cage is much more important than its size. Furthermore, breeding pairs do not require elaborate setups that include natural nesting logs, toys or branches. Most aviculturists provide at least two perches in addition to a nest box and some indestructible food and water bowls. Perches should be wooden, but PVC pipe or cement perches have been used. The lack of fancy additions to the cage is because many pairs are shy and do not respond well to the constant intervention needed to maintain these extraneous items. African parrots are better off left alone if breeding is the desired result.

7.5 Nest Boxes—Design and Placement in the Breeding Cage

Breeders of African parrots commonly use the grandfather clock nesting box. The boxes are tall and narrow with an entrance hole placed somewhere near the top (resembling the face of a grandfather clock). They are constructed from plywood or other cheaper wooden material. Due to the height of the box, a wire or wooden ladder is placed on the inside of the box and extends from the entrance hole down to the nesting chamber at the bottom. Wooden ladders do not last very long as African greys love to chew wood. A ladder helps to prevent the birds from leaping onto the eggs from above, and if chicks are to be fledged, it makes it easier for them to climb out. Inspection doors are placed at the rear-bottom so the keeper can gain access to the eggs or chicks. These doors should be made large enough for the keeper to reach inside the box with a small net. Protective parent birds will destroy eggs or chicks in a hurry so the keeper must be able to work fast at removal time.

Another commonly used box is the shadow, L-shaped or boot style nest. Originally, breeders of African parrots used this style box because it provided a little more privacy for the incubating hen. If sunlight shines into the entrance hole, the nesting chamber itself remains dark. This style box is basically a grandfather style box with an extra chamber attached to the bottom. The extra room is attached to the side and bottom of the box, giving it an L shape. There are several variations to this style, one being the addition of an extra baffle or landing directly below the entrance hole inside the box. This baffle helps to prevent light from shining into the nesting chamber below. I have found that most African parrots will eventually chew this baffle to pieces.

Empty barrels, trash cans, oil drums and natural logs have also been used to breed African birds. In addition, the use of large PVC pipes with caps on the ends have become rather popular with some breeders. The choice of nesting boxes is up to the aviculturist. All of the styles listed above have been used successfully to breed African parrots. Some problems have been noted with the use of the PVC plastic, metal or drum style nests. In areas of the world where the summers are extreme, the internal temperature of these nests may get too hot, and this excessive heat can destroy the eggs or chicks. If young are present, they may dehydrate and die. Common sense is called for when choosing the nest box that is right for your birds. A few pointers that may assist in this decision are listed below. This list is meant to provide input as to safety and functionality.

- Nests should always be kept clean and free of sharp nails, screws or wire.
- Wooden boxes may need to be repaired on a regular basis to prevent escape if nest boxes are placed on the outside of the cage. Birds cannot escape from boxes mounted inside the cage.
- Ladders should always be provided if the nest is deeper than twice the length of the hen's body.
- Inspection doors should be large enough to allow the placement of a small net inside. Keep in mind that if chicks will be pulled from the nest, the door should be large enough to remove them without injury.
- On outdoor cages, the entrance hole should face a direction that prevents the sun from shining into the nesting chamber.
- Use locks or at least two hooks on the inspection door to prevent escape if boxes are hung on the exterior of the cage.
- Birds that chew excessively may need to be provided with a wire-lined box or a metal or PVC cylinder that cannot be destroyed.
- Nesting material should be clean (pine shavings are often used). The use of Five-Seven Dust, a mild insecticide, in the shavings is good to prevent mites or other insects from invading the chicks or eggs.

The placement or location of the nest box within the cage is very important. Since most African species tend to be shy about nesting, it is wise to place the nest box at the furthermost point in the cage and away from the food supply. This location insures the keeper will not disturb the nest when servicing the food and water bowls. Some aviaries are set up in such a way that the nest is directly above the food and water. The birds do eventually become used to this situation, but the opposite end of the cage is preferred whenever possible.

Another factor to consider is that the nest should be located as high as possible within the cage. This gives the birds a sense of security and they will often retreat to the nest when someone enters the aviary or room. A perch located near the entrance to the nest is convenient but not always necessary. The birds do just as well to climb over the wire to get into the box.

7.6 Secrets to Breeding African Parrots—A Breeder's Viewpoint

Although African grey parrots are commonly bred in captivity, many pairs are stubborn and it may seem they will never breed. Over the years, breeders have talked of their experience with breeding certain birds. This has resulted in what I call little secrets that can lead to the successful breeding with stubborn or nervous pairs. These secrets apply to all the African species, not just the grey parrots. African greys, and other African parrots, have the notorious reputation for being difficult to breed in captivity. Following are some tricks of the trade in breeding the birds. They appear in the order of their importance.

Darkness: African birds breed better in dark setups. This may sound absurd, but I assure you it is true. Many breeders have wrapped dark shade cloths around cages housing their African birds. This has resulted in a dramatic increase in production. To further emphasize this point, experiments have been conducted in which pairs of African greys are set up in a dark shed (with little light) while others are set up in the outside sunlight. Amazing as it may sound, the birds provided with dark cages bred almost immediately while the others took almost four years to adjust to their environment. Care should be taken not to deprive the birds of the light needed to synthesize vitamins and minerals in the diet. After the completion of breeding cycles, a full spectrum light or a window allowing sunlight should be installed and used.

Privacy: Along the same line as darkness, privacy seems to be very important to the successful breeding of many African species. Privacy not only refers to the reduction in human intervention or exposure, but also to the birds in adjacent cages. It is not wise to house loud South American birds, such as macaws or conures, in cages that border those of African birds. A quiet area with subtle lighting is preferred.

High fat diets: Contrary to the health kick that is going on in America right now, African birds need a high fat diet to encourage breeding. Pelleted diets and those that include a lot of fresh fruits and vegetables have resulted in breeding success, but the most successful breeders feed their birds peanuts, seeds, nuts and other high fat foods. Higher fat breeder pellets such as ZuPreem's Breeder Diet also act to encourage breeding. Statistics demonstrate that most pairs of African parrots prefer high fat diets, especially during the breeding season.

Calcium supplementation: Mineral blocks or some other source of calcium and phosphorus are very important when breeding African parrots. When consumed, they supplement the needed calcium to balance the breeder diet. The use of high fat diets further increases the importance of calcium supplementation. If the parent birds are allowed to fledge the young, keep a close eye on the calcium supply in order to prevent hypocalcemia in the chicks.

Annual parasite check-ups: African parrots have a propensity to host tape worms and other parasites. It may not be obvious to the keeper, for this reason an annual parasite check by an avian veterinarian is suggested. Worm-infested birds do not breed. If the infestation goes untreated for extended periods of time, the breeder pairs may eventually weaken and become ill.

7.7 The Breeding Diet

As mentioned above, most of the African parrots breed better and thrive well on diets that contain a higher percentage of fat than diets offered to some of the other parrots. This is especially true during the breeding season or when chicks are being fed by the parent birds.

A high fat diet does not mean that improper nutrition is in order. It is still vital that breeding pairs receive the proper amounts of calcium, phosphorus, vitamins and other important elements of nutrition. This balance of nutrition can be accomplished by providing the birds with a variety of foods to choose from. There is no need to feed every food item each and every day. As a matter of fact, this may result in the birds eating the same chosen foods each day and ignoring the ones that are the most important. The result would still be nutritional deficiency even though the diet was well balanced.

Commercial pelleted diets are an excellent base diet for the African parrots. This is, of course, assuming the birds eat the pellets. In addition to pellets, they should be provided with fresh vegetables and fruits, a vitamin and mineral supplement of some sort and nuts and peanuts during breeding. They must be accustomed to eating a variety of foods as difficult as this training might be. The key to getting your birds to try new foods is persistence. It may get to the point where certain foods will have to be provided with no alternatives available. After a few hours or when the birds have tested the new food, a bowl of the normal fare can be added.

During the breeding season the addition of high fat items such as peanuts, sunflower seeds and safflower seeds should be available. For some reason, it has been noticed that breeding is often triggered by the addition of these fatty foods following a period of time when they have not been available. This regime may be similar to conditions in the wild where a seasonal favorite becomes available just before the breeding season.

Calcium is a very important element in the diet of all African parrots. Due to the high incidence of hypocalcemia, a syndrome where blood calcium levels are low and an inability to utilize skeletal calcium results, a daily dietary supplement is recommended. Make sure the calcium supplement contains vitamin D3, as this vitamin is vital to the absorption and use of the available calcium. Symptoms of severe hypocalcemia can include seizures, cracked or broken bones, egg binding, lameness or even death. It is wise to include preventative measures in the diet rather than wait and try to cure the problem after it has occurred. Parent-reared chicks seem to be very susceptible to this problem so the parent birds should be provided with a balanced diet while feeding young.

The subject of diet always creates some controversy. This is likely because so little is really known about the requirements of each species in the parrot family. Nutritional studies on human beings are constantly resulting in changes in our recommended daily allowances; therefore, we can be certain that further study of parrots will result in changes to our suggested feeding regimen. Keep a close eye on the published results of any nutritional testing that may be done by avian nutritional professionals. Incorporate new food items and supplements and try to maintain a good balance that results in the best possible health for your birds.

7.8 The Breeding Season

Parrots kept in captivity often adjust their natural breeding cycles to the most advantageous weather conditions, availability of foods or day-length cycles. This is not true of the African parrots. For some reason they breed during the time period that corresponds to their natural breeding cycles in the wild. Of course, some domestically produced stock, or even a few wild-caught pairs, may breed at any given time of the year or all year long, but this is the exception rather than the rule.

In the wild, African parrots begin to nest around the beginning of October. The breeding season may last as long as six or seven months, ending in late spring or early summer in the Northern Hemisphere. Most captive African birds will breed during this time period no matter what part of the United States the breeder may live in. Since most other parrots nest in the spring and summer, the breeder may welcome the arrival of African parrot chicks in the fall and winter. This keeps the nursery open and in operation year around and provides the breeder with income during the "slow season."

Above: Using the yellow undertail coverts as a dimorphism is not accurate in many cases. This female *Poicephalus senegalus versteri* has yellow undertail coverts—a trait once said to only happen in males. *Photo: Jean Pattison*

Right: Senegal parrots make great companion birds when hand-fed and socialized to humans. This very colorful example is of the subspecies *P. s. versteri*.

Photo: Jan Beatrous

Senegal parrots of the subspecies *P. s. mesotypus* have an orange breast, unlike the other two forms of this species. They originate in the Cameroon region of the African continent. *Photo: Kenneth Nielsen*

Above: Meyer's parrots are not known for their ability to mimic human voice, but they do make great companion birds. This sub-species *P. m. reichenowi* has very little yellow on the head but does have yellow on the bends of the wings.

Photo: David Hancock

Left: There is much confusion over the different subspecies of the Meyer's parrot. Because the abdomen of this bird is splashed with grey, it is probably of the subspecies *damarensis*.

Photo: David Hancock

Right: Given the confusion on subspeciation in the Meyer's parrots, aviculturists should try to match the mates for their birds with the descriptions of the subspecies. This is a typical example of *P. meyeri damarensis*. *Photo: Jan Beatrous*

Below: This imported male Meyer's parrot is probably a pied mutation. If the mutation breeds true, each generation should obtain more and more yellow as the chicks mature. *Photo: Jan Beatrous*

Above: The red-bellied parrot (*P. rufiventris*) demonstrates the most intense dimorphism of all the African parrots. Shown here is a mature male demonstrating the typical red belly of the species.
Photo: Rick Jordan

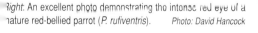

Above: A breeding pair of red-bellied parrots (*P. rufiventris*). The male is below with the female above. Notice the lack of red color in the female's lower abdomen.
Photo: David Hancock

Right: An excellent photo demonstrating the intense red eye of a mature red-bellied parrot (*P. rufiventris*).
Photo: David Hancock

Juvenile red-bellied parrots (*P. rufiventris*) often develop areas of red feathers on the head. This color usually disappears after the first molt. Pictured here are red-bellies at about four weeks of age. *Photo: Jean Pattison*

There are no rules for the juvenile plumage of the red-bellied parrot. Pictured here are newly fledged juveniles, both sporting a red belly—yet, they are both young females. *Photo: Torben Rafn*

The female red-bellied parrot (*P. rufiventris*) lacks the red on the belly once mature. The green on the rump and leg area extends all the way to the upper chest. *Photo: Jan Beatrous*

Virtually unknown in captivity around the world, the yellow-faced parrot (*P. flavifrons*) resembles a Jardine's parrot with yellow on the forecrown. This species originates from Ethiopia and very little is known of its habits. *Photo: Torben Rafn*

Differentiation between the three subspecies of the Jardine's parrot can be difficult. Notice the difference in the intensity of the color found on the heads of the three species of Jardine's parrots. Pictured on the left is *Poicephalus gulielmi gulielmi*, middle is *P. g. massaicus*, and on right is *P. g. fantiensis*. *Photo: Hill Country Aviaries, L.L.C.*

The difference in color and size of the beaks is also noticeable between the three Jardine's species. On the left, *P. g. gulielmi* is a much larger bird with a darker beak and dark red forecrown. In the middle, *P. g. massaicus* has a restricted red-orange crown and a white beak, and on the right, *P. g. fantiensis* shows an orange-yellow forecrown and mottled looking beak. *Photo: Hill Country Aviaries, L.L.C.*

The two forms often called Congo and black-winged Jardine's parrots are compared in this photo. The nominate race *P. g. gulielmi* is on the left, and the Congo or *P. g. massaicus* is pictured on the right. Notice the large amounts of green throughout the wing of the *massaicus* parrot (right) and the dark, almost black appearance of the nominate race *gulielmi* (left). *Photo: Hill Country Aviaries, L.L.C.*

Above: Pictured here is a young black-winged Jardine's parrot (*P. g. gulielmi*). Except for a difference in body weight, babies of all three species of Jardine's often lack the color on the head or it is replaced by chestnut brown. A speckled effect of orange or yellow may be present in young *P. g. fantiensis*.   *Photo: Rick Jordan*

Above: Nestling Jardine's parrots pretty much all look the same. Pictured here are two baby lesser Jardine's, *P. g. fantiensis*.

Photo: Jan Beatrou

Not necessarily a mutation at work, this photo depicts an unusually colored pair of lesser Jardine's parrots (*P. g. fantiensis*).

Photo: Kenneth Nielse

The Cape parrot strongly resembles a large Jardine's parrot. In mature male Cape parrots, typically the pink-red of the forecrown is absent. This is a photo of a male Cape parrot of the species *P. robustus fuscicollis*.

Photo: Jean Pattison

In the subspecies *P. r. fuscicollis*, the female Cape parrots are often more colorful than their male counterparts. Young males may have some pink or red on the head, but it usually disappears with age. A typical female is shown here.

Photo: Jean Pattison

The nominate race of the Cape parrot, *P. r. robustus*, is found in the wild in southern Africa. This race is very rare in the United States and can be differentiated from the other two forms by its brownish head.

Photo: Cherane Pefley

Still quite rare in the United States, Cape parrots of the race *P. r. suahelicus* are often referred to as the silver-headed Cape parrot as it lacks most of the rose-pink markings found in the head of *P. r. fuscicollis*. This race is the largest of the Cape parrots in length and body weight.

Photo: Cherane Pefley

Closely resembling the Meyer's parrot, Ruppell's parrot (*P. rueppellii*) can be easily distinguished by the yellow legs and the bright blue rump of the females.

Photo: Kenneth Nielsen

Left: Because they are not the most colorful parrots, the brown-headed parrot (*P. cryptoxanthus*) had been ignored by aviculturists until only recently. *Photo: Torben Rafn*

Below: Baby brown-headed parrots strongly resemble the young of the other *Poicephalus* parrots. *Photo: Jan Beatrous*

Right: Painting of a yellow-faced parrot by Lyrae Perry.

Known for its ability to mimic human voice and household sounds, the African grey parrot (*Psittacus e. erithacus*) is probably the most common pet African parrot in the world.
Photo: Jan Beatrous

Left: Street vendors in Africa sell grey parrots and Timneh grey parrots in small cages. The brown color in the plumage has been found to be caused by a dietary influence, and it often changes to normal with the next molt.
Photo: Steve Garvin

Below: The Timneh grey parrot (*P. erithacus timneh*) is smaller and darker in color than its cousin the African grey parrot.
Photo: Jean Pattison

Above left: Due to their social nature, it is advantageous to raise baby grey parrots in small groups, where they can identify with each other and with the human hand-feeder.
Photo: Jean Pattison

Above right: Parent rearing of baby grey parrots is encouraged in some situations. In this photo, it is apparent that baby grey parrots often lay on their backs to be fed. When pulled to the nursery, it often takes a few days for the babies to feed in the upright position.
Photo: Jean Pattison

Left: Baby grey parrots that develop abnormal red feathers throughout the plumage, often molt out to be normally colored birds after hand-rearing. In a few cases, the red feathers remain, but breeding specifically for a red grey parrot has not yet been accomplished.
Photo: Jean Pattison

Right: When comparing the grey parrot to the Timneh grey parrot, a noticeable difference in body weight, size of facial area, and beak color becomes evident. The Timneh grey parrot (left) is substantially smaller than the grey parrot on the right.
Photo: R. Jordan, Mark Moore, Scott Stringer

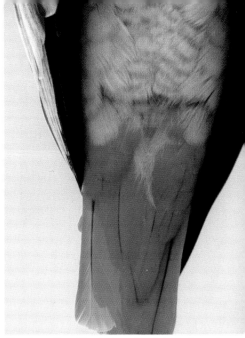

In comparison, the grey parrot has a brighter red tail than that of the Timneh grey parrot. In this photo, the Timneh grey parrot (*P. erithacus timneh*) is on the right, and the grey parrot (*P. e. erithacus*) on the left.

Photo: R. Jordan, Mark Moore, Scott Stringer

Close inspection of the shorter, red, undertail feathers, of a grey parrot (*P. e. erithacus*) reveals faint grey edges on this mature female. Males are generally pure red with no grey edges whatsoever. *Photo: Jan Beatrous*

It is easy to see that the African rose-ringed parakeet (left) is a smaller bird than its Indian cousin, with a more rounded head and a smaller and darker beak. The Indian rose-ringed parakeet (right) is now very common in captivity throughout the world . *Photo: Lyrae Perry*

The Vasa parrot (*Coracopsis vasa*) can be distinguished from the little black parrot by the color of the skin around the eyes and the heavy mandible.

Photo: Jan Beatrous

The little black parrot (*C. nigra*) has dark skin around the eyes and a much smaller, more rounded beak than its larger relative, the Vasa parrot.

Photo: Jan Beatrous

A close-up of the Vasa parrot (*C. vasa*) shows the slight tinge of yellow in the skin and the horn-to white-colored beak of a juvenile.

Photo: John A. Keibe
Advocates for Bird Conservation

Right: Shadow or L-shaped nest boxes seem to be preferred by most African parrots. This is probably due to their shy nature, as these styles prevent the light from shining into the nesting chamber.   *Photo: Rick Jordan*

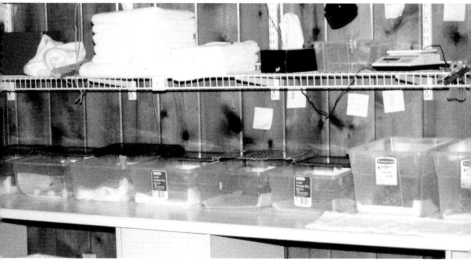

Above: Nursery areas should be kept clean and neat. It is advisable to separate the babies into clutches for the purposes of identification and socialization of the young.   *Photo: Jean Pattison*

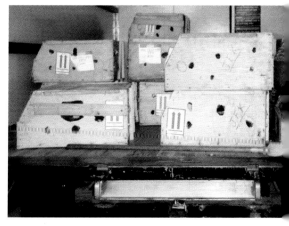

Right. African parrots are shipped from the wild in wooden crates. The International Air Transport Association (IATA) dictates the number of birds that can be packed in one box, and the requirements for food and water, as well as perches. Although seemingly inhumane, mortality rates are very low when IATA rules are followed.
     Photo: Steve Garvin

Three peach-faced lovebirds (*Agapornis roseicollis*). From left to right: Green (normal-natural color), medium green (jade mutation) and dark green (olive mutation).   *Photo: Lee Horton*

Frontal view of the masked lovebird (*A. personata*). This is the normal (naturally occurring) color. This species is also available in several color mutations.
                                    Photo: Lee Horton

Right: Back view of the normally colored masked lovebird (*A. personata*).
                                    Photo: Lee Horton

Below: The Madagascar or grey-headed lovebird (*A. cana*). Male is pictured on the left, and the female is on the right. Notice the strong dimorphism present in this species.   *Photo: Lee Horton*

Left: Blue mutation of the masked lovebird (*A. personata*). This beautiful mutation color is a recessive trait.

Photo: Lee Horton

Right: Fischer's lovebird frontal view (*A. fischeri*). This photo demonstrates the natural color of this species.

Photo: Lee Horton

bove left: A beautiful yellow (dilute) mutation of the Fischer's lovebird (*A. fischeri*).

Photo: Lee Horton

bove center: The Fischer's lovebirds (*A. fischeri*) shown here are lutino mutation eft) and normal green color (right).

Photo: Lee Horton

ight: Although not a colorful mutation, the albino Fischer's lovebird (*A. fischeri*) is ery popular and bred often in captivity.

Photo: Lee Horton

elow: Shown here is a true pair of normally colored Abyssinian or black-winged lovebirds (*A. taranta*). The male is on e left; the female is pictured on the right.

Photo: Lee Horton

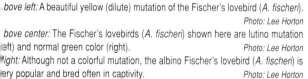

Above: In true pairs of red-faced lovebirds (A. pullaria), the beak and facial area of the female will be slightly ligher in color. Female is on the right.

Photo: Lee Horton

Left: Now quite rare in aviculture here in the United States, the Nyasa lovebird (A. lilianae) is shown here in its natural (normal) color. Photo: Lee Horton

Left: Painting of black-collared lovebird by Lyrae Perry.

Below: Black-cheeked lovebirds (A. nigrigenis) are now available in several color mutations. Pictured here is the normal (natural) color form. Photo: Lee Horton

8 African Rose-ringed Parakeet

8.1 Taxonomy and Distribution

The rose-ringed or ring-necked parakeet is the most widely distributed parrot in the world. (Although they are parrots, they are classified as parakeets because they have long, graduated tails.) The natural range of this species extends from the central and northern African continent, through Afghanistan, India, Nepal, Burma, Pakistan and Sri Lanka. In addition, this species has established feral populations in many other places across the world, including the United Kingdom, the United States, Hong Kong, Singapore, Arabia and South Africa. Some of these feral populations may have been temporary and may no longer exist.

Although rose-ringed parakeets can be found in many different types of habitat, they seem to prefer the edges of Savannah grasslands and areas of woodlands where an adequate supply of trees still exists. The Asian subspecies (*Psittacula krameri manilensis* and *Psittacula k. borealis*) live in the forests but frequent rice paddies and other cultivated areas searching for food. These species, more so than many others, are considered to be agricultural pest species in much of their native habitats.

There are four named subspecies of the rose-ringed parakeet. Of these four subspecies, only two are indigenous to the African continent. There is much debate over the speciation of these two African races as it appears the flocks are interbreeding, resulting in an intermediate form of the

African rose-ringed parakeet. Some people have coined a new form and are calling it "Psittacula krameri centralis," although this name is not scientifically accepted.

Information from persons living in northern Africa seems to suggest that there are feral populations of rose-ringed parakeets breeding in Egypt. These populations are made up of birds from the Asian continent and those of Africa.

In western Africa, extending eastward to Uganda, the nominate race *Psittacula krameri krameri* can be found. This is the smallest of the rose-ringed parakeets and is distinguished from the eastern form by its yellowish to lime green color in the face and underparts. The eastern form, *Psittacula krameri parvirostris*, is a darker green with little yellow in the face and body. The males of both African subspecies develop a pink ring around the neck and a bright blue wash at the back of the nape. Females do not develop this neck ring in any of the four races of this species.

The beaks of both African species are much smaller and have a more dramatic downward curve than the two Indian subspecies. Furthermore, rose-ringed parakeets from Africa have a dark red upper mandible tipped heavily in black, and the lower mandibles are almost entirely black. Indian rose-ringed parakeets have little or no black coloration in the upper mandibles once mature, and their beaks appear to be more orange than red.

8.2 Dimorphism and Physical Notes

In general, rose-ringed parakeets are strongly dimorphic at maturity. Males of all subspecies develop a black "mustache" under the chin (lower mandible) that extends around the side of the lower cheek and forms a broken ring at the back of the head. A line of pink feathers develops below this black ring, from the sides of the cheeks and all the way around the back of the nape. In most species, a blue suffusion is present above this ring, but it is most prominent in the African forms where it can extend forward covering almost half of the facial area behind the eye. A small black line extends from the cere to the eye and is more pronounced in males. Females do not develop the black mustache or pink neck ring of the males. Juveniles resemble females until the first complete molt. In some cases, young males do not develop the full neck ring until the second molt, but they will usually be distinguishable from females by having a few black feathers directly below the lower mandible (beginning the formation of the black mustache).

In captive-bred birds, the process of speciation is often very difficult due to accidental crossbreeding of the subspecies. Most competent aviculturists have managed to keep the African form and the Indian form separate, but the crossbreeding of specimens from continental forms is common due to difficulty in distinguishing between the races.

8.3 International Trade

Although the rose-ringed parakeets are extremely common throughout most of their range, Ghana has listed this species on Appendix III of the Convention on International Trade in Endangered Species (CITES). This was probably done as an effort to keep track of exports originating from that country. No other populations have been listed or are restricted in international trade by CITES. And in many parts of the world, wild-caught birds are still available as pets and breeding stock. Because India no longer allows the mass capture and export of her native birds, many of the Asian forms of this species are being exported from other range countries.

Rose-ringed parakeets appear to be well established in captivity across the world. They are popular caged birds and the need for additional wild-caught bloodlines to supplement captive breeding programs is probably very minimal. The occasional capture of a color mutation that does not exist in captivity does tend to create a demand for wild birds of that color. However, the prolific nature of this bird allows for captive-bred representatives to be available in as little as one year after being taken into captivity. Interestingly, most of the color mutations now kept and bred in captivity are of the two Asian subspecies and not from Africa. To date, there are some twenty-seven or more color variations of the rose-ringed parakeet in aviculture and international trade—many of which were bred from only a few true mutations.

8.4 Avicultural Setups and Husbandry

This species does not require elaborate setups in order to breed freely in captivity. They are strong flyers and should be provided with the largest possible flight cages or areas where they can fly from one perch to another. There is a definite connection between flight space and ability, and subsequent fertility in captive males. It has been noticed that male rose-rings that have less than adequate flight space, or cannot fly at all due to cramped quarters, are poor producers.

Rose-ringed parakeets are a female-aggressive species. This means that the female "rules the roost." She chooses and accepts the nestbox, and she makes the determination as to when the breeding time is right. Females of this species will accept copulation from the male only when breeding is imminent. Additionally, these species rarely establish a lifelong pair bond with each other. They usually pair off just prior to breeding. The male must court the female through elaborate dances and feeding displays before he is accepted as a mate. It is during this time period in captivity, when the male could be killed by an aggressive female. When forming new pairs, it is advisable to watch them closely for any signs of aggression from the hen. The aviculturist may need to house potential mates in cages side by side until they notice a desire to be together. It is not wise to throw two birds together into a cage during the breeding season. Mature females that have spent several years as single birds may never accept a mate. Others may breed and produce fertile eggs in only a few short weeks. The social patterns and behavior of a pair should be observed very closely during their first few days together.

In the United States, and probably in most of the Northern Hemisphere, rose-ringed parakeets begin to breed early in the year, sometimes laying eggs in January. The average clutch size is from three to five eggs, but larger clutches of up to eight are not unheard of. The female tends the nest and does all the incubating. In rare cases, the male is allowed in the nesting box with the female. Incubation does not normally commence until after the second egg is laid, resulting in the first two chicks hatching on the same day. The incubation period is twenty-three days for all forms of this bird.

When chicks are in the nest, the male will feed the female while she remains in the nest box. As well, in some pairs the male will actually assist in the feeding of the young and may spend a lot of time in the box with the female. Breeding pairs should be provided with large amounts of fresh foods such as corn, fruits and fresh legumes. The chicks grow very fast and will fledge from the nest in as little as five or six weeks. They will need to spend a few extra weeks with the parent birds to learn how to eat on their own. It is advisable to remove young birds from the parental cage once they are weaned because fighting is inevitable.

Rose-ringed parakeets can be bred in large colonies. Of course, this type of breeding situation can be problematic as well. In a colony situation, a very large cage will be needed and numerous nesting sites must be provided.

There will still be a certain amount of fighting that takes place, and production is often reduced in the colony versus cage breeding method. As young birds fledge in a colony situation, it is not unusual to see adult males copulating with a newly fledged female, even before she can sit correctly on a perch. Considering this behavior, as would be expected, there is a high incidence of inbreeding within small family groups in the wild and in colony breeding setups.

Both African and Indian parakeets can reproduce successfully at one year. Young males are often fertile even before they develop their neck rings. Females, although physically capable of laying eggs at one year of age, often do not reproduce successfully until their second season.

8.5 Diets in Captivity

As omnivores, like many of the parrot species, rose-ringed parakeets do well if offered a varied diet. Most of them will relish fresh corn on the cob and other fresh fruits and vegetables, but they cannot subsist on fresh foods alone. It is recommended a mixed seed diet and/or a manufactured pelleted parrot diet be offered in addition to fresh fruits and vegetables. Spray millet is also a favorite, particularly of young birds that are weaning and learning to eat on their own.

During the breeding season, it is very important to offer a wide variety of foods to potential parent birds. Without the proper nutrition, females may become egg bound, which means the egg gets stuck in the uterus, or suffer other reproductive diseases caused by vitamin and mineral deficiencies. Legumes, corn and pelleted foods are recommended in addition to the normal parrot fare of mixed seeds. Additional calcium supplementation can be helpful during egg laying, but should not become part of the normal daily diet in the nonbreeding season.

Feeding meat products is not recommended. This is not because these birds will not enjoy them, rather it is due to high risk of contamination and spoilage in these high-protein foods. If served as a treat, meat should be cooked thoroughly. Cooked chicken wings and legs are commonly fed to parrots as a protein supplement. The uneaten portions of such a treat should be removed from the cage within a few hours to avoid bacterial or fungal health problems.

8.6 Hand-rearing Rose-ringed Parakeets (Breeder's Note)

Newly hatched parakeets are very small (4–7 gm) and require frequent feedings and warm brooder temperatures if they are to survive. Baby birds that have not been fed by the parents will require very thin formula, the consistency of milk, for the first seven days in the nursery. For some reason, this species does not do well if formula consistency is too thick during initial hand-feeding. After a week or so, the formula can be thickened to the consistency of applesauce. At any time during hand-feeding if the crop slows or does not empty, it may be helpful to begin feeding very thin formula once again to get the bird's digestive system operating properly. If this does not help, a bacterial culture should be taken by an avian vet immediately and a treatment of antibiotics may be in order.

If a pet quality bird is desired, baby rose-rings will need to be kept in separate containers after about three weeks of age. When raised in clutches or small groups, even baby birds begin to bond with each other and will not remain tame beyond the weaning stage of development. In fact, some get so cranky they refuse to be fed and will fly from the keeper to avoid any human contact. This behavior is not uncommon in smaller parakeets from the Old World.

8.7 Personality Traits and Pet Qualities

One of the most endearing qualities of the rose-ringed parakeet is its ability to mimic. This trait appears to be more prevalent in males that are kept as single pets, but female rose-ringed parakeets have also been known to talk. Wild-caught birds are very difficult to tame. If a pet bird is desired, a hand-fed, newly weaned baby bird should be acquired.

Parakeets should be provided with adequate flight time and space to keep them in top condition. They should be able to fly around freely a few times a day. As well, some birds love to bathe and should be given a large bowl of water or something similar in which to play.

One pet rose-ringed that really sticks out in my mind is Gumby, owned by Debbie Bolander of Pennsylvania. Gumby not only talks and answers questions but also plays tic-tac-toe on a child's plastic playing board. When frustrated, Gumby often clears the board by throwing the playing pieces aside and quitting the game for the day. This bird, although an exceptional representative of the species, is not the only one out there. Recently, while visiting friends, I came across two other pets that were exceptional talkers and had learned tricks, no doubt in an effort to win the attention they wanted or to secure a treat for their antics.

Once tamed and settled into their surroundings, this species exhibits an outgoing personality and a willingness to mimic and learn simple tricks. Keeping with the true nature of parakeets, they will often be a bit boisterous when they want attention or when they are not happy. Strangely enough, very few representatives of this species kept as single pet birds have exhibited neurotic behavior such as self-mutilation or plucking. All in all, the rose-ringed parakeet can make an excellent companion bird but it is suggested that only single birds be kept in one house-hold. If numerous pets are within visible and audible range of each other, they will often bond with each other and will no longer be the best of pets or companions.

9 The Lovebirds

Note: To date, there are many volumes of text available on the subjects of keeping and breeding lovebirds and their mutations.
Lovebirds have become a specialty interest over the past few
decades, and books on their aviculture and mutation breeding
can be quite voluminous. Therefore, for the purposes of this
book, this chapter dealing with the family known as lovebirds is
offered as a very general text. It is not intended to be a complete
guide to the keeping of the genus *Agapornis*.

9.1 Notes on the Genus *Agapornis*

The family of small parrots known as the lovebirds is widely distributed throughout central Africa. Only the species
known as the peach-faced lovebird ranges into southern
Africa, and can be found in the extreme western coastal
area.

With only a few exceptions, lovebirds are common
throughout their range. A total of nine species and nine
subspecies are recognized. For husbandry and taxonomic
reasons, lovebirds are usually categorized into two
groups—those with naked eye-rings (naked skin around
the eye) and those without (feathered around the eye). It is
noteworthy that lovebirds without eye-rings also exhibit
some obvious sexual dimorphisms, and have different nesting habits than those of the naked eye-ring group.

In his book *Parrots of the World*, Joseph Forshaw states
that the lovebirds have been so-named "due to their con-
spicuous indulgence in mutual preening." Contrary to
their implied name, lovebirds can be some of the most
vicious of all caged birds—to each other, that is.
Incompatible pairs or mates have been known to kill or
mutilate one another in the caged environment.

9.2 Taxonomy and Species Identification

As mentioned earlier, members of the genus *Agapornis* are often categorized into two groups—the naked eye-ring species and those with feathered eye-rings. Although categorized differently, some members of the naked eye-ring group have habits of nest building similar to those of the noneye-ring group. Most of the members of the genus with prominent naked eye-rings are not dimorphic and only one or two in this group mimic the nest-building habits of the species without eye-rings. All lovebird species build nests, and egg incubation takes approximately twenty-three days for most species. Reports of shorter incubation on the smaller species, such as the Nyasa lovebird, have been recorded in captivity. The eye-ring group uses down and soft grasses to build nests. They prefer a nesting box in which they build elaborate nests, often filling the entire box with nesting material. On the other hand, the noneye-ring group will most often build only a bottom, opentype (cup) nest within the box before laying commences.

9.2.1 Peach-faced lovebird (*Agapornis roseicollis*)

The species *roseicollis* is probably the most common of all lovebirds now kept in captivity. Two subspecies are recognized, but the second, *Agapornis roseicollis catumbella*, is only found in a restricted area of the range in Southern Angola. The differences in these species is very subtle, *catumbella* being a brighter colored bird with more red suffused into the chest and neck areas.

Hobbyists and enthusiasts have successfully bred peach-faced lovebirds to many generations in captivity and have established numerous color mutations with this species. In the wild, the peach-faced lovebird is found in southwestern Africa, from coastal regions inward. They are still plentiful throughout their range where they usually gather in small flocks, rather than pairs. Peach-faced lovebirds do not have a naked eye-ring.

In normally colored birds, the plumage is generally green with the forehead a light red, extending back behind the eyes. The upper chest is pink extending up to, and including, the throat and cheeks. The rump area is bright blue and the beak is horn colored.

Peach-faced lovebirds are not difficult to breed in captivity. However, due to their willingness to breed in the caged environment, care should be taken to find strong, genetically diverse breeding stocks for captive breeding. Weak or inbred birds will generally not be the most prolific and often hatch-related problems will occur in the nest box.

Breeders have established several color mutations of this species. To date there may be more than thirty colors of peach-faced lovebirds. Color mutations are not hybrids, but instead are pure stock. The different colors are a function of sex-linked, dominant and recessive genes that cause a change in the bird's natural color. Breeding a combination of colors produces even more different color varieties and mutations. Strangely enough, many color mutations have been established from wild-caught stocks. Additionally, color mutations are found in the wild, but this occurrence is rare, probably due to the limited chances of two birds carrying recessive color mutation traits breeding with one another. In captivity and through selective breeding, it only takes one or two generations to get back to the natural "wild" color of the species. It may take a few more generations to get any nonvisual or recessive trait out of the lineage altogether. This is accomplished by breeding colored birds to normal birds for several generations, choosing the normally colored offspring, and breeding them to normally colored mates—in other words, selectively breeding for the natural color instead of the mutation color.

9.2.2 Grey-headed lovebird (*Agapornis cana*)

Sometimes called the Madagascar lovebird, the little grey-headed lovebird is one of the smallest members of the lovebird family. In its natural state, it is only found on the island of Madagascar, but has been introduced on several other islands off the coast of the African continent.

This species is strongly dimorphic and does not have an eye-ring. Males are green and have a light grey head and neck. This grey can extend into the upper chest as well. Females are essentially all green. The beak and feet of both sexes are grey. In both males and females, the underparts are paler than the back and wings, giving the birds a two-toned look. Young birds resemble the adults but may not be as bright in color. The eyes of young birds are not quite as defined and may appear as totally black or dark brown. Once mature, the brown iris of the eye is recognizable.

There are two subspecies of the Madagascar lovebird. The nominate form, *Agapornis cana cana*, is described above. Another subspecies, *Agapornis cana ablectanea*, is noted as having an overall darker plumage with a violet wash to the grey head and chest. These two species do cross habitats in the wild, and surely there are intermediate forms of the grey-headed lovebird on the island of Madagascar.

The grey-headed lovebird is still quite common throughout its natural range. Many birds have been captured for the pet trade and now exist in aviaries across the world. It seemed to take a long time to establish this species in captivity, but this may have been due to sources for birds and the availability of wild stocks during the years of import. Lovebird specialists across the United States and Europe have done well with the grey-headed lovebird.

9.2.3 Black-collared lovebird (*Agapornis swinderniana*)

Originating in western and central Africa, black-collared lovebirds are unknown in captivity and are not considered to be common in the wild. The species *swinderniana* is divided into two additional subspecies, *zenkeri* and *emini*. A slight color differentiation (a red-brown suffusion into the neck and breast) below the collar is used to delineate these species. As well, all three populations are isolated from each other in the wild and probably do not interbreed. The three species are approximately the same size, with an average length of only 13 cm.

Very little is known of this species in its native habitat. Observers of the species claim that it feeds mainly on figs, but has been known to raid cultivated crops of corn and millet. It is speculated that specimens previously taken into captivity have died because of the specialized diet they may require. Field studies of this species are desperately needed as is a feasibility study to assess whether an in situ captive population should be established for observation. To date, there are no records of its nesting habits and we have no egg laying data or hatchling statistics. The pictures in this book were taken of reserved skins collected for museum study.

9.2.4 Red-faced lovebird (*Agapornis pullaria*)

Agapornis pullaria is found in western Uganda, westward through the Ivory Coast and into Guinea and Sierra Leone. It is mainly a bird of the lowland areas, frequenting secondary forests and savanna woodlands (Forshaw). There are indications that the red-faced lovebird is not as common as it once was. Of course, this can be said of most species as humankind continues its encroachment into the natural habitats of most wildlife.

Two subspecies are recognized, but the difference in these two birds is so subtle that one would have to have both species in order to recognize the differences. The nominate form, *Agapornis p. pullaria*, is mainly green with lighter underparts. The forehead is red orange, rump is blue and beak is red, fading to a lighter orange-yellow on the tip. The underwing coverts are black, iris is brown in mature birds and legs are grey. The subspecies *Agapornis pullaria ugandae* is almost identical, with the exception that the blue on the rump is not as bright, and the birds may actually be slightly larger.

In the wild, these lovebirds feed on small seeds, figs, fruits and berries, and have been known to visit cultivated fields of corn or other grain products. Their nesting habits in the wild are also notable. Red-faced lovebirds excavate deep holes (tubes) into the uppermost parts of arboreal termite mounds. Forshaw states that terrestrial mounds are very rarely used for nesting by this species.

The following is a synopsis of some of the observations taken from my personal notebook. During the days of legal importation, I noted that small groups of red-faced lovebirds had been imported and survived to be released from the United States quarantine system. These birds were kept in small holding cages awaiting sale, and there was much fighting and aggression among the birds when housed in such cramped quarters. The fighting was often quite severe and ended in the death of one or more birds on numerous occasions. When tree branches containing numerous green leaves were added to the cages, the fighting seemed to subside, probably due to the fact that the birds now had a place to hide from each other. It was also noted that these birds "hung upside down from the top of the cage at night, and huddled in the corners during most of the daylight hours."

There is a strong dimorphism in this species whereas the males have a "deep red" face, while females are "more pastel colored" in the same area. Also the beak of the males is a deeper orange-red than the females.

The red-faced lovebird is a difficult species to accommodate and breed in captivity. Some breeders have had success breeding wild-caught specimens, but pairing and compatibility seem to play a vital role in this success. It would appear that breeding successes may increase if a larger captive population of birds was available from which to choose.

Because of their nesting habits in the wild (using termite mounds as nest sites), accommodating wild-caught birds in captivity is not easy. The typical wooden lovebird nest box has been offered to many pairs, but only a few have accepted this compromise and have settled in to nest. Perhaps some ingenuity in the design of a nesting box for stubborn captive pairs is in order. Although neither author now keeps this species, we suggest that a nest be designed and built from cement, mimicking the size and shape of a termite mound. Since this species excavates their own nest in the wild, a softer material of plaster of Paris and dried grass could be used to partially "plug" the entrance hole so the birds can dig it out themselves. Additionally, termite mounds are several degrees warmer on the inside than most hollow tree nests. Therefore, perhaps the use of a heating pad or some other source of low heat could be attached to the outside of the cement mound, thereby simulating the warm interior of a natural nest.

9.2.5 Black-winged (Abyssinian) lovebird (*Agapornis taranta*)

The black-winged or, most often called, Abyssinian lovebird strongly resembles the red-faced lovebird. Black-winged lovebirds are slightly larger and a bit less colorful than the red-faced. Male black-winged lovebirds are green with a red forecrown and bright red beak; females lack red on the head altogether. The flight feathers and underwing coverts are black (in mature males) and the tail is green with a black horizontal stripe; it lacks the red striping found in the tail of the red-faced lovebird. The most obvious differentiation would be the black primary feathers, giving this species its common name of "the black-winged lovebird."

Black-winged lovebirds are found in the wild only in Ethiopia. Traditionally, exports from this country have been few and far between. As a result, most of Ethiopia's native birds are not common in captivity outside the country of origin. This is true of the black-winged lovebird as well. In the United States, only a very limited number of breeders have ever seen this species, and even fewer keep it in the aviary. There are a few dedicated lovebird enthusiasts that have been successful with this species, and some offspring are being produced, at least in the United States and Europe. If this bird is to survive in aviculture, there must be some type of official program established and a studbook developed to assist breeders in locating unrelated stocks.

9.2.6 Fischer's lovebird (*Agapornis fischeri*)

The Fischer's lovebird is a beautiful bird. The wings and back of the bird are generally green, but the head is a soft shade of orange that fades into the yellow/green of the upper chest area. The beak is red, nares white and there is a prominent white eye-ring around the dark brown eye. There are several color mutations of this species now established in aviculture around the world.

Fischer's lovebird is found in central and northern Tanzania. Flocks may have been introduced, and are now common, in the coastal regions of Tanzania, as well as that of Kenya and Nairobi. Forshaw calls this species "a widespread resident of the inland plateau." Descriptions of the flocking nature of this species seem to indicate that it has reached potential crop pest proportions where flocks of thousands destroy crops and agriculture in some areas of is natural range.

In captivity, the Fischer's lovebird has always been common. This species is known to be easily accommodated and bred in the captive environment. The Fischer's lovebird freely hybridizes with the masked lovebird (*Agapornis personata*), both in the wild and in captivity. Care should be taken to ensure breeding stocks are not tainted with hybrid genetics.

9.2.7 Masked lovebird (*Agapornis personata*)

The masked lovebird is often confused as being a color mutation of the Fischer's lovebird. Only slightly larger than Fischer's, masked lovebirds have green wings, a dark brownish colored head and neck, yellow upper chest and yellow/green lower abdomen. As in Fischer's, this species has a very prominent white eye-ring and a red beak. Some very beautiful color mutations have been established in this species. The blue masked lovebird is a blue and white version of the normal bird, and once demanded very high prices from collectors. Today, virtually all color mutations of this species are common in captivity.

In the wild, masked lovebirds are found in Tanzania, virtually side by side with the Fischer's lovebird. As mentioned earlier, hybrids are found wherever Fischer's and masked lovebirds live in close proximity. It is the author's opinion that these two species may very well have evolved from similar genetic backgrounds, and are actually color forms of the same bird. Because they breed true, both species should be maintained separately and bloodlines should be kept pure.

9.2.8 Black-cheeked lovebird (*Agapornis nigrigenis*)

Black-cheeked lovebirds are often confused with masked lovebirds. The general plumage is green, with the lower abdominal area being a much lighter yellow/green. The head is brown, cheeks brownish black, beak red and upper breast a pale shade of orange-red.

Like the Fischer's and masked lovebirds, black-cheeked lovebirds have a prominent white eye-ring. The resemblance among these three lovebird species is very strong, and hybrid forms are virtually indistinguishable from each other. It is notable that hybrids between black-cheeked lovebirds and either Fischer's or masked lovebirds result in a bird with a blue rump area. Since the black-cheeked lovebird does not have any blue on the rump in its natural color scheme, crosses can be easily separated from pure birds.

The natural habitat of the black-cheeked lovebird is the smallest of any other lovebird species. Their range is restricted to southwestern Zambia, but specimens have been sighted as far north as northwestern Zimbabwe. This species was not discovered until the early 1900s, and exports for the pet and breeder trade have resulted in a noticeable decrease in wild populations. It is now one of the rarest lovebirds in the wild.

In captivity, the black-cheeked lovebird is not very common except in certain parts of Europe. It is established in the caged bird trade in the United States and other countries, but remains a rarity in England, Germany, and several other leading avicultural countries.

9.2.9 Nyasa lovebird (*Agapornis lilianae*)

The Nyasa lovebird has been described by those who keep it as a "tiny version of the Fischer's lovebird." Adult weights of this species are only about 30–35 grams, as opposed to 40–50 grams, or even more, for the Fischer's lovebird. The general plumage is green, with the head and facial area being orange-red. As in most of the green lovebirds, the underparts are yellow/green and the beak is red. Once again, this species has a very prominent white eyering.

In the wild, Nyasa lovebirds range from southern Tanzania, into northwestern Mozambique and southern Malawi. They can also be found in Zambia and northern Zimbabwe according to Forshaw.

Although it is not considered rare in the wild, the Nyasa lovebird is not well established in captivity in the United States. In fact, this species remains rare in aviculture all over the world. Small consignments of Nyasa lovebirds were imported into the United States in the 1970s and 1980s, but for some reason this species remains uncommon

in the caged bird trade. A lutino or red-eyed yellow mutation was bred from some of this original stock, but has not
been established and only a few still remain. A few more
consignments arrived in the U.S. in the late 1980s, and
have proven a bit more dependable as breeding stock.

9.3 Nutritional Notes and General Diet Tips

Lovebirds are not known to be finicky eaters. Although
they may prefer a diet rich in seeds, they will eat berries,
fruits, vegetables and some greens. In the wild, lovebirds of
several species are known to raid ripening grain fields and
the occasional cornfield.

Today's captive diet should consist of small seeds such
as millet, safflower or sunflower seed, and a combination of
a commercial pelleted diet, fresh fruits and vegetables, and
green foods when they are accepted.

When young are present in the nest box, large amounts
of corn and greens may be consumed. Additionally, spray
millet is favored when chicks are being fed and should be
provided daily. It is important to provide an adequate
amount of all kinds of foods during breeding times and
when chicks are hatched. Lovebirds can be very tempera-
mental and may destroy eggs or chicks if they cannot find
enough food to keep them well fed.

9.4 Husbandry and Breeding Setups

Captive breeders of lovebirds seem to prefer small cages.
Perhaps this has come about only to facilitate the breeder
or a lack of space and not necessarily the birds themselves.
Studies have shown that there is a connection between
flight space and fertility in male birds of many species.
Those given plenty of room to fly, often produced more offspring when housed with healthy, mature females. As a
minimum, cages should measure two feet wide by three
feet long to accommodate flight space and provide a

healthy atmosphere for breeding. Keep in mind that these dimensions are given only as a reference; breeders should provide larger cages whenever possible. Captive birds should never be crowded into small cages.

Lovebirds are cavity nesters. In other words, they build their nests in the hollows of trees or in the case of captive breeding they build nests inside nest boxes provided by the keeper. The standard nest box should measure approximately nine inches square and a one-and-a-half-inch entrance hole should be made to allow access inside the box. An internal wire ladder or some other means of climbing down into the box is desirable to keep the birds from jumping down onto the incubating eggs.

In general, the lovebirds included in the eye-ring group will build elaborate dome-shaped nests within the provided nest box. Noneye-ring species will usually line the bottom of the box with nesting materials, but will not stuff the box in the same way as the eye-ring group does. In any case, all lovebirds enjoy building nests and should be provided with dried grasses, green grasses and other soft nesting materials with which to construct their nest. Some species may even use the seed hulls from millet, oats, wheat and other grains to line the bottom of the box. Most breeders prefer to add a layer of clean, dry, pine shavings to the nest box when first provided. A concave bottom can be used to help keep teh eggs in one area when dealing with species that do not build elaborate nests.

Courtship in lovebirds can be described as "a time of increased activity and vocalization." When the breeding time has arrived, males become more vocal, and both the male and female begin to move about searching for nesting materials. Courtship feeding will increase as well, and copulation may take place several times a day before the eggs are laid.

Most lovebird species now lay fairly large clutches in captivity. Some clutches of seven or eight eggs have been reported, with six being the average. They are generally good parent birds, and if the clutch of chicks is removed, often it will be replaced by another clutch within a few weeks. Incubation lasts about twenty-two to twenty-three days and commences with the laying of the second egg in the clutch.

One of the most common problems with breeding pairs of lovebirds is the plucking of the young in the nest. It is believed this takes place because the female is trying to line the bottom of the nest and keep the babies dry. It is recommended that nesting materials be available even after babies hatch, so the parent birds can repair the nest as needed. Most young, even when heavily plucked, will grow their feathers back a few weeks after leaving the nest box.

Some breeders prefer to colony breed lovebirds. Some species do not do well in colonies and should not be housed in groups. It is suggested that only eye-ring lovebirds and peach-faced lovebirds do well in colonies. If a colony is the goal, the cage used to house the birds must be adequate or fighting will undoubtedly occur. If possible, small trees or shrubs should be placed in the colony cage to provide cover for the more meek specimens. All nest boxes should be placed at the same height within the breeding colony. If boxes are at different heights, a dominant pair will evolve and will defend the right to nest in the highest point within the cage. It is recommended that all babies in the colony be leg banded to help keep track of their genetics. Babies can be banded at the age of eighteen days, and may be too big to band after the age of twenty-five days.

9.5 The Mutation Colors

There are now many color varieties and mutations available in most lovebird species. A mutation is not a difference in species or hybrid, but instead it is a genetic color variation of the same species. In other words, a lutino mutation peach-faced lovebird is still a peach-faced lovebird, but it has a genetic inability to produce the color blue, and therefore appears to be yellow, white and pink. Since the body color of most lovebirds is green, and green is made up of yellow and blue, a mutation is simply the inability to produce one or the other color in the plumage. Yellow and blue are the two main mutations that occur in most species. Other factors such as cinnamon can also change the color of the feathers produced, lightening them considerably. Cinnamon , a mutation color, results from a partial inability to produce blue, black or brown colors in the feathers.

Color mutation breeding in lovebirds and other parrots is a fascinating subject that demands much more detail than would be presented in this text. Many of the mutations are beautiful, and with each new color comes new show standards and a renewed interest in avicultural breeding. There are several good books on this subject, one of which actually teaches you how to predict mutation colors in your birds. This text was written by Fred and Lyrae Perry of California, and is titled *Punnet Square Basics*. Although this text was written for ring-necked parakeets, the way in which it teaches the inheritance modes and color results makes this book a necessity for any mutation breeder.

Since most breeders that keep lovebirds will enjoy breeding the different color versions of these birds, a knowledge of the inheritance modes of each mutation may be beneficial. When dealing with the rarer species, it is always wise to keep some "naturally colored" birds available for future hobbyists to work with. For more information about lovebirds contact the African Lovebird Society.

10 The Vasa and Black Parrots of Africa

10.1 General Notes and Taxonomy

The Vasa and black parrots, within the genus *Coracopsis*, are very strange and exhibit behaviors unlike any other parrots. The Vasa parrot is categorized into three subspecies, and the little black parrot is divided into four subspecific forms. Breeders and pet owners across the world often use the terms greater Vasa parrot and lesser Vasa parrot to identify these two species. But, in actuality, the smaller or lesser Vasa parrot is officially called the black parrot and is not subspecific to the Vasa parrot.

Vasa parrots and black parrots are two of the most unusual Psittacine species found in captivity. In some ways they resemble crows or pigeons, while in others, they are true to form for parrots. As well, they have strange habits, physical characteristics and the shortest incubation periods of any of the other large parrots of the world.

The nominate form of the Vasa parrot, *Coracopsis vasa vasa*, is from the eastern and central regions of Madagascar—a place that many scientists claim has escaped evolution or has evolved on a schedule of its own. This subspecies is the largest of the three forms and measures an average of twenty inches in length, from head to tip of the long tail. *Vasa vasa* and *Coracopsis vasa drouhardi*, also from Madagascar, are probably the two forms most often found in aviculture. The only difference between the two is that *drouhardi* is slightly shorter and has lighter plumage on the underside; some birds may even have light grey to white feathers near the vent area. It should be noted that the ranges of these two subspecies do cross in the wild and imported birds could be of either form.

The third subspecies, *Coracopsis vasa comorensis*, is only found in the Comoro Islands. Taxonomists describe this subspecies as having brown feathers in the undertail coverts. This would definitely set this species apart from its other two subspecific cousins, and make identification of this form rather obvious. There does not appear to be any comorensis in captivity in the United States.

Black parrots inhabit much of the same areas of Africa as do the Vasa parrots. Two forms, *Coracopsis nigra nigra* and *Coracopsis nigra libs*, are found on the island of Madagascar. Of the two remaining subspecies, *Coracopsis nigra sibilans* is found in the Comoro Islands, and *Coracopsis nigra barklyi* is from Praslin Island in the Seychelles. *Barklyi*, the subspecies from the Seychelles, is now listed as endangered despite the fact that it is probably not distinct from *sibilans*, found in the Comoro Islands. If history were known, we would probably find that *sibilans* was introduced to the Seychelles and has been classified as a separate subspecies simply due to regional variations that occurred because of food supply availability.

Vasa and black parrots are both fairly common throughout their native habitats. Of course, given the numbers of these parrots in trade during the decade of the 1980s, and the fact that they are island species, certainly populations have declined dramatically in recent years. Black parrots were never as common in international trade as were the Vasa parrots. Today, there are very few pairs of the little black parrot that remain in American aviculture; however, both of the larger forms of Vasa parrots from Madagascar are maintained and breeders are working to establish them in captivity.

10.2 Vasa Parrots—Prehistoric Birds of Africa

The Vasa parrot is a long-tailed, dark grey parrot, totally different from other parrots. It does, however, resemble the closely related little black parrots. Vasa parrots can have varying degrees of brown feathers, and some even have whitish feathers in the vent area. But, for the most part, they are dark grey in color. During the nonbreeding season, the beak is also dark grey, but will turn to horn color when the bird comes into breeding condition. Iris is brown and the legs and feet are flesh colored.

In the United States and Europe, most of the Vasa parrots are of the nominate race, *Coracopsis vasa vasa*. This is probably due to availability from the wild and the preference of the trappers in the area. A few representatives in captivity may be of the subspecies *Coracopsis vasa drouhardi*, and hopefully aviculturists are aware of the differences in these subspecies and are trying to keep the bloodlines pure. Both of these birds are very similar, making identification difficult to determine. In some cases, this could explain the size difference between some males and females of captive pairs. Breeders should take the time and initiative to determine that they have two birds of the same subspecies before attempting to breed them.

10.3 Avicultural Notes and Breeding of the Vasa Parrot

Captive Vasa parrots should be kept in large cages that are at least two or three meters long. In the wild, these birds fly high and strong, and they should be afforded flight cages in the captive environment to keep them in top breeding and physical condition. Privacy seems to be another issue that needs to be addressed when keeping this species in captivity. Vasa parrots can be shy and often prefer being isolated from other parrots or human intervention. Captive-bred birds may act differently, but those breeders who are working with wild-caught stocks should be aware that privacy may mean the difference between success and failure when attempting to breed this species.

In captivity, the Vasa parrot does not appear to be a fussy eater. They will accept seeds, fruits, vegetables, legumes and even a pelleted diet. Since this species does not sport a colorful plumage, vitamin deficiencies and other signs of malnutrition may not be apparent in the feathers. Anytime a Vasa parrot develops large amounts of white, odd or nonuniform black feathers, some type of nutritional supplementation may need to be incorporated into the diet. The strange loss of feathers during breeding will compound any dietary deficiency that develops from inadequate rations.

Of all the Psittacines now kept in captivity, the Vasa and little black parrot are the only two species known to lose their head feathers when they come into breeding condition. These birds actually go bald, and the skin on the top of the head then turns bright yellow. As well, the color seems to drain from the beak and it turns from grey to a light horn color. These are absolute signs that birds are in breeding condition, even if they are not setup with a mate at the time.

Another strange phenomenon occurs in the male Vasa or black parrot during the breeding season. Males develop an elongated prolapse of the vent, resembling, in some ways, a penis. Strangely enough, this prolapse is only present when males are in breeding condition. Stranger still, females that are maintained without a male present may come into breeding condition and will exhibit this prolapse as well. In females, the prolapse is not as pronounced or obvious as in the male birds. In more than one case study, two females kept together have both come into breeding condition and have developed this slight prolapse. One of the females then assumed the role of the male and mounted the other female as if trying to mate with her. To date, no fertile eggs have been produced from these female-female pairs, but it does make one wonder about this practice as a technique to survival.

Vasa parrots have been bred in many different types of nesting boxes. Most breeders use the grandfather clock box, but boot boxes and L-shaped nests have also been used successfully. Breeding season for these birds varies in the captive environment. Some pairs attempt to nest in the late fall, while others breed in the spring or summer of the year.

The average clutch size for the Vasa parrot is two or three eggs. Incubation commences with the laying of the first egg. Vasa eggs hatch in eighteen days. With the exception of the budgerigar, this is the shortest incubation time of any other Psittacine.

There does not seem to be any special requirements for rearing of the young. Captive breeders have used their homemade formulas of human baby's foods and primate chows as well as commercially prepared hand-rearing formulas to raise Vasa parrots. The chicks grow fast and are usually weaning by the age of eight to ten weeks.

10.4 Black Parrots

Black parrots appear to be nothing more than miniature versions of their larger cousins, the Vasa parrots. This is probably why most aviculturists refer to this species as the lesser Vasa parrot. Adult black parrots average about fourteen inches in length and are generally petite birds.

Like the Vasa, the only subspecies that are represented in aviculture in the United States are the two forms found on the island of Madagascar. A lack of interest in this species has led to its sudden rarity among captive breeders. Probably due to its rather dull plumage, breeders more or less ignored the little black parrot during the days of importation, and now few pairs exist in the captive environment in the United States and probably Europe as well. This lack of interest may be compounded by the fact that the subspecies originating from the Seychelles is now controlled in the U.S. as an endangered species, and permits are required for commercial transactions across any state lines. Breeders are very wary of this new requirement due to the difficulty in identifying the different subspecies of the black parrot. The misidentification of the more common black parrot by an official of the government could result in a federal criminal charge.

Although not particularly difficult to breed, the gene pool of available birds in the U.S. is very limited. Compatible pairs have demonstrated a willingness to breed in captivity, and several breeders have been successful in rearing black parrots. Captive-bred birds are shy but are not as nervous as wild-caught birds of the same species. The keeping of this species as a pet is not recommended, due mainly to its rarity and the need to establish this bird in captivity. As companion birds, both the Vasa and the black parrot are very limited in their ability to mimic human voice. Their natural calls consist of whistling sounds and purrs, which may contribute to their inability to talk.

11 Basic Husbandry & Breeding Tips

11.1 African Parrots in the Nest Box—What Can You Expect?

When dealing with any of the *Poicephalus* parrots or greys, and after pairs have settled into their new environment, there are a few things the breeder should keep in mind if breeding does occur.

For the most part, grey parrots and many of the members of the *Poicephalus* genus are attentive parents. They are known for keeping chicks well fed and warm during their brooding period. In areas where the temperature drops suddenly, most African parrots can be trusted to keep eggs or chicks well brooded even during a spell of sub-freezing weather. If chicks are large (ten days old or older), they may not fit tightly under the parent birds and should be pulled for hand-rearing during these unexpected cold spells. Larger clutches of eggs or a combination of large babies and a few unhatched eggs may also present a problem. Experienced parent birds with a proven track record should be fine and will usually succeed in keeping the nest warm.

As chicks mature and sprout their own down, they are capable of handling cooler temperatures and can often stay with the parents for short periods of inclimate weather. These older chicks have also learned not to make too much noise if someone approaches the nest box. They huddle close to their parents and wait for danger to depart. It is wise to speak softly or make some sort of soft noise before you check a nest box containing eggs or chicks. This gives the parent birds a warning that you are coming and they may be less apt to toss eggs or chicks across the box in their panic to escape the box. During the breeding season, nest boxes should be checked often. Of course, caution is in order—you must know the birds and how they will react. If parent birds are nervous, you may not want to bother them as often, and a schedule of nest box checks can be made once a week. Some pairs will attack anything in the box in displaced aggression when a human intervenes with the nesting process. This is usually noticed with some of the *Poicephalus* parrots, and not generally the African grey parrots.

When nesting occurs, it often appears that some African parrot parents never leave the box to eat. This may cause the breeder to panic, often thinking that chicks will not be fed properly. However, in most cases this is not true, as many hens will sneak out when no one is looking to eat, drink and defecate. The opposite can often be true; there are other pairs that seem to never be in the box tending to the chicks. As the breeding pairs become more and more adjusted to their environment, they will spend more time out of the box. By the time they have raised four or five clutches, they should be experts and will know exactly how much time they must spend tending to the clutch.

Since many of the birds now raised in captivity are destined for pet homes, it may become necessary to pull them for hand-rearing. If this is the plan, it is best if chicks are pulled at about twenty-one days of age so they can be leg banded and hand-reared. At this age, their eyes are wide open and they are aware of what is going on. If parent birds are very attentive, chicks can be left with them for several more weeks and they can be pulled just before they fledge the box. Pulling the chicks of this age may make hand-feeding difficult for the first day or two, but they often adjust to their new human parents in short order and grow up to be as healthy and adjusted as chicks pulled at a younger age. A note of caution is in order here. Nervous, crazy parent birds will often produce nervous chicks if they remain with the parents for more than a few days. There will be a marked difference in the temperament, hand-fed chicks being more calm and less nervous in chicks pulled at five days of age, and those left with the parents until after their eyes are open.

11.2 Pulling Eggs or Chicks from the Nest

Taking chicks from the nest for hand-rearing can be a stressful experience for the keeper as well as the parent birds and chicks. Ideally, the parent birds should not be in the nest with the chicks when it is time to pull babies. This often creates a fiasco of flying shavings, growling and stress for the chicks that are being pulled as well as the parent stock. Always be prepared for a battle at the nest box. Take a flashlight, a small hand towel, a divider of some sort and a container in which to place the chicks.

If parents refuse to leave the box even after gentle tapping and soft persuasion, the chicks will have to be pulled out from under them. This is not the ideal situation; it can lead to nervous, growling chicks if they are old enough to realize what is going on. It is believed that a stressful pull from the nest results in chicks that are nervous and not as sweet as those that did not experience this stress. After removal from the box, inspect the chicks for injuries after they are in the house or nursery. Chicks that seem more frightened than others may have sustained injuries during the confusion in the nest box. A severe injury, such as a fractured leg or wing, will need to be tended to by a qualified avian veterinarian.

If some sort of incubation regime is set up and running, eggs can be pulled and hatched. This situation reduces the stress on young chicks and will often result in the parent birds replacing the lost clutch. Chicks being hand-fed from day one require extra time and effort on the part of the keeper. This is not a practice that is to be taken lightly.

11.3 Problem Pairs and Incompatibility

Nobody wants to hear that a pair of birds is incompatible and will probably never produce viable young. Members of the genus *Poicephalus* are notorious for being picky or incompatible with each other. Seasoned breeders know that, in a stable environment, pairs that consistently trash their eggs or kill or mutilate chicks in the nest will probably never produce young (without some human intervention into the nesting process). Additionally, these pairs are prime candidates for mate annihilation. Eventually one mate or the other will make a kill. This is a sad but true fact about the smaller African parrots, and a fact that must be known and understood by the breeder. The best management technique for an incompatible pair of birds is to break them up and try to find them mates that they both accept and breed with.

Although African grey parrots are not known for killing mates, they can be very fussy about birds with which they will breed. The wise breeder will give a pair a fair amount of time to breed and, if there have been no attempts, will offer other mates until a compatible pair is formed.

11.4 Mate Annihilation—How Can It Be Avoided?

As mentioned above, some pairs simply do not belong together. Some breeders are untroubled about purchasing a male and a female of a certain species, throwing them into a cage together and calling them a pair. Unfortunately, the birds themselves do not always appreciate the choice of mates. When dealing with the *Poicephalus* parrots, this can mean death to one of the pair. A true sign of total compatibility is a pair that will breed, lay eggs, incubate them and hatch and feed the young. As well, compatible pairs often sit together, preen each other and court or copulate on a regular basis. Any pairs that bicker and screech at each other all the time, and trash eggs or chicks may need to be split up and new mates offered to each partner. If bickering occurs in young birds not yet old enough to breed (less than three years of age), a separation of a year or a breeding season may result in a better pair bond when they are reintroduced to each other.

12 Incubation Techniques & Methodology

12.1 Parental Habits—What Can Happen in the Nest Box

In aviculture there are no guarantees, and, unfortunately, no one can predict what will happen in the nest box. The best parent birds in the aviary may suddenly destroy a clutch of eggs for no apparent reason. Poor parental habits have made it necessary for the aviculturist to learn the dynamics of artificial incubation and hand-rearing in order to maximize the survival rate of eggs and chicks.

When someone mentions parental habits, with regard to the African parrots, the first thing that comes to mind is the chewing of a chick's toes or wing tips. For some strange reason African parrots will occasionally chew off the toes or wing tips of a chick in the nest. In many cases they do this as soon as the chicks have hatched. This does not give the aviculturist much time to decide the disposition of the remaining eggs or offspring that may be in the nest at the time. Another interesting note is that if a pair of birds does chew their chicks' toes, they will often do it with every clutch, but not necessarily with every chick. This action results in crippled birds or birds that cannot grip a perch upon fledging. It is highly suggested the eggs be removed from the nest and hatched in the incubator if the breeding pair has exhibited this bad habit. The re-pairing of birds with this habit has been known to help.

Wild-caught African parrots can be very nervous at nesting time. This can result in broken eggs in the nest box. When dealing with pairs that throw most of the nesting material out of the box and leave the eggs on the solid wooden bottom, this problem is magnified. Placing a new layer of nesting material under the eggs may solve the problem with some pairs, but there are always those that will remove the new material each time it is replaced. The best course of action in this case is to provide the parent birds with plenty of privacy if they are to set the clutch and hatch the eggs. If possible, eggs should be removed from these pairs and hatched in the incubator. If this scenario is repeated each time the pair nests, a deeper, and subsequently darker, nest box may solve the problem.

Another problem that sometimes surfaces in the nest box is a calcium deficiency that leaves the chicks crippled or deformed. This is not necessarily due to poor parental habits; rather it is a fairly common nutritional problem that occurs in many African parrots in captivity. Hypocalcemia, as it is called, may also be prevalent in the wild populations, but little field work has been accomplished that would provide us with this answer. In the wild, crippled or deformed chicks would become prey for predators and would not be noticed in the flock.

Many breeders have tried to solve the mystery of these calcium problems by providing a balanced diet to parent birds during the nesting season. In some cases, a boost in good nutrition for the parent birds has resulted in a lowered incidence of the problem in the chicks. In other cases, it does not seem to be a function of the food that is being fed and could possibly be a hereditary problem passed on to chicks from parent birds. With some breeders, the increased incidence of this problem has led to a protocol wherein most African parrot chicks are not allowed to remain with the parents for more than twenty-one days. They are usually pulled for hand-rearing at this stage and this has resulted in a much lower percentage of chicks that develop calcium and skeletal problems. Nutritional study on the African parrots is needed to uncover the mystery of hypocalcemia in these birds. Aviculturists can assist in this project by keeping good records of the young that are raised, the diets fed and any supplementation that resulted in a lower or higher incidence of this disease in the nest box.

12.2 Artificial Incubation for Increased Production

Captive breeders are constantly seeking the best way to increase production without discouraging future breeding attempts. Some believe pulling every clutch of eggs that is laid will cause the breeding pair to stop producing. This has proven not to be true. Birds in the wild are continuously faced with danger and lost eggs or chicks. Over the course of history and through the marvels of evolution, female birds have developed the ability to lay several clutches of eggs in order to complete a successful breeding season and perpetuate the species. Only old or weak hens will be debilitated by this natural cycling and replacement of eggs.

It is now common practice for many breeders to pull the eggs from the parental nest after the clutch is complete. This has not resulted in the parent birds abandoning the nest and refusing to breed again. If a potential situation like this occurs, it may be wise to replace the nest box with a new one or move it to another area of the cage. In the wild, when a nest fails the breeding pair may seek a new nesting site and try again. In captivity, however, it appears that most of the time, breeding pairs are very willing to nest in the same box again and again, despite the failure of that location. Most birds have a strong instinct to nest and reproduce. Caged pairs are no exception to this rule, and usually multiple clutches can be expected from most breeding hens.

Artificial incubation has made it possible to double or triple the number of chicks that can be produced by one pair in any given year. This is accomplished by pulling the eggs as they are laid or pulling the entire clutch of eggs once the hen begins to incubate. If even one egg is allowed to remain in the nest, the hen will begin to incubate and will normally not replace lost eggs (in the present clutch). Increased productivity only occurs if all of the eggs are removed for incubation.

The number of clutches that any given hen will lay in one year varies from bird to bird. This number is partially dependent on the age of the laying hen, as hens in their prime, approximately six to twenty-five years of age, may lay three or four clutches per breeding season. Keep in mind that young hens of only a few years of age and those that are breeding for the first time, may only lay one clutch, even if the eggs are removed.

12.3 A Functional System for Incubation

Choosing an incubator can be a frustrating task. Which one is the best to incubate parrot eggs? Which one provides the highest hatch rate? And the costs—some of them are very expensive while others seem to be too cheap to do the job. The ones that are extremely cheap will usually provide a cheap service as well. In most cases, the actual protocol and incubation regimen is more important than the machine itself.

Hatching parrot eggs successfully requires some knowledge of the egg itself, the process of incubation and the development of the growing embryos. Through candling of the eggs, the aviculturist may be able to make the necessary adjustments to the machines to result in high hatch

117

rates. Any eggs that fail to hatch should be opened and examined to see if there are signs of the cause of failure.

Having spent some ten years opening eggs and exploring the cause of death in parrot embryos, I feel the main cause of death has to do with high humidity. We were all taught to believe that parrots are all tropical in nature and that they exist in an extremely high humidity environment. This is true of some, but even so, they do not nest during the most humid times of the year. In addition, the incubating parent birds have a way of controlling the humidity. This is accomplished through bathing or the purposeful cracking of eggs. Yes, that's right, some parent birds purposely crack eggs in the nest. At first this theory sounds absurd and totally out of line. After watching the incubation habits of pairs that have been subjected to high humidity in the nest and then to humidity of very low levels, there does seem to be some truth to this theory. It is not, however, an invitation for aviculturists to start breaking eggs during incubation.

We may never know all the secrets to incubating eggs. Our only recourse is to continue doing what works and keeping notes on the conditions under which the eggs hatch the best. Keeping in mind that a high humidity environment can destroy incubating embryos, the use of multiple incubators may help to reduce mortality. At the very least, two incubators should be purchased, one to be used as an incubator and one as a hatching unit. This system is suggested because the humidity requirements for incubation are very different from those for hatching eggs.

The use of human infant incubators has become popular with some parrot people. These units make excellent brooders for the chicks, but are not the best machines to use for the incubation of eggs. They are usually equipped with an accurate thermostat and some even have a good air flow system, but the commercially produced egg incubators still do a better job with the eggs with regard to hatchability rates. Relatively inexpensive plastic or Styrofoam incubators work well if a close eye is kept on the variation that may take place in the temperature. This variation is often caused by an increase or decrease in the room temperature where the machine is located. Controlling the room temperature may make the management of a plastic or Styrofoam incubator easier. Humidity is also difficult to control in any machine. The use of a room dehumidifier can be beneficial no matter which incubator is being used. It is much easier to add water, and subsequently humidity, than it is to remove it from the air that circulates through the machines.

The commercial trade in pet parrots has brought about the development of several new models of incubators to choose from. Some of them offer solid state or computer thermostatic controls that are accurate to within one degree of the chosen setting. Some of them have turning units that gently roll the eggs while others use tilt trays or sliding trays to reposition the eggs each hour. The best incubator will be one with dependable temperature control, easy humidity determination and a turning unit that allows some adjustments to be made in order to customize the turning process to the time schedule preferred by the breeder. This type of incubator may be cost prohibitive for the small breeder or hobbyist, but, usually, the increase in productivity helps to offset this one-time setup cost.

Always choose an incubator that has been proven by other breeders. If possible, try to choose the one that allows you to vary the temperature settings and the amount of turns the automatic turner makes in one day. Since many machines come with a preset turning mechanism, ask the manufacturer if they can modify this unit to turn every four hours. If this cannot be done, you may want to turn the eggs by hand for the first few weeks before engaging the automatic turning mechanism or simply choose another machine. No matter which incubator you choose, the amount of attention that is provided to the eggs and hatching chicks will make the difference between a good choice and a bad one. Any incubator that can hold a temperature of 99°F can be used to incubate parrot eggs. Attention to detail, monitoring of the heat and humidity and candling of the eggs are the most important parts of the incubation regimen and proper management.

12.4 Temperature and Humidity

Literally all Psittacine eggs incubate at approximately the same temperature. They do, however, develop at different rates even at this constant setting. This results in each species having its own incubation period or amount of time that it takes the embryo to fully develop and complete the hatch process. To a certain degree, this incubation period may vary between eggs of the same species, but the difference in time is often a function of the heat that has been applied during incubation.

Fertile eggs develop at a rate that is consistent with the temperature at which they are incubated. This means that it is possible, through temperature manipulation, to cause an egg to develop too fast or too slow. Development, other than at the normal rate, causes weakness in the embryos and chicks. Through trial and error aviculturists have established a temperature range that causes embryonic development to take place at approximately the same rate as it would under natural conditions. The proof of this is that the eggs of several different species, incubated at the same time, will hatch on the exact day they would if allowed to remain with the parent birds. The proper temperature setting results in strong, viable chicks that thrive well in the nursery.

Many different temperature settings have been tried on the eggs of many different species. The resulting recommendation for incubation temperature is between

98.5°F and 99.5°F. The lower temperatures are often beneficial when dealing with the eggs of inattentive parents. In other words, if the female frequently leaves the nest to search for food, her eggs seem to respond to a lower setting in the artificial incubation environment. Since most species of parrots either take turns during incubation or the male feeds the female while she continues her incubation duties, the lowest setting is not often used. A majority of bird breeders now set their machines at approximately 99.2°F (37.3°C). This setting can be used for all Psittacine eggs.

In the nest, incubating eggs go through periods of cooling when the parent birds leave the clutch for short periods of time. It has been noticed that these cooling periods become more frequent and increase in time as the eggs near the hatching point. This phenomenon is probably one of the unknown secrets to proper incubation methodology. It is difficult to incorporate this cooling period into the artificial system because we have all been taught to believe that the eggs must be kept warm at all times or they will not hatch. After many years of observation, this rumor has been disproved, and there is no need to panic if eggs become slightly chilled during the later stages of development. In fact, it may actually have a beneficial effect on the embryo inside. Some breeders have incorporated cooling periods into the incubation regimen by means of opening the incubator doors for a short period of time each day or by turning the machines off. A note of caution is warranted here: do not forget to close the door or turn the machine on again!

Humidity is another matter all together. It would be so much easier if the humidity setting could remain constant over the incubation period. Unfortunately, this is not recommended and could result in a low hatch rate or a high incidence of problem hatches. It appears that one of the most common mistakes that is made is the use of high humidity settings to incubate eggs. High humidity causes the eggs to retain more fluids than needed and hatching becomes laborious and difficult, resulting in many dead-in-shell chicks. The recommendation of lower humidity settings has changed this scenario drastically and has resulted in higher hatch rates and chicks that are stronger from the very start.

The relative humidity in the incubation environment controls the amount of fluid that can transpire through the eggshell and into the surrounding air. Only so much moisture can be absorbed by the heated air before it becomes saturated and can absorb no more. When bowls of water or full water reservoirs are present inside the incubator, the air becomes saturated by this water supply and the eggs cannot shed the moisture that is necessary. The result is an overweight chick that has trouble moving its head into the hatch position. When the time arrives for the chick to break into the aircell and breathe air, it is not possible to do so and the chick dies. This is a very prevalent problem with the larger, thick-shelled eggs of many species.

The most important time to keep the humidity low is in the first two weeks of incubation. It is during this time period that the aviculturist should notice the growing aircell within the egg. Earlier recommendations of 50 percent relative humidity are borderline in effect and new, lower settings are now being used. The more eggs that are being incubated at the same time, the higher the humidity will become simply from the transpired moisture of all of those eggs. It is often very difficult to control the humidity within the machine and the use of an outside dehumidifier may be necessary. This provides a dryer air that is drawn into the machines and passed across the eggs. The dry air has the potential of absorbing greater amounts of moisture to be carried out of the incubator vents and into the dehumidifier unit, starting the cycle over again. A system such as this works very well and the resulting hatch rates have been boosted dramatically.

During the first two weeks of incubation, the relative humidity setting can be set as low as 38–42 percent. Be sure that no cracked or compromised eggs are present in the incubator. Cracked or compromised eggs should be incubated at a humidity level of 60 percent or higher. A low setting could cause a fast dehydration and early death to the growing embryo if the eggshell is cracked. After all of the eggs are about fourteen days of age, the moisture level can be increased to 46–48 percent relative humidity. The final few days of incubation present no real high humidity dangers and the moisture level can be boosted as high as possible for the hatch. If all of the eggs in the machine are in the final week of development, turn off the dehumidifier and add water to the incubator tanks. This will provide a better environment for hatching.

The aviculturist must learn methods of candling eggs in order to properly control the humidity settings for incubation. Candling eggs is a procedure that cannot be taught in a book. The only way to gain experience with this procedure is to take every opportunity to practice it. Candle eggs that are in the early stages of development and those that have been incubating for extended periods of time. Keep notes on the vascular development, aircell sizes and shapes, and any other noticeable internal characteristic. It is wise to record the hatch rates of eggs that have been observed during the incubation process as well. This will eventually lead to the development of good judgment and experience with the eggs that are to be incubated in the future.

12.5 Position and Turning of the Eggs

Probably the second-most prevalent cause of death in the incubator is the malpositioning of chicks within the egg. Chicks will sometimes position themselves upside down or even sideways within the fluid portion of the egg. When hatch time arrives, they cannot reach the aircell area and may die trying to breathe air for the first time.

The way in which the egg rests on the incubator tray can influence the final position of the embryo. Sometime during the third week of development, the embryo begins to position itself for the hatch. It is imperative that the chick turn into the proper position during this limited time frame as it will be impossible to rotate once the embryo grows much larger. Gravity appears to be the mechanism that guides the chick into the right position. This means that the eggs must remain in a position wherein the large end of the egg (aircell end) rests slightly higher than the small end. If the egg is positioned in the incubator with the small end upward, the chick will position its head away from the pull of gravity. Thus, it will be upside down within the egg. When hatch time arrives, there will be no aircell for the chick to break into and take its first breath. The only hope for most upside down chicks is hatch assistance by the aviculturist. Left unassisted, only about 50 percent of these malpositions manage to escape the egg alive. Those that do hatch on their own do so by pipping the shell and drawing air in from the outside.

Hatch assistance is a tedious and nerve-wracking experience. The slightest mistake can cause death to the chick being assisted. Over the past decade, hatch assistance has become an accepted practice and much has been learned about the hatching process and the chicks themselves. First-time attempts at hatch assistance should be performed under the supervision of an experienced aviculturist. The biggest problem is knowing exactly when to intervene. If the egg is disrupted too early, the blood vessels that support the embryo will be broken and death will be rapid. If too much time passes, the chick may suffocate and die from lack of oxygen. Timing is vital and requires the experience of a seasoned aviculturist.

Turning of the eggs is necessary for proper development of the embryo. Eggs left unturned will develop in only the upper portion of the egg and the chick will not survive. This is because the yolk, containing the ovum, floats to the top position within the shell walls of the egg. Each time the egg is turned, the yolk will begin to float upward and will rest against the inside top of the eggshell.

The ideal frequency of turning has not yet been established for each species of the parrot family. However, increased hatchability rates have been noticed over the past few years by reducing the once recommended number of turns per day. Most incubators that come equipped with automatic turning units will turn the eggs once each hour. For many species, this is too often and the embryo may not develop in the lower portions of the egg. Upon candling, large areas of undeveloped albumen are noticeable in the small end of the egg. Reduce the turning to approximately once every four hours and hatch rates should increase.

Eggs are rotated on their sides. Do not turn eggs end over end as this may cause the liquid to shift into the air-cell and rupture the inner shell membranes. Once this membrane is broken, the chick will die as many blood vessels lie directly beneath this thin membrane and carry the blood supply to the embryo. A gentle quarter turn (lightly rolling the eggs on their sides) about every four hours will do the job.

When turning eggs, a complete turn of 180 degrees is not recommended. It is best to turn the egg only one quarter of a turn or about 90 degrees on the circle. Always turn in the same direction to make sure the blood vessels distribute themselves throughout the egg. Turning back and forth may result in areas of undeveloped albumen and could cause death to the embryo. If automatic turning units turn eggs back and forth, be sure to turn the eggs at least one full turn (180 degrees) by hand each day, in addition to the turning accomplished by the automatic unit. As with most of the actions required of artificial incubation, turning is most important in the first two weeks of life. After about the third week, the embryo should already be well established and turning becomes less important, although it is still necessary.

12.6 The Hatch

If all goes well, the hatch usually begins approximately three days prior to the emergence of the chick from the egg. The first step to hatching is the puncture of the internal membrane, which allows the chick to breathe air. The chick moves its head up toward the aircell causing the shape of the aircell to change. This is called internal pip or drawdown. Unfortunately, this process is one that cannot be assisted, the chick must do this on its own or it will not survive. During drawdown or internal pip, while candling the egg, you will notice that the perfectly circular shape of the aircell has changed and now appears to have grown considerably in only a few hours. This signifies that the chick has begun to move and is trying to shift its body into the hatch position. In cases where the humidity was too high or the position of the egg was not right for extended periods of time, the chick may not be able to maneuver its body into the hatch position. These are the problem hatches and many will require hatch assistance.

During the normal course of action, the chick punctures the inner membrane with its tiny egg tooth, located at the very tip of the beak. This egg tooth is very sharp and is used to push a small wedge outward on the eggshell. The breaking outward of the eggshell is called external pip and indicates the chick has successfully made an airhole through the egg. In many cases, directly after pip time, the chick rests while continuing to absorb the remaining portion of its yolk sac in preparation for hatch.

Sometime during the next twenty-four to forty-eight hours, the chick will begin to rotate within the egg and push outward with its egg tooth. This causes a line of breaks in the shell, which becomes very noticeable from the outside. When the chick has turned all the way around within the egg and has cracked the shell in a complete circle, it will push with its feet and neck muscles to pop the top off the egg.

The hatch process is very physically demanding on the chick. After the hatch, many chicks will rest for hours before they will stand to solicit feeding. During the hatch, elevation of the humidity in the incubator or hatcher unit is recommended. Once the chick has managed to pip the shell, air can be drawn into the egg and will often dry the inner shell membranes, making it difficult to move. If the membranes become too dry, they stick to the skin of the chick and prevent it from completing the hatching process. Once exhausted from the physical labor, the chick will die. When the first external pip mark is noticed, the humidity in the incubator should be elevated to make the hatch easier. Recommended humidity levels are in excess of 75 percent relative. This can be accomplished by adding water to the tanks or by placing wide bowls of water inside the unit. After hatch, the water can be removed so it does not have a negative effect on the eggs that are still in the incubation stage.

12.7 The African Parrots—Statistics on Incubation

The amount of time it takes the eggs to fully develop and hatch is usually expressed as the incubation period. Some books break this time period down into two segments, the incubation period and the period from pip to hatch. This method is used for several reasons. Many species vary in the amount of time it takes to hatch after the chick has pipped the shell. Generally, this time period is between thirty-six and seventy-two hours; therefore, the incubation periods below are given as total incubation and hatching time from the start of incubation to the hatch of the chick.

As a rule, you can expect the chick to pip the shell about thirty-six to seventy-two hours before the listed days to hatch time is reached below. The average time from pip to hatch is forty-eight hours.

Species	Latin	Days to Hatch
grey parrot	*Psittacus erithacus erithacus*	28
Timneh grey parrot	*Psittacus erithacus timneh*	27–28
Senegal parrot	*Poicephalus senegalus*	23–24
Meyer's parrot	*Poicephalus meyeri*	23–24
Jardine's parrot	*Poicephalus gulielmi*	23–24
Cape parrot	*Poicephalus robustus*	27–28
red-bellied parrot	*Poicephalus rufiventris*	24
brown-headed parrot	*Poicephalus cryptoxanthus*	24
most lovebird species	*Agapornis*	23

13 Hand-rearing

13.1 Hand-rearing—Concepts and Practices

In a text of this fashion, it would be impossible to provide everything you need to know to hand-rear your first clutch of baby African parrots. The actual action of hand-feeding itself is not difficult, but the instincts and observations that come with experience are difficult to relay in writing.

There is more to hand-rearing than simply feeding the chicks. The keeper must learn to recognize the signs of illness, adjust brooding temperatures as needed and feed at the frequency and volume that is right for each chick. This experience does not come easily. A few good books have been written on this subject and if you plan to hand feed your young it would be wise to invest in them.

Basic hand-rearing concepts consist of brooding, feeding and weaning. The young chicks must be brooded at a temperature that is appropriate for their stage of life. Very young chicks must be kept at high temperatures similar to that of incubation. As they grow and mature these brooding temperatures can be lowered because the chick will have a better ability to regulate its own body temperature. Brooding is very important! Improper temperatures can cause slowed digestion that will, in turn, cause the chick to be stunted or die. Learn to observe the behavior and attitude of the chicks. When they are too hot they will often flap their wings in an attempt to cool the air. In addition, clutches brooded in the same container will not rest against each other, but instead will retreat to the farthest point away from each other in an attempt to cool themselves a bit. When they are cold they will roll themselves into a tight ball to try to conserve body temperature, often piling on top of each other in a group container.

In an attempt to explain proper brooding temperature and food consumption, we can look at the stages of development in four different increments of age. The first being the neonatal stage where the chick is newly hatched and has very little down (down feathers). At this stage of life, the chick requires high temperature heat (about 94–96°F) and frequent feedings. Very young chicks will have to be fed about every hour or two during the day and night. Hand-rearing formulas are available through your pet store or wholesale food distributor. These preparations must be made very thin and watery for chicks in the first stage of development. The secret is to feed the food very thin on an hourly basis. Be cautious, some instant hand-rearing formulas will thicken after standing for only a minute or two. You must allow this thickening to occur before feeding and then thin the formula once again. If the food is fed to the chick and it thickens in the crop, the chick may be unable to digest the heavy consistency and the crop will remain full or may sour.

When the chick has grown a bit and begins developing its second down feathers, it is entering the second stage of development. At this stage the temperature of the brooder can be lowered to between 86–92°F. (Note: Anytime you adjust the brooder to a lower temperature and the chick's digestion stops, you must elevate the temperature once again and slowly lower it to the desired setting.) In the second stage of development, the chick should be eating more food at each feeding. This means the frequency of feeding has been reduced as well. It will no longer be necessary to feed during the night. One last feed at 11 P.M. and the first one at 6 or 7 A.M. will suffice. Food consistency can be thickened to that of canned tomato sauce or a little thicker.

The third stage of development is when the bird actually begins to sprout real feathers. For most African parrot babies that are growing normally, this is about three to four weeks of age. For the smaller *Poicephalus* parrots, it may be a bit earlier. This stage continues until the feathers cover most of the body and the tail is about half its adult length. Chicks of this age are quite hardy. They will only require a brooding temperature of about 80°F and are often comfortable at room temperature. If you are raising a clutch of babies together they will undoubtedly not need additional heat or brooding. If they are cold they will keep each other warm by huddling together. The food can be thickened to the point where it takes four to six hours to empty from the crop. Consistency can be described as that of normal catsup (thin enough that it still rolls off a tipped spoon).

In the forth or last stage, the chick is almost fully feathered and is ready to be introduced to normal parrot foods. Be cautious during the weaning process! Some birds will starve to death if hand feeding is suddenly stopped before they know how to eat. I suggest that you offer fresh foods, pelleted diets and seeds but continue to feed the hand-rearing formula at least twice a day. You may want to feed only half of the normal amount to allow the bird to try eating on its own. Place the young birds into a small parrot cage with a perch mounted very close to the floor of the cage. Young birds will experiment with perching but may not have the balance of an adult bird.

Once the young birds are consuming enough food to maintain their weight, the hand feeding can be reduced and eventually discontinued. This is a very slow process and there are a few rules that should be observed during this stage of hand-rearing. These rules are meant as a general guideline to ensure the chick is developing and growing at a normal rate.

- Chicks should gain weight each day during the first three stages of life.
- During weaning it is okay to lose a little weight, but do not allow them to starve.

- If the crop does not empty in the normal amount of time, and nothing else has changed (environmentally) they may need medical attention. Crop stasis, not caused by thick food or improper brooding, can be the first sign of a health problem.

- Extremely cold or hot conditions can cause crop stasis.

- The maximum amount of hand-rearing formula needed will be reached during stage two or three. With African grey parrots, the crop is tight and overfilling will cause vomiting. The maximum recommended amount is about 50–60 cc.

- It is easier to allow the parents to start feeding the chicks. The best time for ease of feeding would be to pull them from the nest at stage two of development (about fifteen to twenty-one days of age).

13.2 Before the Chicks Arrive

Aviculturists should always be prepared to hand-rear chicks even if this is not part of the planned protocol for the collection. Often things go wrong in the parental nest; chicks will have to be pulled and hand-reared if they are to survive. This means that a nursery setup of some sort should be in working order and organized at all times.

The basic equipment needed to rear chicks includes a brooder, feeding syringes or tools, formula, thermometers and, if possible, a good set of scales or balances. There are several models of commercially produced brooders on the market. The best types are those that keep their set temperature within a couple of degrees of accuracy. Fluctuations of more than three or four degrees can cause problems with very young chicks and may cause digestion to slow. Prices are competitive, so make certain you get the most for your money.

Commercially prepared instant formulas are also available from most bird specialty pet stores. These formulas, in powder form, will keep for at least a year if frozen. This is your best defense against being caught off guard by an unexpected hatchling. Be sure to rotate stock and always use the older stock first.

Food and heat are the two most important elements for successful hand rearing but many other supplies come in handy when supplying a nursery. Clean-up supplies, disinfectants, cotton swabs, tissues, small brooding dishes, distilled water, back-up power sources, hot water bottles, tweezers, scissors and a note pad will probably be needed at one point or another.

13.3 Partial Parent Rearing

It is always easier to feed a chick that has been fed by the parents for a couple of weeks. At this stage in life they are larger, require fewer feedings and can usually be kept at lower brooder temperatures with no problems. Parent rearing also presents some problems, especially with many captive pairs of African parrots. Some parent birds are nervous and will do strange things to the chicks, such as nipping off toes and wing tips.

In Europe and some other parts of the world, parent rearing has become very popular again. This is likely due to the discovery that there is no truth to the rumors that parent-reared chicks will breed at younger ages in the aviary. Actually, some parent-reared species are so nervous, they make very poor aviary breeders and many spend their day flying back and forth within the cage trying to get away from the human keeper. The stress these birds experience is equivalent to placing totally wild birds in a cage.

Partially hand-reared chicks will grow up and become dependable breeders at exactly the same age as those that were fledged by parent birds. In fact, hand-reared birds will be more calm and are less likely to destroy eggs or chicks in the nest. The key to successful breeding of captive-reared African parrots is patience, exactly the same as if you were waiting for a wild pair to nest.

Socialization plays an important role in captive breeding potential. Young birds in the weaning stages of life must have access to each other and must be allowed to interact. In some cases this may result in a bird that nips at human fingers, but in the long run they are more dependable breeders because they know more about their own kind. Parent birds do not educate the young as much as does the socialization between young birds of the same species.

13.4 Hand-rearing from Day One

Rearing a chick from the egg is a time-consuming task. Newly hatched chicks must be fed frequently or they will not survive. Generally, feeding about every hour will be required for at least a full week. These feedings should be continued throughout the night as well. The total time a chick spends with an empty crop will determine its fate. Empty crops equal weight loss and weakness.

Formulas for newly hatched chicks and chicks that are less than a week old should be very thin, like evaporated milk. Thick formula tends to slow or stop the crop and will eventually lead to dehydration and death. A thin formula in combination with the very small size of the crop is the reason that chicks must be fed so frequently. Keep food in the crop at all times during that first week or two and the chicks will be assured a strong start in life. Keep formula temperatures between 104–108°F. High temperatures can cause many physical problems and could cause severe burns within the system of the chick.

Brooding temperatures are also critical at this stage of development. Chicks must be maintained at a temperature just slightly lower than that of incubation. The usual temperature used for the first week is between 94 and 96°F.

After the chicks have begun to grow and develop small spots where down feathers will erupt, the temperature can be lowered a degree every other day or so. Never make a dramatic adjustment in brooding temperature or the consistency of the formula.

Crop motility and weight gains are the keys to assessing the health and well being of a chick. As long as the food is being digested at a fairly steady rate, the chick should be growing at a steady rate. This growth may be minute at the beginning, but as the crop size increases and the chick itself grows, weight gains will begin to increase dramatically. It is best to weigh chicks each day using a scale that measures in grams. Healthy, well-fed chicks will gain weight each day. A loss in weight is an indication that feeding is not frequent enough or in sufficient amounts. Keep note of times fed and the amounts of formula digested; when weight gains level off, increase the amounts fed and record the differences. In this way, you can teach yourself the proper way to hand rear the chicks. Every chick will be different and will take different amounts of food. This is the reason for the exclusion of a feeding chart in this book. Day-one chicks may take only a quarter of a cc of food while those that are beginning to wean (about seven to eight weeks) will take up to 60 ccs.

13.5 Disease Prevention in the Nursery

The nursery area, whether it be a corner of the kitchen or a separate room of the house, must be kept clean. The biggest disease risk occurs from a dirty facility or dirty food containers. Once disease has entered the nursery, it is often spread by physical contact either between birds, off the equipment or from the hands of the keeper.

Certain species of birds have been assigned a risk factor associated with their propensity to carry hidden disease such as polyoma virus. For this reason it is unwise to house birds together in a nursery, brooder or weaning cage unless they are clutch mates or have been raised together since they entered the nursery. Some birds can carry a lethal virus and not shed it to others until they become stressed at weaning time or until they become ill themselves. The simple truth about disease prevention in the nursery is that all birds should be housed separately, handled with clean hands, and provided with their own personal food and water bowls, their own cages and their own perches. Although this is not an easy way to manage the nursery, it is the most effective method to prevent the spread of disease.

Furthermore, a clean facility and environment are imperative. The counters, floors, walls and all equipment should be disinfected regularly. Soak food bowls and water containers in some type of disinfectant when they are not being used and keep all hand-rearing equipment clean. Dirty brooder bowls or cages should be removed from the nursery for cleaning. This will help eliminate the spread of viruses that may be present in the feces of some birds. Always disinfect anything that is to be given back to the bird or used with another bird.

13.6 Feeding Methodology

It can be quite intimidating to try to feed a newly hatched parrot chick. Slower is usually better with young hatchlings. The use of syringes, spoons and feeding tubes (gavages) are common. The type of instrument that you are most comfortable with will be the best one for you.

For the first few weeks, a spoon or small syringe will probably be the best answer. Small spoons with the edges bent slightly upward to simulate the lower mandible of the parents work well for the first-time feeder. Slowly introduce the warm food into the beak of the chick. It may be helpful to use the forefinger and thumb of the other hand to lightly grip the tip of the beak on the chick. This will often cause the feeding response to become stronger. A feeding response is the little jerking motion and noise the chicks make when they are actually swallowing food. To introduce food into a chick's beak when it is not swallowing can cause it to inhale the food and die.

Formula temperature remains basically the same throughout the entire hand-rearing process. African grey chicks will often prefer it a little warmer than other parrots. Proper temperature is between 104–108°F. If food is warmer than 110°F, tissue damage may occur in the mouth, throat or crop. Once the tissue is burned, it will become inflamed and will produce large amounts of pink liquid, giving the impression the crop is always full. Crop burns are serious and must be attended to by an experienced avian veterinarian. If chicks will swallow cooler food, it is best to err on the lower side of the temperature scale.

Generally, chicks that are cold will not eat. It is important to make sure that brooder temperatures are comfortable for the chick and that it is not panting or flailing its wings. These two actions are indicative of an overly warm and incorrect brooding temperature. Cold chicks are very inactive and will usually roll themselves into a tight ball within the brooding dish. The wing tips and beak will be cool to the touch.

As the parrots get a little older they will begin to mouth or taste the food they are being fed. This is a trying time for the feeder as some chicks will throw food all over the place. Many experienced breeders switch feeding instruments to a syringe or feeding tube at this point. Still, chicks can easily regurgitate some of the crop contents and will taste it and throw it around the brooder. Grey parrot chicks are famous for this!

The method in which a baby bird is fed is a personal choice until it affects the next person who may purchase that bird. Tube feeding, using a rubber hose, and gavage feeding, using a metal hose, have received some very bad press of late. This has probably been the result of someone purchasing a tube-fed chick that would not eat from a syringe or spoon. It is very important that chicks be reared in such a way that they can be fed by almost any method. It is true that tube-fed babies may not solicit feeding in the normal way. But, those that are tube fed most of the time and syringe or spoon fed prior to being transferred to someone else may eat better for the new owner. It is very important that aviculturists pass feeding information on to the next consumer.

13.7 Hand-rearing Formulas for African Parrots

The African parrots originate from the Old World. Most neonates of the Old World do not require the high fat, high protein formulas as do parrots of the New World. This makes formula preparation for African species rather simple. Most of the hand-feeding formulas available on the market today are available in different fat levels. If a commercial formula is to be used, choose one that contains a fat level of 8–10 percent. Elevated fat levels can cause slow digestion or even physical problems such as liver disease.

Homemade formulas are usually made using a standard base. In Europe human baby foods are used as the base. We have found that this is usually not sufficient nutrition for many parrot types. In the United States, the use of monkey or primate chow as a formula base is very common and works very well. Choose one that is not oily to the touch to avoid contaminants in the food. To this food, the usual additives include peanut butter, creamed corn, green vegetables (jars of baby food) or some type of vegetable oil that may not be necessary when feeding Old World chicks.

A standard recipe would be to soak twenty-five monkey or primate biscuits in hot water. When they are soft all the way through, cover again in warm water and microwave until almost boiling (about ten minutes minimum). Remove from microwave and stir until almost smooth. Add two heaping tablespoons of smooth peanut butter, one six-ounce jar of creamed corn and one four-ounce jar of garden or green vegetables. Stir the formula, place small amounts in blender and blend until totally smooth. After preparation, the addition of a tablespoon of wheat grass powder or spiralina (algae) powder can also be used. Be sure to add these last two ingredients after the mixture has cooled to avoid cooking out their beneficial vitamins. The same holds true for the addition of avian vitamin supplements. Always add vitamin products right before feeding. This recipe makes a blender full; it can be frozen for up to two weeks.

Homemade formulas can be frozen in ice cube trays to accommodate the preparation of smaller amounts. After the cubes are frozen, place them in air-tight plastic bags to keep ice crystals from forming. When needed, take one or two cubes out of the freezer and microwave to the proper temperature. (Whenever a microwave is used to heat formula, be sure to stir the food and check for consistency of temperatures to avoid hot spots that could burn a chick's crop.) Add vitamins or natural supplements and feed. Do not add additional vitamins to commercially prepared instant formulas. These preparations already have the necessary vitamins and minerals in the mixture. Oversupplementation may occur with the addition of more vitamins causing severe physical problems, sickness and possibly death.

13.8 The Weaning Process

When do you introduce normal food to a growing chick? What kind of foods do you offer first? These are the most commonly asked questions with regard to the weaning process. The time period when a young bird is learning to eat normal foods and become less reliant on hand-feeding is a stressful time. Weight losses, depression and frustration are perfectly normal during this time. (Sometimes the keeper also experiences these emotions!)

African parrots are not notoriously difficult birds to wean. Due to their intelligent and curious nature they may sample foods at a very young age. The proper time to begin weaning cannot be expressed in terms of age itself. Each and every bird will mature differently despite the same feeding regimen and the exact same treatment in the nursery. Young birds can be moved into small cages with low-mounted perches and begin the weaning process when they are almost fully feathered. The last area of the body to feather is usually the crop or upper chest. When small pin-feathers begin to appear in this area and the remainder of the bird's body is already fairly well feathered, they can begin to be weaned.

The first step to weaning is to introduce chicks to foods other than the hand-rearing formula. At first, soft foods are best offered because these chicks are not normally drinking water and may experience an impacted crop if they ingest large amounts of dry, hard food. Introduce fresh or canned corn kernels, mixed vegetables, soaked primate biscuits, soaked pelleted foods, fruits, baby foods or even a small bowl of warm hand-feeding formula. Do not expect the bird to walk over and immediately begin to eat, although stranger things have happened! One very successful secret to weaning is to place small amounts of the weaning foods directly into the beak of the bird and solicit the feeding response. This directs the attention of the bird toward the food that is being offered.

It may be several days before the chicks even look at the weaning foods. During these first few days, the keeper must continue hand feeding, although frequency and quantities should be reduced. A chick with a full crop has no need to eat other food. As the chick begins to play with

the offered foods, cut the earliest feeding of the day completely out of the schedule. Continue to offer the foods that
are accepted and slowly eliminate all hand feeding. Be sure
that chicks do not lose too much weight. A loss of more
than 20 percent of their beginning weight is too much and
hand feeding must begin again to supplement the chick.

If other birds in the nursery are already weaned, it may
be helpful to place their cage next to the cage of a bird that
is just beginning to learn and is being socialized in the
same manner. Young birds often observe the behavior of
others and may learn to eat much faster if a role model is
available. Once your chick is eating large amounts of soft
foods, offer it a bowl of water and the normal dry foods such
as seed, pellets and primate biscuits. Below is a list of the
foods to offer weaning birds. It is meant to provide you
with some new ideas and is not necessarily a complete list
of foods that can be offered.

13.8.1 Weaning Foods

Stage 1: You can offer fresh vegetables and fruits,
steamed or cooked vegetables and fruits, apple sauce,
creamy baby foods of any flavor (including meats, but they
are not recommended) bread, spray millet, soaked pelleted
foods, soaked primate biscuits, corn on the cob, dry baked
potato, baked sweet potato, dishes of hand-rearing formula, cooked pasta or toast with peanut butter and a little
jelly.

Stage 2: Offer all foods listed above plus, normal parrot
seed mixtures, dry pelleted foods, water, nuts—literally
anything an adult parrot can eat!

13.9 Socialization of the Young

Why are some hand-fed baby birds easy to handle and
sweet while others are shy, nippy or even nasty? A great
deal of these personality traits can be learned while the
chicks are in the weaning process. This is why socializing

the chicks with either humans or other birds is so important. Birds that are to become pets need to be handled by human keepers on a daily basis.

Raising young African parrots for the pet trade means a friendly, sweet bird is in order. Raising birds for future breeding stock can mean the opposite—sweet, lovable birds are not necessary for breeding, and are often not even preferred. How then can the nursery manager assure the customer that their purchase will be socialized properly for the role it is to play in the future?

Young parrots become very social just about the time they begin to wean. They learn the difference between biting and tasting, between talking or screaming and between birds and humans. This is the time in their life where they must be given the education that will form their personality for the future. Of course, this does not mean they will be either nice or nasty, there is a middle road. One can also socialize a bird toward other birds and humans.

Birds that are destined to be breeders in the future must be given access to other young birds of their own species, or at least their own genus. It is best to raise these chicks with each other and allow them to play, eat, argue and socialize together. The amount of human intervention should be kept to a minimum. Talking, playing, hugging, kissing and speech training will not be necessary for this future breeding stock. The keeper should not hold these birds and should actually avoid talking to them when they are servicing the cage or feeding. The result will be birds that prefer the company of another bird rather than the keeper or another human.

On the other hand, keeping baby birds tame and sweet requires quite the opposite behavior. If possible, visual barriers should be placed between the weaning cages of babies of the same species. The only playing and interaction that they should be subjected to is that of the keeper or other people. Handling, talking, holding and other social interaction should be with humans and not with birds of their own kind. Be sure to let the pet store owner know how you have socialized the birds so the store owner will continue to keep them separated from other birds. Once they learn their normal behavior from another bird, they will begin to make that transition from a human-bonded bird to that of a normally socialized one. They will often become very independent and if allowed to progress, they may even growl if someone reaches to pick them up.

The socialization of young birds is an important management technique with which to experiment. Some birds will not respond as well to the pet style of socializing as others. On the same note, some birds that are not handled during their socialization period may enjoy being handled by many people. If they were properly socialized with members of their own kind they will eventually resort to interaction with other birds when the human factor is reduced or eliminated.

References

Forshaw, Joseph M. 1973. *Parrots of the World*. Lansdowne Editions, Melbourne, Australia.

Jordan, Rick. 1989. *Parrot Incubation Procedures*. Silvio Mattacchione & Co., Canada.

Low, Rosemary. 1992. *Parrots in Aviculture, A Photo Reference Guide*. Silvio Mattacchione & Co., Canada.

Monroe, Burt L. Jr., and Charles G. Sibley. 1993. *A World Checklist of Birds*. Edwards Brothers Inc. Ann Arbor, Michigan, U.S.A.

Voren, Howard, and Rick Jordan. 1992. *Parrots: Hand-feeding and Nursery Management*. Silvio Mattacchione & Co., Canada.

Index

A Practical

The
Administrator's
Handbook

Robert L. Bradley, EdD
Editor

School Administrators Association of New York State
Kevin S. Casey, *Executive Director*
Donald J. Nickson, *Deputy Executive Director*

This handbook is intended to provide general responses to questions of
interest to school leaders. The answers do not address specific situations that
a school leader may be encountering. While every effort has been made to
ensure the accuracy of the responses, they may not address all nuances of a
specific situation. Also, laws are changed during each session of Congress and
the state legislature; the courts are continually handing down interpretations
of existing laws; and local district policies often have a significant impact on
how an issue should be resolved. School leaders are encouraged to review
local policies, and when legal interpretations are involved, they are urged to
work with the superintendent, school attorney, and professional association
to obtain appropriate legal counsel. This is especially important relative to
the principal and teacher evaluation (APPR) laws and regulations, which
continue to evolve. Visit engageny.org for ongoing updates in this area.

Send all inquiries to:
School Administrators Association of New York State
8 Airport Park Boulevard
Latham, New York 12110

Contents

Acknowledgments

This is the third edition of *The Administrator's Handbook*, a vision of SAANYS to provide a service to its members. Don Nickson has played an important leadership role with the publication of all three editions. Executive Director Kevin Casey gave valuable input in the development of the original edition and his support with the next two editions ensured that the project would continue for SAANYS members. The third edition also continues the vision that Jim Torrance and Dick Thomas had to provide a practical resource for school administrators.

This project has been successful because of the dedicated work of many people. Mark Dunn played a significant role in organizing focus group meetings of school administrators and consolidating feedback from the meetings for this handbook. The outstanding SAANYS team attended to many details and provided oversight during the processes of editing, review, and publishing. This edition, like the first two, relied on Michelle Hebert's organization and expertise in communications and publishing, including current technology, which assured a careful process to prepare the handbook. Sharon Caruso gave important attention to the organization, layout, and cover design of the handbook. Barbara Kelly added careful proofreading that strengthened the document. The SAANYS legal department provided critical support for the review and editing of the content.

Our writers who worked on developing answers have extensive experience as school administrators and working with districts through BOCES. Their thoughtful and attentive work included careful research for the answers and topics of the various chapters.

Writers

Joyce Carr, Supervisor of Special Education and Student Support Services, Elmira City School District

Kathleen Chaucer, EdD, Principal, Milton Terrace Elementary School, Ballston Spa Central School District

Christy Colangelo, Safety Coordinator, Oneida-Madison-Herkimer BOCES

Mark Dunn, Retired Principal, Hughes Elementary School, New Hartford Central School District

Richard M. Evans, EdD, Principal, Stevens Elementary School, Burnt Hills-Ballston Lake Central Schools
Maureen Futscher, EdD, Principal, Bradley Elementary School, New Hartford Central School District
Jeffrey Gordon, Assistant Superintendent for Personnel, Fayetteville-Manlius Central School District
Maryellen Symer, Assistant Superintendent for Instruction, Burnt Hills-Ballston Lake Central Schools
Robert Bradley, EdD, Doctor in Educational Leadership Program, The Sage Colleges

Robert L. Bradley,
Editor

Introduction

This handbook is unique because it contains questions that have been designed by practicing administrators who are actively involved in the daily work of school leadership. Mark Dunn, a veteran school administrator, met with several groups of administrators using a format similar to the 2007 and 2012 projects to gather their feedback. Their work together helped to eliminate questions from the second edition that were no longer relevant and to revise questions that needed refreshing. They identified new questions that have emerged since the second edition was published. As a result, the questions in this handbook have come from a cross section of administrators including principals, assistant principals, CSE chairpeople, and athletic directors. Our writers who developed the answers to the questions have extensive experience as school administrators and/or working with school districts through BOCES.

The introduction in the first edition of this handbook in 2007 noted:

> The issues of the twenty-first century challenging educators are complicated and reflect the highly regulatory nature of our schools... Professional educators need to have access to a vast body of information to address these issues in a thoughtful manner. Yet, the day-to-day demands of school administrators do not always permit the time for in-depth research that may provide the information base to solve a problem, to build a shared vision, or to create a new approach.
>
> (Bradley, ed., 2007, p. ii)

The 2012 edition reflected how the landscape for school administrators had continued to shift after the publication of the 2007 edition. The 2012 edition addressed a variety of issues that showed how the work of school leaders had become more challenging and complex, adding new topics that included NCLB, DASA, RTI, cyberbullying, APPR, and safety issues.

Reflecting the changes that school leaders and their schools are facing, this new edition includes over 25 new questions. Answers have been revised to show changes in regulations and current thinking about educational subjects. Some of the new questions address issues such as ESSA, reauthorization of the McKinney-Vento Homeless Assistance Act, opioids, lead testing, concussions, and personal electronic devices. The content also reinforces the importance and accountability of schools and their leaders to provide students and staff with a safe and supportive environment free from discrimination, intimidation, harassment, and bullying in schools and at school functions. These changes and challenges are set in a context with limited resources to meet the needs of students and expectations for accountability.

The answers to the questions are arranged to accomplish three purposes. First, the answers are designed to include succinct and informative responses. Second, the answers have practical advice or suggestions when they may be helpful. Finally, whenever possible, the answers include sources where additional information can be found. Although every question does not allow for a three-part answer, most of them will point the reader to another resource if additional information is needed. The answers in some cases are deliberately general or refer the reader to local policies that should be in place since some questions depend on the context or the individual school setting.

This handbook is divided into sections based on topic:

- In sections one and five, there are questions that relate to a wide range of student matters that include discipline and extracurricular activities.
- The second section is on health and safety, an area that is highly regulated and is emerging as one that takes the time and attention of administrators.
- Questions that relate to school and home relationships are addressed in section three.
- Section four has questions about curriculum and instruction.
- Supervision of staff and evaluation is covered in section six. A new subsection about professional development has been added to this section.
- Section seven includes the greatest number of questions in this handbook since it covers the highly regulated areas of special education and Section 504.
- The last section includes questions that relate to transportation.

In addition to sources that are cited in answers to questions, SAANYS has included some websites in an appendix that will provide additional resources.

Many answers reference a website. Many of them are located at the New York State Education Department website at http://www.nysed.gov/. Accessing this site can retrieve a great deal of helpful information. For example, the texts of decisions of the Commissioner of Education since July 1991 are available at the site for the Office of Counsel of the New York State Education Department. Many of the answers in this handbook cite decisions that have been made in legal appeals to the Commissioner of Education. The decisions also provide a logical rationale and a legal foundation that can help administrators address both complicated and straightforward problems. Another website of note is http://engageny.org/, which has resources to support the New York State Education Department's reform agenda.

The process of revising this handbook brought Mark Dunn and me into contact with many excellent school administrators and the staff at SAANYS. We continue to be impressed with their abilities and passion to identify, respond to, and to provide leadership for the critical issues that face our students and schools. We have heard them express their steadfast belief in the importance of education and their commitment to students. It has reinforced our continued admiration for the dedication of the school administrators in New York State and the understanding that "leadership is second only to classroom instruction among all school-related factors that contribute to what students learn at school" (Leithwood, Louis, Anderson, and Wahlstrom, 2004).

Robert L. Bradley, *Editor*

References

Bradley, R. (Ed.) (2007). *The Administrator's Handbook*. Albany, NY: School Administrators Association of New York State.

Leithwood, K.; Louis, K.; Anderson, S.; and Wahlstrom, K. (2004).

How to Use This Handbook

This handbook was designed to provide school leaders in New York State with a desktop reference to assist in getting quick answers to issues and questions that arise frequently. It is arranged by major topic with each topic containing answers to a series of questions and guidance for additional research. The index identifies key terms and refers the reader to specific questions and answers that deal with those issues. That reference is given by the question number. The first part of the number refers the user to the chapter and the second part to the specific question in that chapter. For example, to find question 4-5, the user would go to chapter 4 and then to the fifth question in the chapter.

Many questions include acronyms that are routinely used in the field. We recognize that some of these may not be known to all users, so we have included a glossary of acronyms.

Section 1A
Student Discipline

1-1. What is a code of conduct? Is a code of conduct required for each school building in New York State? What are the requirements that must be contained in a code of conduct?

A board of education is required by Section 100.2(1)(2) of Commissioner's Regulations to adopt a code of conduct that provides for the maintenance of order on school property and at school functions, as defined in Education Law 2801. The code governs the conduct of students, teachers, school personnel, and visitors. It must be developed collaboratively with student, teacher, administrator, and parent organizations. School safety personnel and other school personnel must be consulted.

The code includes, but is not limited to:

- Provisions that address conduct, dress, language, civil and respectful treatment of students, personnel, and visitors.
- Descriptions of the roles of teachers, administrators, other school personnel, parents, and the board of education.
- Disciplinary actions to be taken for violations of the code.
- Standards and procedures to ensure safety and security of students and school personnel.
- Provisions for removal from school buildings of people who violate the code.
- The time period when a student may be removed from a classroom according to Education Law 3214 (3-a)(c) and a description of the continued education for these students.
- Disciplinary measures that follow student possession or use of illegal substances or weapons, use of physical force, vandalism, violation of another student's civil rights, harassment, threats of violence, bullying, and discrimination.
- Procedures to report violations of the code and disciplinary actions in response to them.
- Procedures to ensure compliance with laws for students with disabilities.
- Provisions for reporting code violations that are criminal actions to law enforcement agencies, for notifying parents

about violations, for filing complaints or petitions in courts, and for making referrals to appropriate human services agencies.

- Minimum suspension periods for students who are substantially disruptive according to Education Law 3214 (3-a) and who are defined as "violent pupils" according to Education Law 3214 (2-a)(a).
- Requirements for notification of the community, parents, students, teachers, and other school personnel.
- A bill of rights and responsibilities of students, which focuses on positive student behavior. The document shall be annually publicized and explained to students.
- Procedures for responding to acts of harassment, bullying, and/or discrimination that creates a hostile school environment by conduct, or by threats, intimidation, or abuse, including cyberbullying as defined by Education Law 11(8).
- Guidelines and programs for in-service education programs for all district staff members to ensure effective implementation of school policy on school conduct and discipline.
- Provisions for responding to acts of harassment, bullying, and/or discrimination against students by employees or students pursuant to Section 100.2 (l) (2) (b). With respect to such acts against students by students, these provisions incorporate a progressive model of student discipline that includes measured, balanced, and age-appropriate remedies and procedures that make appropriate use of prevention, education, intervention, and discipline. The provisions consider, among other things, the nature and severity of the offending student's behavior(s), the developmental age of the student, the previous disciplinary record of the student and other extenuating circumstances, and the impact the student's behaviors had on the individual(s) who was physically injured and/or emotionally harmed. Responses shall be reasonably calculated to end the harassment, bullying, and/or discrimination; prevent recurrence; and eliminate the hostile environment. This progressive model

of student discipline shall be consistent with the other provisions of the code of conduct.

A code of conduct is an appropriate policy to include key provisions of the Dignity for All Students Act (DASA). See http://www.p12.nysed.gov/dignityact/.

A board of education shall annually review and update, if necessary, the district's code, taking into consideration the effectiveness of provisions in the code and the fairness and consistency of its application. It is helpful to establish a process that ensures annual reviews with collaboration of the required groups. More information can be found in the Commissioner's Regulations and education laws that are noted.

1-2. What requirements in the code of conduct must be sent to parents?

Commissioner's Regulation 100.2 (1)(2) requires that "a plain language summary of the code be mailed to all parents, or those in parental relation to students" before the start of a school year. The summary and the entire code must be available for review upon request from parents. In addition, the Commissioner's Regulations require the complete code of conduct to be posted on the website, if any, of the school district or the BOCES, including annual updates to the code.

The Commissioner's decision in *Appeal of K.M.*, 51 Ed Dept Rep, Decision No. 16,320 states that in the case of "abridged versions" of the codes, parents and students should be clearly apprised that they need to refer to the code for a complete statement of district policies relating to student conduct and discipline.

1-3. What are the requirements for notifying parents regarding matters of discipline?

The district's code of conduct must describe how persons in parental relation will be notified when a student violates the school's code of conduct. Commissioner's Regulation (Section 100.2 (l)(2)(ii) (m)) holds that the code of conduct adopted by a board of education shall include the circumstances under which notification must occur and also the procedures for notifying those in parental relation to the student about any code violations.

1-4. What information may a principal release regarding a matter of school discipline and a student? Is it mandatory for a principal to put the name of another student involved on the disciplinary form?

The principal should always follow the Family Educational Rights and Privacy Act (FERPA). This act prohibits the release of personally identifiable information (see also question 1-37.) When possible, it is a helpful practice to avoid sharing information with a third party that may identify or provide information about another student. If the principal has a question about how to prepare a disciplinary form for an incident that involves another student, that question should be discussed with counsel in order to find a way not to violate FERPA.

1-5. What are the proper procedures an administrator must follow when suspending a student?

Education Law 3214(3)(a) authorizes a board of education, board of trustees, sole trustee, superintendent of schools, district superintendent, or principal of a school to suspend a "pupil who is insubordinate or disorderly or violent or disruptive, or whose conduct otherwise endangers the safety, morals, health or welfare of others." The statute does not authorize an assistant principal to suspend students, nor does it authorize the principal to delegate his authority to suspend (*Appeal of C.R.*, 45 Ed Dept Rep 303, Decision No. 15,330). Although Education Law 3214 allows principals to suspend students for five days or less, suspensions in excess of five days require a process that involves a hearing according to Education Law 3214. See question 1-6.

Education Law 3214(3)(b) governs the assignment of an out-of-school suspension for less than five days, a short-term suspension. This law requires that the suspending authority give notice to the student of the charged misconduct. That authority shall give an explanation if the student denies the misconduct. There is also an opportunity for the student and parent to have an informal conference with the principal in order to give the student's version of the events and to question complaining witnesses. The notice and opportunity for the informal conference must take place prior to the suspension unless the student's presence in school poses a continuing danger to people or property or an ongoing threat of disruption to the academic process. In that case, the law allows the conference to take place as soon as reasonably practical.

There is also a requirement of notice to parents according to Section 100.2(l)(4) of the Commissioner's Regulations for suspensions of five days or less. The regulation states that "school district officials shall immediately notify the parents or the persons in parental relation in writing that the student may be suspended from school." The notice must be sent within 24 hours of the decision to propose a suspension by personal delivery, express mail delivery, or equivalent means that would reasonably assure receipt of the notice within the 24-hour period. The notice shall also be provided by telephone if the school has a telephone number for the parent. Oral communication with a parent regarding a suspension is not a substitute for the required written notification (*Appeal of J.Z.*, 47 Ed Dept Rep 243, Decision No. 15,681; *Appeal of a Student with a Disability*, 47 id. 19, Decision No. 15,608). Additionally, the Commissioner's decisions have repeatedly held that sending the written notice by regular mail does not satisfy the regulation (*Appeal of B.B.*, 49 Ed Dept Rep 253, Decision No. 16,017).

The notice and informal conference must be in the dominant language used by those in parental relation to the student. The notice shall include a description of the incident and of the rights of the parents to request the informal conference according to the provisions of the Education Law (*Appeal of V.R. and C.R.*, 43 Ed Dept Rep 99, Decision No. 14,934). The purpose of the written notice requirement is to ensure that parents of, or persons in parental relation to, a student suspended for five days or less are made aware of the statutory right provided in Education Law Section 3214(3) (b) (1) to question the complaining witnesses in the presence of the principal who imposed the suspension in the first instance, and who has authority to terminate or reduce the suspension. This procedure affords the principal the opportunity to decide whether his or her original decision to suspend was correct or should be modified (*Appeal of F.W.*, 48 Ed Dept Rep 399, Decision No. 15,897). It is insufficient to provide merely an opportunity to speak with the principal without the complaining witnesses present, or an opportunity to speak with complaining witnesses without the principal present (*Appeal of B.B.*, 49 Ed Dept 253, Decision No. 16,017; *Appeal of Doyle*, 53 Ed Dept Rep, Decision No. 16,439).

It is important for administrators to review the district's policies and practices regarding suspension procedures to make sure that they reflect state law and Commissioner's Regulations. A standard procedure for notification to parents should be in place so that the process is not challenged when a decision is made to suspend a student.

1-6. What are the reasons for a superintendent's hearing? What is the role of the administrator in a superintendent's hearing?

Education Law 3214(3)(c) is used to determine whether an out-of-school suspension will be for more than five days. According to this law, a student may be suspended "who is insubordinate or disorderly or violent or disruptive or whose conduct otherwise endangers the safety, morals, health or welfare of others." The law describes the right of a student to a fair hearing and describes the process, notice, and procedures for such a hearing. The superintendent may serve as the hearing officer or may choose to designate an impartial hearing officer who will make findings of fact and recommendations to the superintendent.

It generally falls to the principal or another building administrator to present the case at the hearing on behalf of the district since the misconduct would have caused the principal or another building administrator taking disciplinary action in the matter and since the superintendent will be making the decision about the length of a suspension. The building administrator will need to develop a charge statement for the particular infraction and an anecdotal record that contains the disciplinary record of the student. These will be considered if the hearing officer determines that the charged misconduct by the student did occur. According to the Commissioner (*Appeal of J.D.*, 39 Ed Dept Rep 593, Decision No. 14,322), the charges for the charge statement "need only be sufficiently specific to advise the student and counsel of the activities or incidents which have given rise to the proceedings and which will form the basis for the hearing."

The administrator must also be prepared to present witnesses and any other evidence including pictures or video, to substantiate the charged misconduct. In the case of a student disciplinary hearing, "it is improper for the hearing officer to consider a witness's written statement unless the witness is available for cross examination" (*Appeal of R.Y.*, Ed Dept 336, Decision No. 16,046). It is helpful that the letter of notification indicate the opportunity to present witness testimony and the need to have such witnesses physically present at the hearing.

It is important that the facts and steps taken during the determination of disciplinary action are reviewed with counsel for the district before the hearing.

1-7. What is the proper wording of a suspension letter?

The notice provided to parents must include a description of the alleged misconduct and information about the parents' right to request an immediate informal conference with the principal in the event of a short- term suspension of five days or less to present the student's version of the incident and to ask questions of the complaining witnesses. There is no specific language for the letter in the statutes, but Section 100.2 (1)(4) states:

> Such notice shall provide a description of the incident(s) for which suspension is proposed and shall inform the parents or persons in parental relation of their right to request an immediate informal conference with the principal in accordance with the provisions of Education Law, section 3214(3)(b). Such notice and informal conference shall be in the dominant language or mode of communication used by the parents or persons in parental relation to the pupil.

It is important for schools within a district to be consistent with the format of the letter that is used to notify parents about a suspension. Education Law 3214 (3)(b)(1) and Section 100.2 (1)(4) of Commissioner's Regulations provide these statutory requirements.

1-8. When is suspension appropriate for elementary students and secondary students?

The decision to suspend a student is a local school decision that should reflect the philosophy of the school district as developed in the code of conduct. An annual review of the code is required. This process provides an opportunity to review and discuss the district's philosophy concerning suspension as a disciplinary option. The code includes a range of disciplinary measures that may be assigned for violations of the code. The code must also include provisions for removal of a student from a classroom and suspension of students, consistent with applicable laws. A code is required to include a minimum suspension period for any student who "repeatedly is substantially disruptive of the educational process or substantially interferes with the teacher's authority over the classroom." "Repeatedly" is defined in the Regulation as removal of the student from the classroom for four or more times in a semester or three or more times in a trimester.

See questions 7-62 and 7-64 for information about a suspension for a student with a disability.

1-9. What role does in-school suspension have in the range of disciplinary consequences?

The process for assigning in-school suspension must be fair and give students and parents the opportunity to discuss the conduct being reviewed with the person or body authorized to impose the in-school suspension (*Appeal of M.C.*, 43 Ed Dept Rep 276, Decision No. 14,993). Additional procedures to follow, including notifying parents, are found in the district's code of conduct.

The use of an in-school suspension is generally regarded as a less serious penalty than an out-of-school suspension. An out-of-school suspension requires procedures that are consistent with education law and the Commissioner's Regulations. An in-school suspension is an administrative consequence, and the procedures used to determine its use must be fair and give students and parents the opportunity to discuss the conduct that is being reviewed with the person or body authorized to impose the discipline (*Appeal of G.H.L.*, 46 id. 571, Decision No. 15,598).

The code of conduct development and review is an appropriate place to discuss and to determine situations in which in-school suspension can be an option in the range of disciplinary consequences. The code should provide fairness and flexibility in determining its use. The administrator should make sure that the in-school suspension program is designed both for punishment if the student needs to be removed from a classroom and for prevention of future incidents. Both academic support and counseling might be provided as part of the program.

1-10. What procedures should be considered for an in-school suspension?

In-school suspensions are not governed by Education Law 3214. "While Education Law 3214 prohibits an assistant principal from imposing an out-of-school suspension, it does not prohibit an assistant principal from imposing an in-school suspension" (*Appeal of M.C.*, 43 Ed Dept Rep 276, Decision No. 14,993).

In-school suspensions and suspensions from extracurricular activities are not governed by Education Law 3214 and do not require a full hearing (*Appeal of N.C.*, 42 Ed Dept Rep 119, Decision No. 14,794). Procedures governing in-school suspensions and suspensions from extracurricular privileges need only be fair and give students and parents an opportunity to discuss the conduct being reviewed with the person or body authorized to impose the discipline. (*Appeal of G.H.L.*, 46 id. 571, Decision No. 15,598)

1-11. How may a student be removed from class? Can a student be removed from class and left unattended in a hallway?

A teacher may remove a "disruptive pupil" from class according to the provisions of Education Law 3214 and the district's code of conduct. Education Law 3214 notes that such a student "is an elementary or secondary student under twenty-one years of age who is substantially disruptive of the educational process or substantially interferes with the teacher's authority over the classroom." A student should not be left unattended in the hallway. A student removed from class should be sent to the building administrator to ensure that there is compliance with the law and that there is supervision of the student. Education Law 3214 also requires that the teacher give reasons for the removal to the student and principal.

Procedures for removing a student from class must be described in the code of conduct. The principal must inform the parents of the pupil about the removal and the reasons for it within 24 hours. The principal cannot change the removal unless the principal finds that the evidence does not support the charges, there is a violation of law, or the conduct warrants a suspension according to the procedures of Education Law 3214. A hearing according to Education Law 3214 must be held if there is consideration of removal of the student from class for more than five days. Education Law 3214 (3-a) addresses the removal of a student from a classroom.

The code of conduct must include provisions that describe how a student may be removed from a classroom for a specific incident. The code must also include procedures for continued educational programming for the student in the event of removal from class. A teacher's removal of a student from a classroom and suspension of a student from class are both categories that are reported on the VADIR form that is sent to SED.

Education Law 3214(3-a) (b) requires that the principal, or a designated school district administrator, inform the parent of the removal and the reasons therefore within 24 hours of the removal. The law also provides that the student and the parent shall, upon request, be given an opportunity for an informal conference within 48 hours of the removal with the principal to discuss the reasons for the removal. If the student denies the charges, the principal is required to provide an explanation of the basis for the removal and allow the parent and the student to present the student's version of the events (*Appeal of K.M.*, 49 Ed Dept Rep, Decision No. 16,015).

The principal can set aside the removal from class under certain circumstances. Education Law 3214 (3-a)(c) states:

> The principal shall not set aside the discipline imposed by the teacher unless the principal finds that the charges against the pupil are not supported by substantial evidence or that the pupil's removal is otherwise in violation of law or that the conduct warrants suspension from school pursuant to this section and a suspension will be imposed.

Education Law 3214 (3-a)(d) also states that "the principal may, in his or her discretion, designate a school district administrator, to carry out the functions required of the principal under this subdivision."

1-12. What steps should be taken if a student is suspected of being in possession or under the influence of an illegal substance?

The administrator should follow disciplinary procedures for incidents that involve the use or possession of illegal substances that are required to be in a code of conduct for such events. Since the incident involves an illegal substance, it is important to coordinate with the local law enforcement agency in order to provide evidence that the substance is illegal and to address violations of law. The code of conduct must have provisions for notifying law enforcement personnel about violations of the code that are a crime.

It is also important to protect any evidence, take a picture of the evidence, and document the chain of custody for evidence that will be presented in a hearing.

1-13. What rights does a suspended child have to an education?

A student who is of compulsory attendance age and who has been suspended has a right to receive alternative education. Education Law 3214 (3)(e) requires school districts to take immediate steps to provide alternative instruction to students of compulsory school ages who are suspended. "The term 'immediate' does not mean instantaneously, but it does mean that a school district must act promptly" (*Appeal of M.K. and S.K.*, 45 Ed Dept Rep 424, Decision No. 15,373). The Commissioner has found that a delay of four days was unreasonable (*Appeal of Bridges*, 34 Ed Dept Rep 232, Decision No. 13,291).

The instruction "must be substantially equivalent to the student's regular classroom program" and the district must "act reasonably promptly, with due regard for the nature and circumstances of the particular case" (*Appeal of Camille S.*, 39 Ed Dept Rep 574, Decision No. 14,316). That decision also held that the definition of "substantially equivalent instruction" would be decided on a case-by-case basis. The Commissioner has held that two hours of instruction per day are sufficient to meet a district's obligations under the education law in the cases of suspended students (*Appeal of Camille S.*, 39 id. 574, Decision No. 14,316).

In addition, Subdivision (l) of Section 100.2 of the Regulations of the Commissioner of Education requires provisions in the code of conduct for continued educational programming for students who are removed from the classroom or suspended from school. These educational programs must be "appropriate to individual student needs."

It should be noted that Commissioner's Regulation 175.21, which applies to hospitals and other institutions that provide for care, custody, and treatment of children for state aid, and that provide instruction for students, holds that each elementary pupil shall receive those services for five hours of instruction per week and, to the extent possible, one hour per day. The same regulation requires ten hours of instruction per week at the secondary school level and, to the extent possible, two hours per day. See also http://www.p12.nysed.gov/sss/lawsregs/ContractsForInstructionQandA.pdf for more information about districts entering into contracts for the instruction of suspended students.

1-14. What constitutes harassment, sex offenses, bullying,

and teasing? Are there any reporting procedures?

"Harassment," "sex offenses," and "bullying" are terms that are included in the Summary of Violent and Disruptive Incidents report form, which must be submitted to the State Education Department. These terms are explained in the Glossary of Terms Used in Reporting Violent and Disruptive Incidents (see http://www.p12.nysed.gov/sss/ssae/schoolsafety/vadir/glossary201718.html).

Commissioner's Regulation 100.2 (kk) states:

Harassment or bullying means the creation of a hostile environment by conduct or by threats, intimidation, or abuse, including cyberbullying as defined in Education Law Section 11(8), that either:

a. has or would have the effect of unreasonably and substantially interfering with a student's educational performance, opportunities or benefits, or mental, emotional and/or physical well-being, including conduct, threats, intimidation or abuse that reasonably causes or would reasonably be expected to cause emotional harm; or

b. reasonably causes or would reasonably be expected to cause physical injury to a student or to cause a student to fear for his or her physical safety.

Teasing and name calling or verbal bullying are considered forms of bullying (see https://www.stopbullying.gov/what-is-bullying/definitionindex.html).

The Dignity for All Students Act makes it clear in public school policy that no student shall be subject to discrimination, harassment, or bullying based upon a person's actual or perceived race, color, weight, national origin, ethnic group, religion, religious practice, disability, sexual orientation, gender, or sex by school students or employees. School districts are required to adopt a policy to be included in the code of conduct that addresses training for employees, identifying one staff person to handle human relations in the previously referenced areas, and instruction in tolerance, respect for others, and dignity. See http://www.p12.nysed.gov/dignityact/ for more information about the Dignity Act, including resources to combat harassment, bullying, discrimination and cyberbullying. There is also information about creating a safe and supportive environment for transgender and nonconforming students. See also 1-15, 1-16, 1-17, 1-18, and 1-36.

See http://www.p12.nysed.gov/dignityact/documents/Prevent

BullyingInYourSchool_Nov2016.pdf about addressing bullying including cyberbullying, intimidation, harassment, and discrimination in schools.

Incidents are reportable whether or not the perpetrator was disciplined or referred to law enforcement. Incidents are reported differently if the perpetrator is suspended, removed as a disruptive student according to Education Law 3214, referred to a counseling or treatment program, transferred to alternative education, or referred to law enforcement or the juvenile justice system, according to the code of conduct. Incidents are also reported in the case of an employee who is disciplined or referred to law enforcement.

1-15. What regulations govern bullying, harassment, and discrimination in schools?

The Dignity for All Students Act requires schools to provide students with a safe and supportive environment free from discrimination, intimidation, taunting, harassment, and bullying while at school or at a school function. Schools are required to develop a code of conduct and train students and staff to recognize and report incidences of bullying, harassment, and discrimination to an appointed Dignity Act coordinator. All incidents must be dealt with accordingly and reported to SED. The State Education website has resources and guidance available to help schools develop a program: http://www.p12.nysed.gov/dignityact/.

1-16. What are considerations for school leaders with regard to transgender students?

The State Education Department provides guidance for school districts at https://bit.ly/1CSy1ZC. This document serves as the foundation for this answer.

A school administrator provides leadership to all public school students, including transgender and gender nonconforming (GNC) students, with an environment that is free from discrimination and harassment, fosters civility in public schools, and ensures that every student has equal access to educational programs and activities.

School leaders in their efforts to promote a positive school culture should become familiar with applicable law, regulations, guidance, and related resources, and communicate and model respect for the gender identity of all students.

Both DASA, including its implementing regulations and guidance, and this guidance document reflect the reality that transgender and GNC students are enrolled in New York's public schools. These students, because of the possibility of misunderstanding and lack of knowledge about their lives, may be at a higher risk for peer ostracism, victimization, and bullying. Educators play an essential role in advocating for the well-being of students and creating a supportive school culture. (p. 4)

New York State Education Law 3201-a prohibits discrimination based on sex with respect to admission into or inclusion in courses of instruction and athletic teams in public schools. Furthermore, DASA specifically provides that "no student shall be subjected to harassment or bullying by employees or students on school property or at a school function; nor shall any student be subjected to discrimination based on a person's actual or perceived race, color, weight, national origin, ethnic group, religion, religious practice, disability, sexual orientation, gender (including gender identity or expression), or sex by school employees or students on school property or at a school function." DASA includes gender as a protected category and defines gender as "a person's actual or perceived sex and includes a person's gender identity or expression." (p. 1)

School administrators should consult the guidance from SED as it relates to gender identity, gender transition, use of names and pronouns, and student privacy and communication with families. SED also recommends that understanding the common terminology associated with gender identity is important to providing a safe and supportive school environment for students (p. 2).

The guidance also states that school districts are encouraged to provide the guidance document and other resources, such as trainings and information sessions, to the school community including, but not limited to, parents, students, staff, and residents (p.11). The school leader plays a leadership role with these activities.

The school administrator should review policies and practices with the school attorney that relate to gender-based activities to ensure compliance with Title IX and DASA. See 1-48, 4-21, and 5-14.

1-17. What is an administrator's responsibility for Internet bullying at home or after school?

The administrator should provide leadership to ensure that a district takes a comprehensive approach to the issues of cyberbullying, sexting, and the use of social networking by both students and staff through the district's Internet safety policy (see http://www.nysed.gov/edtech/internet-safety-and-cyberbullying-0) and the annual review of its code of conduct. The administrator should make sure that the district's legal counsel is consulted concerning specific questions about Internet safety and the Acceptable Use Policy.

It is important that this comprehensive approach be ongoing in order to consider the evolution of technology. It is also important that education be provided for students and professional development for staff about cyberbullying. The New York State Education Law on Internet Safety and Appropriate Use allows for education of students for safe and appropriate use of Internet technology and resources (http://www.nysed.gov/edtech/internet-safety-and-cyberbullying-0). See also 1-14 and 1-18.

The Commissioner has clearly stated, in a case that involved the use of email, that students may be disciplined for off-campus behavior that may "endanger the health or safety of pupils within the educational system or adversely affect the educative process" (*Appeal of Ravick*, 40 Ed Dept Rep 262, Decision No. 14,477). If there is not a connection between the safety of students and the educational process, it may be a matter that must be handled by the local police agency. See also question 1-21 about off-campus student behavior as it relates to school consequences. A school resource officer (SRO) may be helpful in ending Internet harassment.

The State Education Department, in its document The New York State Dignity for All Students Act: A Resource and Promising Practices Guide for School Administrators and Faculty, notes:

> Students who are targeted often become alienated due to the fact that they are simply unsure of the appropriate steps to take to address the situation. To ensure that these circumstances do not occur, school administrators are strongly encouraged to provide support for students through guidance, social work, and/or psychological services in the district. (p. 48)

The document from the State Education Department also adds:

> The Code of Conduct should also include statements that make it abundantly clear that cyberbullying is a form of harassment and bullying and that both it and sexting are unacceptable and inappropriate and [will not be tolerated] on school grounds or at school-sponsored events or functions, using either school or personal technology. (p. 50)

The Dignity Act includes a definition of cyberbullying and related conduct that occurs off school property, but could create a "risk of substantial disruption within the school environment, when it is foreseeable that the conduct, threats, intimidation, or abuse might reach school property (Education Law 11 (7))" (http://www.p12.nysed.gov/dignityact/documents/FINALDignityForAllStudentsActGuidanceDec2017.pdf). The Guide also notes that "districts are urged to review each fact pattern with their school attorney to determine the proper bounds of school responsibility and/or authority in a particular case."

1-18. What rights does the school have to restrict or ban student use of cell phones and other personal electronic devices in schools?

The code of conduct, through its development and review, is an appropriate place to discuss the extent of restriction of electronic devices in the school and outside of classroom settings. Considerations about whether to ban or simply restrict use in schools include disruptions to the educational process, ability of the school personnel to enforce the policy and any parental concerns for communication and safety. Language concerning a policy restricting use of electronic devices should be reviewed with a policy specialist or an attorney. Any language to restrict use or to ban such devices should connect restricted use of such devices with their impact on the educational process. The policy should clarify how an administrator will respond when there is a violation of the policy. The Commissioner has ruled that a school district has the right to prohibit or restrict cell phone usage throughout its buildings (*Appeal and Application of Rosten*, 49 Ed Dept Rep 237, Decision No. 16,014).

Additionally, the State Education Department states:

The Dignity Act [DASA] defines "cyberbullying" as harassment or bullying that occurs through any form of electronic communication (Education Law §11[8]). Cyberbullying can include, among other things, harassment by way of email, instant messaging, blogs, chat rooms, pagers, cell phones, gaming systems, tweeting, or social media websites. It is important to note that the regulation of off-campus conduct that is in the form of verbal or written speech – whether communicated face-to-face, in writing or electronically – may implicate the First Amendment rights of the speaker. The extent of a school's responsibility and/or authority to address off-campus harassment or bullying in the form of speech depends upon the specific facts of each unique situation. As a result, this guidance cannot establish bright-line rules. Rather, districts are urged to review each fact pattern with their school attorney to determine the proper bounds of school responsibility and/or authority in a particular case (http://www.p12.nysed.gov/dignityact/documents/ FINALDignityForAllStudentsActGuidanceDec2017.pdf).

In addition, the State Education Department's policy for all secondary-level state exams does not allow students to bring any communication device to a state exam. The School Administrator's Manual includes a list of prohibited devices that must be read to the students before beginning the examination. If a principal determines that a student was using a communication device, during the administration of the test, and the determination was made using due process procedures, the test must be invalidated with no score calculated for the student. Any testing irregularity involving the use of the device must be reported by the principal to the Office of State Assessment. Proctors must read a statement about the policy to students at the start of an exam (http://www.p12.nysed.gov/assessment/sam/secondary/ section2-15.pdf). See also question 1-17.

1-19 What is the law regarding student dress In New York State schools? What are the regulations for mandating a dress code for students?

The Commissioner's Regulations (Subdivision (l)(2)(i) of Section 100.2) state that the district code of conduct shall include provisions for appropriate and acceptable, as well as unacceptable and inappropriate, dress on school property and at school functions. See 1-1 for more information about the collaborative process to develop the code of conduct that shall be approved by a board of education.

The Commissioner has held that "a school board may regulate student dress where there are legitimate educational reasons to do so, such as teaching students socially appropriate behavior, eliminating potential health or safety hazards, preserving the integrity of the educational process or avoiding school violence" (*Appeal of Conley*, 34 Ed Dept Rep 376, Decision No. 13,349). A school board may not use fashion or taste as the sole criterion in regulating student appearance (*Appeal of Pintka*, 33 Ed Dept Rep 228, Decision No. 13,034).

The Pintka case also notes that it is important that the dress code be developed locally in consultation with teachers, administrators, school-related professionals, students, and parents so that the policy reflects the current standards of the community with regard to "decorum and deportment." The Commissioner has also stated that significant policy decisions that may impact on student rights, including student dress, require "careful consideration and thoughtful discussion within the school community, including parents, teachers, and student" (*Appeal of Phillips*, 38 Ed Dept 297, Decision No. 14,038).

1-20. What is VADIR? Who in the school district is responsible for reporting discipline statistics to the New York State Education Department? What types of discipline issues need to be reported? Does the State Education Department define discipline actions that must be reported?

VADIR refers to the Uniform Violent and Disruptive Incident Reporting System that is required as a result of the SAVE Act. A summary of violent and disruptive incidents for each school in a district must be completed and submitted to the State Education Department. The superintendent is required to certify the data for each school. It is important for each building principal to review all data and to ensure that there is a uniform system for reporting all required incidents since information about VADIR is reported to the public. Two years of VADIR data are used to determine whether a school is designated as "persistently dangerous" (http://www.p12.nysed.gov/irs/school_safety/school_safety_accountability.html).

The Glossary of Terms Used in Reporting Violent and Disruptive Incidents defines the terms for the incident categories that are contained on the report form that is sent to the State Education Department. The glossary is available at the Information and Reporting Services webpage at the State Education Department (see question 1-14). See also questions 1-11, 1-27, 1-28, and 1-36.

1-21. What jurisdiction does a principal have when students fight off school grounds at student activities or in the community?

Education Law 2801 (1) ensures that codes of conduct apply to school-sponsored or school-authorized events and activities regardless of where they take place, including in another state. This makes it clear that the code of conduct and the jurisdiction of the principal apply to student behavior at student activities that take place off school grounds.

Prior Commissioner's decisions have upheld the suspension of students for off-campus conduct (*Appeal of W.T.*, 46 Ed Dept Rep 363, Decision No. 15,534; *Appeal of C.R.*, 45 id. 303, Decision No. 15,330). In addition, the Commissioner has held that students may be disciplined for behavior that occurs outside of school in cases that may endanger the health or safety of students within the school or adversely affect the education process (*Appeal of A.F. and T.P.*, 56 Ed Dept Rep, Decision No. 16,997). It is important for the administrator to be able to establish a connection between the off-campus behavior and either the health or safety of students or the educational process. These cases are often complicated and it is helpful to review the facts with counsel for the school district.

1-22. What parameters should an administrator consider when physically intervening in a fight among students?

The Commissioner's Regulations (Section 100.2 (l) (3)) that address corporal punishment also provide guidance for these situations. That regulation defines corporal punishment so as not to include "the use of reasonable physical force for any of the following purposes:

(a) to protect oneself from physical injury;
(b) to protect another pupil or teacher or any other person from physical injury;
(c) to protect the property of school or of others; or
(d) to restrain or remove a pupil whose behavior is interfering with the orderly exercise and performance of school district

functions, powers or duties, if that pupil has refused to comply with a request to refrain from further disruptive acts; provided that alternative procedures and methods not involving the use of physical force cannot reasonably be employed to achieve the purposes set forth in clauses (a) through (d) of this subparagraph."

The last clause is particularly important since it notes that a request must first be made to stop the disruptive behavior and it also points out the need to be clear that, if physical force were used, alternative strategies would not work.

1-23. When a fight occurs, when is it appropriate to differentiate discipline between combatants?

It is possible to differentiate discipline depending on the facts of the matter and the participation of the students. Differentiation may occur after a thorough investigation and appropriate due process to determine the facts. The investigation and due process may reveal that there were different levels of involvement by the students or that one student had a documented history of fighting with prior notice that similar incidents in the future would be treated more seriously. Some of the decisions of the Commissioner relate to this approach.

The Commissioner has held that "in cases of student discipline, the sanction imposed must be proportionate to the severity of the offense involved" (*Appeal of M.F. and J.F.*, 43 Ed Dept Rep 174, Decision No. 14,960). In *Appeal of Bussfield*, 34 Ed Dept Rep 383, Decision No. 13,352, the Commissioner stated that there may be discipline of a student only when the record shows that there has been proof of misconduct and a reasonable degree of certainty that the student participated in the misconduct. The Commissioner has noted that "the decision to suspend a student from school must be based on competent and substantial evidence that the student actually participated in the conduct charged" (*Appeal of Aldith L.*, 30 Ed Dept Rep 291, Decision No. 14,241).

The fact that another student may have received a lesser penalty or no discipline in a case does not provide a basis for nullifying the penalty as long as the student engaged in the conduct and received an appropriate penalty (*Appeal of R.Y.*, 49 Ed Dept Rep 336, Decision No. 16,046). The Commissioner has also ruled (*Appeal of C.V.*, 56 Ed

Dept, Decision No. 17,016) that the fact that other students involved in an incident may have received different or lesser penalties, or no disciplinary measures at all, does not, of itself, provide a basis for nullifying the discipline imposed on another student, provided that the record establishes that the student engaged in the misconduct and the penalty imposed is therefore appropriate (*Appeal of L.T.*, 51 Ed Dept Rep, Decision No. 16,242; *Appeal of R.Y.*, 49 id. 336, Decision No. 16,046).

1-24. How should an administrator deal with a student who instigates a fight but is not involved?

The administrator needs to establish the facts through a thorough investigation and using due process procedures. The administrator should be able to establish a connection between the facts of the case, the student's behavior, and the code of conduct. As a result, any discipline would be based on evidence and the code of conduct. The Commissioner has held that "in order for a student to be disciplined for misconduct, there must be competent and substantial evidence that the student participated in the objectionable conduct" (*Appeal of Doris J.*, 31 Ed Dept Rep 153, Decision No. 12,602). It is important to remember that the discipline taken in such a matter must be proportionate to the severity of the offense (*Appeal of R.C.*, 41 Ed Dept Rep 446, Decision No. 14,741).

It should be added that Education Law 3214(3) provides that "[a] pupil who is insubordinate or disorderly, or whose conduct otherwise endangers the safety, morals, health or welfare of others" may be suspended from required attendance. The administrator should consider if there is a connection between instigation of a fight and endangering the safety of others. A code of conduct may include "inciting violence" as a prohibited conduct. See *Appeal of R.A.*, 47 Ed Dept Rep 504, Decision No. 15,767; *Appeal of R.A.*, 48 Ed Dept Rep 520, Decision No. 15,935.

1-25. May an administrator use community service as a punishment for students who break school rules? May a board of education authorize participation in counseling as a condition for a student's early return to school?

The Commissioner has held that community service cannot be imposed for a suspension according to Education Law 3214

(*Appeal of L.H.*, 43 Ed Dept Rep 315, Decision No. 15,005). That does not prevent an administrator from using community service as a disciplinary option that is not imposed as a result of a hearing held according to Education Law 3214. In that case, it would be helpful to have community service or school service listed as an option at the appropriate place in the code of conduct. As with any disciplinary action, it should be assigned following appropriate investigative and due process procedures to determine the facts of the matter.

Education Law 3214 gives a board of education, pursuant to 3214 procedures, the authority to condition a student's early return to school and revocation of suspension on the basis of voluntary participation in counseling or, where appropriate, specialized classes for anger management or dispute resolution. See *Appeal of K.H.*, 49 Ed Dept Rep 210, Decision No. 16,004.

1-26. Are any forms of group punishment an acceptable practice?

The Commissioner has held that there must be proof of misconduct and a reasonable amount of certainty that a student participated in misconduct before assigning a disciplinary penalty. In addition, the Commissioner has stated that the threatened punishment of several students because one may have been guilty would not have a rational basis and would be arbitrary (*Appeal of Bussfield*, 34 Ed Dept Rep 383, Decision No. 13,352). On the other hand, this decision by the Commissioner would not prevent similar punishment from being used for students in a case in which several students had been found to participate in the same act of misconduct.

1-27. What procedures should be followed when a student pulls a fire alarm in a school?

Once a fire alarm is pulled, the building must be evacuated. According to the attorney general, firefighters must enter the school and remain there until they have determined that the fire is out. The school cannot be occupied until the firefighting service determines that the fire is out and/or declares that the school is safe for occupancy. An investigation would follow to determine the facts and find out who pulled the fire alarm, utilizing due process procedures. See http://www.p12.nysed.gov/facplan/articles/H01_fire_alarms.html for more information about the attorney general's informal opinion #81-13.

It is important for school officials to work with law enforcement authorities during the investigation. It is a violation of the New York State Penal Law to falsely pull a fire alarm. The school needs to consider carefully all of the facts, in view of the seriousness of falsely activating a fire alarm and causing a school to be evacuated, before determining the action that should be taken. The police department should be involved in this process, and school disciplinary policies should be observed. If a suspension for more than five days is considered, then the procedures for a hearing according to Education Law 3214 must be followed. Falsely activating a fire alarm is also an incident category that requires VADIR reporting.

1-28. What type of evidence should be gathered, and what are educationally appropriate punishments for defacing school property?

Disciplinary measures for vandalism to school property should be included in a code of conduct. These measures should include a range of options for disciplinary consideration by the administrator, depending on the extent of the act and whether the student has a prior disciplinary record. Disciplinary options that may be found in a code of conduct include restitution, suspension, and a 3214 hearing for consideration of a suspension that exceeds five days. The act may also be one that is criminal and would be referred to a law enforcement agency.

The crime scene should be preserved until law enforcement personnel can investigate it. This would include acts of graffiti, which should not be removed until they have been recorded or law enforcement personnel have investigated them. A helpful practice is to ensure that pictures are taken of the graffiti or act of vandalism.

Intentional or reckless damaging of school property is listed on the VADIR form and has a range of reportable consequences.

1-29. What are the laws, regulations, and recommended policies related to locker searches, backpack searches, strip searches, and canine searches?

A search of a locker by a school official requires that the "reasonable cause" or "reasonable suspicion" standard be met. If a search is conducted by a law enforcement official, the higher standard of "probable cause" must be met. Searches by drug-sniffing dogs in hallways with lockers have generally not been held to need reasonable suspicion. However, reasonable and individualized suspicion would be needed to sniff individual items of a particular student.

An administrator needs reasonable cause that evidence will be found that would violate a law or the school's code of conduct in order to search a student's property such as a student's backpack. A law enforcement official must meet the higher standard of probable cause that evidence will be found that would violate a law in order to conduct a search. A search of a backpack, since it is a personal possession, should be conducted on the basis of individualized suspicion that there is evidence associated with that particular backpack or its owner.

Strip searches have been considered by the courts to be too intrusive to an individual to justify on the grounds of reasonable suspicion. If one is being considered due to imminent danger to the health and safety of building occupants, there should be an immediate call to counsel for the school district to review the matter. Involvement of law enforcement to conduct the search should be considered if time permits.

The administrator is better protected and more consistent with searches of student property if there is a board of education policy concerning searches. The code of conduct is an appropriate place to include procedures for searches.

School officials do not need probable cause or a warrant. They do, however, need reasonable suspicion. The Commissioner's decision in *Appeal of a Student with a Disability*, 50 Ed Dept Rep, Decision No. 16,168 includes the following clarifying information:

> The Fourth Amendment to the United States Constitution prohibits government officials from conducting unreasonable searches and seizures. In *New Jersey v. T.L.O.* (469 U.S. 325; "T.L.O."), the United States Supreme Court held that the prohibition extends to searches by public school officials. However, the Court also recognized the uniqueness of the school setting and the need to balance a student's legitimate expectation of privacy against the substantial interest of teachers and administrators in maintaining discipline in the classroom and on school grounds (id.). The legality of a search depends upon the reasonableness, under all circumstances, of the search (id.; see also *Appeal of J.R. and N.R.*, 48 Ed Dept Rep 239, Decision No. 15,848).

Determining reasonableness involves a two-fold inquiry: 1) whether the search was "justified at its inception", that is, whether there are reasonable grounds for suspecting that the search will reveal evidence that the student has violated or is violating either the law or the rules of the school; and 2) whether the search as actually conducted "was reasonably related in scope to the circumstances which justified [it] ... in the first place" (T.L.O. at 341, citing *Terry v. Ohio*, 392 U.S. 1). The Court stated that the search will be permissible in scope when the measures adopted are reasonably related to the objectives of the search and not excessively intrusive in light of the age and sex of the student and the nature of the infraction (T.L.O. at 342; see also *Appeal of J.R. and N.R.*, 48 Ed Dept Rep 239, Decision No. 15,848).

Among the factors to be considered in determining the sufficiency of cause to search a student are the child's age, history and record in school, the prevalence and seriousness of the problem in the school to which the search is directed and, of course, the exigency to make the search without delay (see also *Appeal of J.R. and N.R.*, 48 Ed Dept Rep 239, Decision No. 15,848).

The Commissioner's decision in *Appeal of J.R. and N.R.*, 48 Ed Dept Rep 239, Decision No. 15,848 notes that "a request to empty pockets has been deemed to be the equivalent of searching the pockets themselves (*Matter of Bernard G.*, 247 AD2d 91)." In that same decision, the Commissioner decided that search was justified and that the request that P.R. empty his pockets was minimally intrusive and reasonably related in scope to the circumstances presented.

1-30. What is a proper procedure when an administrator must search a locker?

The administrator should have someone designated by the school administration and/or a law enforcement officer present as a witness when a locker is being searched. It is better to conduct the search while classes are in session and not at a time when large groups of people are in the area of the locker in order to minimize disruption and to maintain student privacy as much as possible. If a law enforcement officer or school resource officer is present, and that person is not employed by the school, it is preferable to have the administrator conduct the search with the law enforcement personnel present in a supportive role. However, the law enforcement official would be available in the event that evidence was found that violated a law.

While courts have generally held that lockers are the property of schools, it is advisable to give notice at the start of the school year that lockers are the property of the school and that there may be general searches during the school year. It is important to consider the administrative guidelines noted above, including the reasonable cause standard for a general search. It is always important to review such considerations in advance with counsel for the school district.

1-31. What constitutes a weapon in a school building?

The New York State Education Department's Glossary of Terms Used in Reporting Violent and Disruptive Incidents from the New York State Education Department contains a number of definitions of weapons that are used for the Violent and Disruptive Incidents report (see also question 1-14). Education Law 3214 defines a "violent pupil" as one who possesses or displays, while on school district property, "a gun, knife, explosive or incendiary bomb or other dangerous instrument capable of causing physical injury or death" or who "threatens, while on school district property, to use any instrument that appears capable of causing physical injury or death."

The Federal Gun-Free Schools Act of 1994 defines "weapon" as a firearm as identified in Section 921 of Title 18, United States Code. A firearm, according to this code, includes any weapon that can expel, or be converted to expel, a projectile by action of an explosive or other propellant. A weapon, also means a "destructive device" that is explosive, incendiary, or poisonous gas. Antique firearms are not included in this definition. In cases that involve potential weapons, it is important to review the definitions in this code and to consult with the school attorney and law enforcement agency. Since a one-year suspension is mandated for a student who violates this act, Education Law 3214 requires that a hearing be held for any student who has been charged with bringing a weapon to school according to the Gun-Free Schools Act.

It is helpful to consult with law enforcement agencies to understand how they apply laws to items that can be considered weapons, so that there is a thoughtful basis for the definition of "weapon" that is used by a district.

The definition of "weapon" should be addressed in the school code of conduct. (For more information about definitions of "weapon" in a code of conduct, see *Appeal of J.R. and N.R.,* 48 Ed Dept Rep 239, Decision No. 15,848). The code of conduct provides notice that weapons are not allowed in school and explains the possible consequences for having a weapon (*Appeal of M.G.,* 41 Ed Dept Rep 58, Decision No. 14,614). The Commissioner has upheld decisions in which districts included BB guns and knives in the definitions of "weapons" in their codes of conduct.

1-32. What right does a student have to drive to school? What right does a student have regarding parking on school property?

A student does not have a right to drive to school. A board of education has the discretion to determine the use of school property (*Matter of Hollister,* 33 Ed Dept Rep 294, Decision No. 13,053). It is good practice to have a policy adopted by the board of education that provides a basis for decisions concerning parking by students on school property and the issue of students driving to school. The policy should carefully consider the matter of students driving to school and the ability to enforce any provisions of such a policy, since it is possible in some circumstances for students to drive to school, but not park on school grounds.

1-33. If a student is given the privilege of driving to school and leaving early, what are the legal ramifications to the school district?

A district should have a policy that addresses the matter of students driving to and from school. The district should carefully assess the need for granting this privilege. There should also be a policy that addresses the early dismissal of students and includes criteria for this privilege such as a note from a parent, participation in a college course, and the impact on the student's academic program. A reasonable policy and procedure should be developed with input from staff, attorneys, and the district's insurance carrier to address any practical and legal concerns if the district has identified a need to allow an early release with students being able to drive. There should be strict procedures in the policy for this practice, such as no other students in the car. It is important that administrators ensure that a process is in place to review this policy each year. Such a process will allow emerging questions and issues about student attendance to be addressed with a thoughtful, timely, and planned approach.

1-34. What is an order of protection and how does it apply to a school?

An order of protection is a legal order to stop violent or harassing behavior. It is issued by a civil court, such as family court, or a criminal court. A "restraining order" is called an order of protection in New York State statute. An order can apply to either minors or to adults. If there are questions about how an order applies to a school, the administrator should seek a copy of the order from the court or through the school's attorney. There may be questions about how the order applies to school, and it is a good practice to seek clarification from the court or from the court through the school attorney about the interpretation and application of an order. The school administrator should follow the order.

1-35. What are the definitions of cheating/plagiarism? Are there recommended consequences for such acts?

Both cheating and plagiarism need to be included in student grading policies. Cheating usually applies to examinations. Cheating involves using information unfairly to gain an advantage over other students and compromises the integrity of an examination. The Commissioner has upheld the use of a zero in such cases when there has been a full investigation by the district of the circumstances and when students have been given an opportunity to present their versions of the matter. In those cases, the Commissioner has ruled that giving a zero was not arbitrary or capricious since the integrity of the examination had been compromised and a due process procedure had been followed (see *Appeal of Megan M.*, 38 Ed Dept Rep 807, Decision No. 14,149).

Plagiarism has become a growing issue for schools with increased use of the Internet. The act of plagiarism involves intentionally using the ideas or words of another person without referencing the other person or giving credit to that person. Judgment concerning plagiarism is challenging for teachers and principals since, in some cases, the student has unintentionally misused or left out reference sources.

"Plagiarism" should have a clear definition and policy for application that has been collaboratively developed with teachers.

The definition and consequences need to be clearly communicated to students so that they understand what plagiarism means and the implications for it. Some of the writing style manuals, such as the *Publication Manual of the American Psychological Association* and the *MLA Handbook for Writers of Research Papers*, provide definitions and information about plagiarism that may be helpful for discussion when developing guidelines for students. Some schools contract for commercially developed software programs to detect plagiarism or hire substitute teachers to check sources on major papers. A discussion to develop a policy for plagiarism will also be helpful for teachers in refining written assignments and teaching strategies so that the potential for plagiarism is minimized.

A Commissioner's decision has ruled that plagiarism on a test compromised the integrity of an exam and not regrading the exam would allow a student to benefit from his or her conduct to the disadvantage of other students who took the exam (*Appeal of Baker-Stein*, 37 Ed Dept 401, Decision No. 13,889).

The Commissioner has also noted that a student's misconduct must be related to academic performance to warrant an academic sanction (*Appeal of Wilhelm and Lynn R.*, 31 Ed Dept Rep 509, Decision No. 12,716).

If there is cheating on a Regents exam, the section on fraud in the School Administrator's Manual, Secondary Level Examinations, should be consulted. There is a section about obtaining information from or giving information to other students. There is also a section on fraud. The section states:

> Under Section 8.5 of the Rules of the Board of Regents, fraud shall include the use of unfair means to pass an examination, attempting to give aid to, or obtain aid from, another person in any examination, alteration of any Regents Examination credential, and intentional misrepresentation in connection with Regents Examinations or credentials.

The section also notes that fraud on Regents examinations is a misdemeanor by whoever committed it according to Education Law 225. The procedures to be followed by the principal in such cases are explained, and include meeting with the student and sending a report to the New York State Education Department.

1-36. Does a student's discipline history appear in the student's permanent record?

The "permanent record card" for all students, required by the New York State Archives and Records Administration publication Records Retention and Disposition Schedule ED-1" (http://www.archives.nysed.gov/common/archives/files/mr_pub_ed1.pdf), must include, but is not limited to, information on school entry, withdrawal and graduation, subjects taken, and grades received from examinations. This cumulative education file is required to be kept permanently.

Records Retention and Disposition Schedule ED-1 also requires that "major" disciplinary actions, including suspensions, must be kept for three years after the end of the school year, but no less than three years after the student reaches the age of 18. "Minor" disciplinary records are required to be kept for three years after the end of the school year. The schedule notes that school districts may wish to retain some or all of the minor disciplinary records for longer periods of time, especially in case of potential litigation involving an unrecognized learning disability since the litigation could begin any time before the student reaches the age of 21.

In addition, VADIR data must be maintained. Violent and disruptive incident reports and summary records, including copies of summary information sent to SED, must be kept until the youngest person in the incident is 27 years old. Summary records may be required to be kept longer, even permanently, if they document school violence or if a school has been designated a persistently dangerous school. Additionally, persistently dangerous school designation records must be retained permanently (see "Questions and Answers" at http://www.p12.nysed.gov/sss/ssae/schoolsafety/vadir/SSECQandA.html). Note that violent and disruptive data received back from SED only has to be retained until the data are confirmed and any corrections completed.

Schedule ED-1 gives minimum lengths of time that the records must be kept, but they may be kept longer. The district's records management officer should have a procedure for any records maintained that exceed the minimum time required for maintenance by the State Education Department. The FERPA guidelines should be followed for any requests for a student's records. Note also that the schedule for ED-1 Special Education provides guidance about records relating to special education services.

1-37. May discipline records be shared with teachers and parents?

A school should be clear about practices that relate to the sharing of any information that relates to a student. The Family Educational Rights and Privacy Act (FERPA) gives access to student records for school officials who have a legitimate educational interest. Not all school officials have reason to have access to the records of a specific student, and it is important for schools to be viewed as protecting the confidentiality of student records and information. See http://www2. ed.gov/policy/gen/guid/fpco/ferpa/index.html for more information.

The district's code of conduct must describe procedures for contacting parents about violations of the code, so communication with parents about discipline matters is expected. In addition, FERPA gives parents the right to inspect and to review the student's educational records maintained by the school. A procedure to do so should be clear to employees and parents.

1-38. What rights do the police have to come into schools to interview students?

It is advisable to have a board of education policy in place to describe the conditions under which law enforcement authorities will be present in the schools to speak with students and to address how parents will be contacted in those cases. It is important to review periodically with law enforcement agencies the understandings of how the schools will work with them on investigations that relate to school matters and investigations that relate to nonschool-related matters.

An administrator should be clear about whether the matter in question is a school or a nonschool matter. For example, police may be invited into schools by school officials to conduct an investigation or search relating to a school issue. On the other hand, many investigations of nonschool-related cases can be conducted outside of the school setting, and arrests in such cases can take place apart from the school setting. Police also may have a warrant from a judge to arrest a student or conduct a search in school.

1-39. What are the legal reasons for being absent or tardy as defined by the New York State Education Department?

Section 104.1 of Commissioner's Regulations requires that each school district adopt a comprehensive student attendance policy. Local school districts determine the definitions for "excused" and "unexcused" absences. According to "Questions and Answers on the Attendance Regulation, Commissioner's Regulation 104.1" from the State Education Department, schools can determine their guidelines for unexcused and excused absences, tardies, and early departures that are reflective of local education needs, community needs, philosophy, and priorities (http://www.p12.nysed.gov/sss/pps/attendance/attendanceQ-A.html).

The Commissioner's Regulation also requires that the policy be developed collaboratively with board of education representatives, administrators, teachers, parents, students, and community members. The development of the required comprehensive attendance policy through a collaborative effort provides the process to develop the definitions for unexcused and excused absences.

1-40. What are the consequences when a student has an unexcused absence?

The comprehensive attendance policy defines what constitutes unexcused and excused absences. That policy includes a description of disciplinary sanctions used to discourage unexcused absences, tardies, and early departures and the policy regarding student attendance and course credit. See question 1-39 for more information.

It is important that administrators ensure that a process is in place to review this policy each year. Such a process will allow emerging questions and issues about student attendance to be addressed with a thoughtful, timely, and planned approach.

1-41. What procedures should be followed when a student is reported as missing or leaves school grounds without permission?

The parents, or those in parental relation, should be notified. The required comprehensive attendance policy shall incorporate "a description of the notice to be provided to the parent(s) of or person(s) in parental relation to pupils who are absent, tardy or depart early without proper excuse." See Section 104.1 (i) of Commissioner's Regulations for information about this policy.

Section 3213 (2) (c-d) of the Commissioner's Regulations

specifically references elementary students and requires that parents of elementary students be informed about their right to be notified when their child is "deemed absent" from school without prior notification and consent to such absence by the person in parental relation. If parents wish such notification, they must forward a request in writing to the principal of the school with their telephone number or other information that would allow communication to take place. Even if the parents have not requested contact in such situations, notification is important. The administrator should make sure that a system is in place so that communication in these instances will take place.

1-42. How should the use or possession of electronic cigarettes be addressed?

The use of electronic cigarettes and vaping should be considered within the context of the code of conduct as it relates to smoking. If these practices are not part of the code of conduct, the administrator should make sure that they are considered during the process of revising the policy. The Commissioner has ruled on a case that involved the use of electronic cigarettes and nicotine solution. In that case, the use of electronic cigarettes and nicotine solution was included in the district's code of conduct and the Commissioner did not comment on the policy. See *Appeal of M.W. and K.W.*, 55 Ed Dept Rep, Decision No. 16,903.

1-43. What rights do the media have to access a school building?

The Commissioner has cited Education Law 1709(2) and (33) in several cases that give authority to school boards to establish rules and regulations about order and discipline in schools. These cases involved procedures and restrictions for classroom visitation and parents escorting their children to their classrooms. See *Appeal of Canazon*, 33 Ed Dept Rep 124, Decision No. 12,997; *Appeal of Keller*, 32 Ed Dept Rep 47, Decision No. 12,753; and *Appeal of Havens*, 42 Ed Dept Rep 13, Decision No. 14,758. See also question 3-5.

The media does not have the right to enter school grounds without permission. The school administrator should consult with the board of education policies that govern requests from the media for access to schools and students. The district should ensure that the policy addresses contacting parents when students are interviewed.

It is important to be fair and to work with media who plan to do a story that involves the school so that the school's perspective is part of the story. It is also important to explain to journalists the considerations that a school has for the presence of the media to be disruptive to the educational process and, if necessary, to provide alternative ways to cover a story. For example, students, with parent permission, or teachers could be available during lunch or free time for some topics and schools could make the determination about who speaks to the media. Students can be interviewed off school grounds without permission of the schools. Generally, schools allow media personnel to cover athletic and other extracurricular activities without advance permission. To plan for media coverage of a crisis, the district's crisis plan should include provision for a designated spokesperson and procedures for providing information to the media.

Section 1B
Student Activities

1-44. What responsibility does a school district have to maintain order and discipline at school events?

Education Law 2801 (1) mandates codes of conduct for school districts and states that codes of conduct apply to school-sponsored and school-authorized activities, regardless of where they take place. The statute specifically states that this definition includes any event or activity that may take place in another state. In addition, a board of education has the responsibility, according to Education Law 2503 (2), for the discipline of its schools and "of all the educational, social or recreational activities and other interests under its charge or direction."

The Commissioner's decision in *Appeal of Lore*, 33 Ed Dept Rep 144, Decision No. 13,004, states: "While a school is not an insurer of the safety of its students, it will be held liable in damages for a foreseeable injury proximately related to the absence of supervision."

The code of conduct, during its annual review, should be considered for its application to school-sponsored events including those that occur off campus. Planning for such events should consider any information that would be a factor in the school's responsibility for supervision. See also question 1-21.

1-45. What are the proper procedures to follow when organizing a class trip?

The New York State Police have a field trip attendance system that is available at http://troopers.ny.gov/Schools_and_Communities/Field_Trip/System_Description. The system is designed to provide advice concerning student management on trips, including the monitoring and tracking of students and dealing with medical emergencies and bus accidents.

If the trip is outside the area, it is important to contact local law enforcement to determine if there are any safety concerns in the area of the trip. If there is a safety or security office at the site of the trip, it is also important to check with that office.

The administrator should also consider providing adequate

chaperones for students as well as information for parents. Procedures for administrative approval of a trip and related policies will vary from district to district.

There are travel advisories from the United States Department of State about other countries at https://travel.state.gov/content/passports/en/alertswarnings.html. There are also travel advisories for countries by the CDC at https://wwwnc.cdc.gov/travel/notices.

1-46. Can teacher-chaperones take their children on a school-sponsored trip?

This is a decision that individual school districts must make. A policy should be developed in advance to address such circumstances. There are several factors to consider. Questions about liability should be reviewed with the district insurance carrier to determine both district responsibilities for the chaperone's children and the concern that a chaperone might be distracted from full supervisory attention with the chaperone's children on the trip. There should be consideration in advance of any potential that some students might not be allowed to go on a trip that a chaperone's children are permitted to attend. Questions to consider are whether there are enough chaperones who are not taking children and if the availability of chaperones for overnight trips is affected by conflicts with family supervision responsibilities. It is also important to consider the ages of the children of the teacher and whether they are of school age.

1-47. What is the role of student government in school governance?

There are a variety of roles that student government can play in the functioning of a school. These include, but are not limited to: advisory, conflict resolution, student leadership, community and school service, responsibility for student elections, coordinating student activities, and coordinating fundraising. Two organizations that support student councils and student leadership are the National Association of Student Councils and the New York State Council on Leadership and Student Activities.

The National Association of Student Councils represents middle and high school councils and is a program of NASSP. Its goal has been to help all student councils become more effective. For more information, see https://www.natstuco.org/.

The New York State Council on Leadership and Student Activities supports leadership development among middle and high school students (http://www.nysclsa.org/index.html).

Education laws permit a student to serve on a board of education as an ex officio and nonvoting member if there has been voter approval. The law describes procedures to follow to determine the student representative if voter approval has been given. The law does not require a school district to have a student representative. It also does not prevent a locally developed model for student representation in school governance. For more information, see Education Laws 1702, 1804, and 1901.

1-48. Do students have the right to request a religious club or an LGBT (lesbian, gay, bisexual, and transgender) club in a school?

Students may request a student club. The decision of a district to allow a particular club should follow its own policy, which must be based on the Equal Access Act and related court cases, such as *Westside Community Board of Education v. Mergens*, 496 U.S. 226 (1990), which interpret the law.

All student groups are expected to be treated equitably under the law. There is a "limited open forum" if school policy allows noncurriculum-related clubs or groups to meet. In that situation, other noncurriculum-related groups must have similar access. If a school allows access only to curriculum-related student groups or clubs, a "closed forum" exists, and the school does not have to grant access to noncurriculum-related clubs. A curriculum-related club must directly relate to the curriculum or courses offered by a school. It is important to consult with the school district's counsel when there are questions about requests for clubs. It is also important to be clear about the criteria used to determine whether a club is related to the curriculum of a school if a closed forum is in place.

The Supreme Court case related to this issue is *Westside Community Board of Education v. Mergens*, 496 U.S. 226 (1990).

1-49. What role does the principal play in monitoring the contents of the school newspaper or yearbook?

The principal's authority with regard to student newspapers is determined by whether the newspaper is a voluntary extracurricular activity or whether the newspaper is part of the regular school curriculum. The Commissioner has held that a board of education has greater authority to regulate a school newspaper that is part of a class, but that authority is more restricted when it is part of a voluntary extracurricular activity (*Appeal of the Board of Education of the Wappingers Central School District*, Decision No. 13,327). He added, "School newspapers which are extracurricular activities should reflect the policy and judgment of the student editors. While student newspapers should observe the normal rules of responsible journalism, students are free to editorialize."

Administrators should develop a policy with standards and criteria that can be used to judge editorial pieces that may be published in student newspapers. The policy should be reviewed with school counsel. The federal case that provides more guidance in this area is *Hazelwood School District v. Kuhlmeir*, 484 U.S. 260 (1988).

The school yearbook is usually an extracurricular activity; the advisor is usually paid a stipend by the school district. Final approval for the publishing of the yearbook may come from the advisor and/or the principal. One of the issues that sometimes face a yearbook advisor and principal is advertisements and their wording. A clear policy for advertisements that the school attorney has reviewed is helpful.

1-50. How does an administrator evaluate extracurricular activities?

The school leader should review the purpose and efficacy of extracurricular activities on a regular basis. An administrator should consider several questions and factors when evaluating an extracurricular program. One set of questions involves the level of participation among students. Do participation rates justify the activities? Is there a comprehensive range of options for all students? Do the participation rates reflect accessibility for all students regardless of race, gender, or disabilities? Are the activities open and accessible to all students?

Other questions include the relationship of the activities to the mission of the school. Is the extracurricular program based upon a limited open forum or a closed forum (see question 1-48) with regard to the Equal Access Act? Are the activities consistent with the mission and beliefs of the school? Do the activities help improve student attendance, academic performance, and school culture? Do the activities encourage students to be connected with the school? Does one activity conflict with other activities or academic requirements?

In order to evaluate the activities, there should be data available on participation rates. Surveys and questionnaires can provide other information that would be helpful in evaluating the total program or an individual activity.

1-51. What are the parameters of fundraising for clubs, activities, and teams in New York State schools?

A school administrator should be familiar with regulations that affect fundraising activities in schools. Regents Rule 19.6 states, "Direct solicitation of charitable funds from children in the public schools shall not be permitted on school property during school hours." The Commissioner, in *Appeal of Ponte*, 38 Ed Dept Rep 280, Decision No. 14,033, notes that the rule does not prevent recruitment of children during school hours for activities that occur off school grounds or after school hours. The rule does not prohibit arm's-length transactions where the contributor receives recompense for a donation that goes to charity such as a ticket for a social event, or indirect forms of charitable solicitation such as a bin placed in a common area for donation of food, clothing, or money.

More detailed information about solicitation of charitable donations from schoolchildren may be found at http://www.counsel.nysed.gov/questions/ques. This information from the New York State Education Department Office of Counsel explains how the school and school personnel may not be a conduit to collect money from students that was earned on behalf of a charity. The document clarifies how students may participate in a food or clothing drive involving the donation of goods to the needy. It describes conditions under which school clubs may engage in fundraising for charitable purposes such as an extracurricular activity. The information addresses the solicitation of funds for a fellow student who is ill or for a memorial scholarship. It notes that Rule 19.6 does not apply to a community service program in which high school students "receive credit for providing services to a charitable organization, provided that there is no solicitation of donations from students while they are attending school."

School property may not be used for a private commercial purpose. In *Appeal of Citizens for Responsible Fiscal and Educational Policy, et al.*, 40 Ed Dept Rep 315, Decision No. 14,489, the Commissioner stated that "school personnel may not participate during school hours or on school grounds in the solicitation of orders, distribution of advertising materials or collection of charges for sale of products." The Commissioner has previously ruled that commercial products that serve a legitimate school purpose such as class rings and yearbook photographs may be sold on school grounds when specific criteria are followed (*Appeal of Gary Credit Corporation*, 26 Ed Dept Rep 414; *Appeal of Tarolli*, Ed Dept Rep 60, Decision No. 13,982).

In addition, an administrator should consult any board policies that relate to fundraising. A well-developed policy can help an administrator achieve equitable resources for all activities. Inequality of resources may result because some organizations have greater ability to raise funds than others. The policy should also specify the purposes for which funds can be used and ensure that a tax-paying public is not overly solicited for school activities that the public may think should fall within the scope of a school budget.

1-52. How does the administration establish financial oversight of extracurricular activities? What are the proper accounting procedures for handling money with regard to student fees and extracurricular accounts?

Extraclassroom activity accounts are operated by and for students. The administrator needs to review the rules and regulations for the operation and accounting of extracurricular accounts that a board of education is required to have in place. The administrator should also make sure that the recommended procedures developed by the State Education Department to safeguard funds and protect a learning experience for students are followed. Section 172 of Commissioner's Regulations explains the required financial accounting of extraclassroom activity accounts in school districts with less than one million students. See http://www.p12.nysed.gov/mgtserv/accounting/docs/ExtraclassroomActivitiesJanuary2015.pdf for the finance pamphlet that describes guidelines for safeguarding, accounting, and auditing extraclassroom activity funds.

These activities generate cash funds, and the administrator should be attentive to the procedures for handling funds including admissions, dues, sales by student groups, inventory control, donations, deposits, purchasing, the petty cash fund for these accounts, and record keeping. The staff treasurer for the extraclassroom accounts should be bonded by the board of education. It is also important to be aware of the possible taxability for items that are sold by student organizations and to make sure that faculty advisors are informed. In addition, some payments for services rendered may require that IRS guidelines be followed. The annual independent audit of school district finances may include an audit of the extraclassroom accounts and should be reviewed annually at the time of the audit.

The financing of extracurricular activities makes it necessary for the administrator to communicate with the school business official. It is helpful for advisors, others who work with extracurricular activities, and the staff treasurer for extracurricular activities to meet annually with the school business official or district treasurer to review procedures.

Section 2
Health and Safety

2-1. What elements of school safety are required/recommended in New York State schools?

Key elements include comprehensive emergency plans at both the district and building levels; a written code of conduct for students, staff, and visitors; annual violence prevention/intervention and mental health training for staff (https://safeschools.ny.gov/mental-health-resources-educators); a uniform violent incident reporting system; character education; child abuse reporting; and drills to practice emergency response.

In addition, a threat assessment team should be created to evaluate student threats against others or themselves, and develop plans to intervene and prevent violence against students and staff. For more information see the National Association of School Psychologists webpage https://www.nasponline.org/resources-and-publications/resources/school-safety-and-crisis.

The New York State Education Department has additional resources and information about school safety and the most recent changes to the emergency response regulations, at http://www.p12.nysed.gov/sss/ssae/schoolsafety/save.

2-2. Who is responsible for building-level emergency response planning? What are the team's responsibilities?

Education Law 2801-a and Commissioner's Regulation 155.17 require each school building to have a building-level emergency response team that is responsible for developing a response plan and appointing an emergency response and post-incident response team. The building-level emergency response team should consist of administrators, teachers, and a parent organization representative, as well as law enforcement officers, fire officials, and any other emergency management personnel who may be needed. See http://www.p12.nysed.gov/sss/documents/QuickGuideEmerPlanningNov2016_final.pdf.

The building-level emergency response plan must be developed using the state-provided template. It must be kept confidential and requires an annual review by the team no later than September 1. A copy of the plan needs to be submitted to the New York State Police and local law enforcement by October 15 each year. To request a plan template or to submit a plan to the state, see https://safeschools.ny.gov.

2-3. Who should be on the emergency response team for a school building? What is the role of the members and who leads the team?

The emergency response team (ERT) is appointed by the building-level emergency response team and is made up of trained personnel who are familiar with the building and can be freed from student supervision. The ERT may conduct suspicious object searches, preclear evacuation routes and shelter sites, direct students and staff during evacuations, help check attendance, and facilitate communication. The principal, acting as the incident commander, may not be able to participate on the ERT but can give direction to the team in the command center (most often the main office). The incident commander has the overall responsibility for managing an incident by establishing goals, planning strategies, and implementing tactics. The incident commander position must always be staffed.

For assistance with emergency response planning, contact your BOCES health and safety coordinator/risk management program or your New York State Police community outreach coordinator.

2-4. Should building-level emergency response team members receive any specialized emergency management training? If so, what is required?

Each public school district is required to develop school safety plans in coordination with local emergency managers and use the incident command system (ICS) format to define the chain of command. Given these requirements, all staff likely to be involved in emergency management activities should take the Introduction to National Incident Management System (NIMS) (IS-700) and Introduction to the Incident Command System (IS-100SCa) courses. These classes are offered free online by FEMA at http://training.fema.gov/IS/NIMS.asp. Training may also be arranged through BOCES health and safety coordinators.

The ICS is a nationally recognized system for managing emergencies. This system utilizes a structure with well-defined roles and functions for personnel to follow.

First responders (i.e., fire, rescue, and law enforcement) are using NIMS as a framework for compatibility when responding to incidents. Since school districts are generally the recipient of these services, it is imperative for school personnel to understand their roles during an incident to ensure that these services are delivered in a timely, effective manner.

2-5. What emergency responses are required to be used with staff and students?

The standardized building-level emergency response plan template contains the SHELL terminology/responses and definitions that are required to be used in New York State schools:

- Shelter in place
- Hold in place
- Evacuate
- Lockout
- Lockdown

A quick reference to the emergency response terms, including their definitions and instructions, is available at http://www.p12.nysed.gov/sss/documents/QuickReferenceCardv102-13-15.pdf.

2-6. What are the requirements for emergency drills in New York State schools?

Section 807 of Education Law requires that schools conduct 12 emergency response drills annually: eight (8) evacuation/fire drills and four (4) lockdown drills. Any combination of eight (8) of these drills needs to be completed by December 31 and the remaining four (4) by the end of the school year.

Two additional drills must be conducted during summer school; one of these should be held in the first week. Schools must practice at least one drill during the lunch period or time of assembly, unless they have given instruction to students on how to respond.

Although not required, instruction should be given to students and staff regarding the remaining emergency response terms: shelter in place, hold in place, and lockout.

According to Commissioner's Regulation 155.17, a "go home" drill must be conducted annually to practice sheltering in place and early dismissal. Parents must be notified at least one week in advance of this district-wide drill and students can only be released 15 minutes early.

Many resources are available for guidance when preparing and conducting these drills. Assistance may be arranged through BOCES health and safety coordinators, local law enforcement, and the New York State Police community outreach coordinators.

2-7. What are some general guidelines an administrator should follow in maintaining building safety throughout the school day (arrival, dismissal, entrances, etc.)?

Controlling admission to a school building will help reduce the risk of unauthorized visitors and promote building safety. Key elements to access control include maintaining single point of entry with signage, arrival/dismissal procedures, and visitor sign in/out procedures (including visitor badges or color-coded stickers.) Educating staff, students, and parents about these procedures is essential to building a culture of safety. Staff should be encouraged to greet and challenge strangers and to report any unsafe situations to the administration (e.g., doors being propped open, graffiti). Continued training including drills (e.g., lockdowns and tabletop exercises that simulate emergency situations) will also contribute to building safety by developing staff confidence in knowing their roles during an emergency. See question 2-6 regarding the requirements for drills.

2-8. What are the functions of a post-incident response team? What community members may be on the team? What role can community religious leaders play on the team?

The post-incident response team (in the past this team has also been referred to as the crisis team) provides emotional and psychological support during and following an emergency. Every school building is required to have a building-level emergency response plan that includes a plan for dealing with the aftereffects of an incident. The plan should be developed and practiced by the team. The team includes nurses, social workers, school psychologists, administrators, and others who have appropriate skills and training. Depending upon the nature and scope of the crisis, the team may be expanded to include resources from the community including mental health personnel and religious leaders.

Because the post-incident response team may be activated while an emergency is in progress, its members should be different from the members of the emergency response team. It should be able to function without the leadership of the building administrator who is responsible for managing the incident.

The post-incident response team may be activated for incidents that occur off campus when the students and staff of the home district may be affected. See question 2-9 for more information.

2-9. Is there a recommended procedure for student/staff/ community tragedies?

Prior to the Project SAVE legislation, many schools developed post-incident response or crisis teams and plans to deal with the psychological effects of emergencies such as the death of a student or staff member. The post-incident response or school crisis plan was usually written and practiced by a team of school and community health, mental health, and social services personnel. In the event of a tragedy affecting students and/or staff, the post-incident response team was activated. The post-incident response plan is required to be part of the building-level emergency response plan. Due to the skills necessary to deal with the emotional effect of the emergency, and the need for others to manage the physical aspect of the incident, the members of the post-incident response team may differ from those on the building's emergency response team.

Administrators should notify neighboring schools and local BOCES when a tragedy occurs that might affect students in other districts.

See https://www.nasponline.org/resources-and-publications/ resources/school-safety-and-crisis/social-media-and-school-crises.

2-10. Is there a recommended procedure for bus accidents?

The building-level emergency response plan must include procedures for bus accidents. The building administrator may be expected to report to the scene and collaborate with emergency response personnel. Student accounting and parent notification are essential to the response. The administrator must also be prepared to respond to questions from the media about an accident. Depending on the nature of the accident, the post-incident response team may be activated for support during and after the emergency.

2-11. What requirements are in place for a principal in the event of a bomb threat? What emergency response should be taken by the building administrator?

The district procedures for bomb threats must be included in the building-level emergency plan. Depending upon the nature of the threat, administrators may choose to shelter in a precleared area of the building or evacuate to an external site. The administrator should consider carefully any decision to send students home since this action may encourage subsequent threats.

Contact local law enforcement immediately in the event of a bomb threat. Bomb dogs (sometimes referred to as "explosives detection canines" by law enforcement agencies) may be dispatched to the scene to assist the building-level emergency response team in a search for suspicious materials and objects.

Cards printed by the New York State Police have guidance questions (https://troopers.ny.gov/Publications/Crime_Prevention/bombcard. pdf) to ask a caller delivering a bomb threat that should be located by all staff telephones. Front-desk personnel should be trained to respond to a bomb threat call. Written bomb threats such as notes or writing on walls should be preserved until fully investigated. Making a false bomb threat toward a school is a felony.

All bomb threats must be reported to the State Education Department.

2-12. In the case of a bomb threat, who searches the building with the police?

The emergency response team for the school building may assist the police in a "suspicious object" search. The team members must have received prior training in order to conduct such a search. Participation is voluntary. If a suspicious object is found, it will be investigated by law enforcement. Team members should never handle a suspect object.

The emergency response team should be made up of staff members who are familiar with the building and readily available in the event of a threat. Custodial staff, administrators, and guidance counselors are typical ERT members. See question 2-3 for more information.

2-13. What is the role of the school resource officer (SRO)? How can the administration use information about students from the officer?

According to the National Association of School Resource Officers, the SRO has three main roles: educator (i.e., guest lecturer), informal counselor/mentor, and law enforcement officer. The SRO is trained to prevent, intervene, and respond to school emergencies but should not be considered the school disciplinarian. School rule violations should be addressed by the administration. While the SRO's authority exceeds that of the school's authority when it is necessary to use force or make an arrest, the SRO is also limited by the law in areas where the school has more latitude, such as searches.

In order for the SRO program to be most effective, building administrators, counselors, teachers, and the SRO need to work as a team with well-defined roles. In order to establish good rapport with students and maintain a positive school climate, the SRO may choose to keep some discussions confidential, but can be expected to share any information crucial to the safety and security of the school.

2-14. At what point or under what circumstances should police be called into a school?

In the event of a suspected or actual criminal act, law enforcement should be notified immediately using the 911 system, where available. Such acts may include bomb threats, threats of violence (including social media), intruders, suspicious objects or persons, violent acts against staff or students, burglary, arson, and other crime or attempted crime. The responding officer(s) can assist in the containment and investigation of the incident.

2-15. What procedures should be followed in the event of an emergency during administration of state tests?

The State Education Department, in conjunction with the New York State Police, has developed guidelines for responding to bomb threats that occur prior to the administration of state exams. A team of school personnel and law enforcement officers, including a bomb dog if available, may preclear the building following set procedures. Doors must be monitored and entry and exit from the building controlled. Once the preclearance is completed, the exam may be held as scheduled.

Provisions for evacuation during emergencies are included in the latest version of the School Administrator's Manual, Secondary Level Examinations (http://www.p12.nysed.gov/assessment/sam/secondary/section2-15.pdf). If the principal deems it necessary to evacuate students for their safety, students should be supervised insofar as possible. The exam time may be extended to accommodate the interruption.

In addition, according to the School Administrator's Manual, Secondary Level Examinations, New York State exams may not be given when severe weather warrants the closing of school and cancellation of normal bus transportation.

2-16. Are there any special considerations for students on field trips?

The State Education Department recommends that schools use the field trip attendance system developed by the New York State Police to help monitor students and staff on field trips. Information is available at https://www.troopers.ny.gov/Schools_and_Communities/Field_Trip/System_Description/. See also questions 1-45 and 2-42.

2-17. Who must be fingerprinted in a school district? How do the regulations apply to volunteers?

Under Part 87 of Commissioner's Regulations, the State Education Department requires that prospective school employees and applicants for certification be fingerprinted. This includes all employees who are expected to have face-to-face communication with students. The State Education Department states that "volunteers, individuals who worked in the school district the previous year and employees who have no direct contact with students are examples of individuals who are exempt." Clearances are provided to school districts by the State Education Department, as are changes in the status of the employee's criminal record if deemed necessary by the Department.

School bus drivers and attendants are fingerprinted under New York State Vehicle and Traffic Law and are entered into the Division of Criminal Justice Services records. Any person entering the employ of a school district must be fingerprinted unless they have been previously recorded in the State Education Department's system.

District policies for volunteers' roles and required supervision should be reviewed by administrators prior to their working with students. Further information regarding the state's fingerprinting requirements may be found at http://www.highered.nysed.gov/tsei/ospra/fpprocess.html.

2-18. What are the requirements of a school employee who suspects a child is a victim of abuse?

Article 23-B of Education Law requires that all teachers, nurses, counselors, psychologists, social workers, administrators, and other certified school personnel receive training in recognizing and reporting suspected cases of abuse that occur in the school or on school grounds and are committed by an employee or volunteer. The building principal is responsible for reviewing the written report and determining the appropriate course of action consistent with Section 100.2 of Commissioner's Regulations.

Section 413 of New York State Social Services Law includes educational staff as mandated reporters for all suspected cases of child abuse. This law includes penalties for failure to report and immunity from liability. A staff member must notify the principal or the principal's designee. There should be a board of education policy that establishes procedures for investigating and reporting suspected cases.

2-19. What and how much information must a school district release regarding a convicted sex offender residing in the community?

There is no requirement that a school district release such information to the community. Information about convicted sex offenders is released to local law enforcement agencies. Depending on the level of risk assigned by the courts, the law enforcement agency can release information to the community. The school may not want to be a conduit for information that can be better addressed by law enforcement personnel. The district should have a policy in place to determine how the information will be disseminated to school staff members who should be aware of the information. More information is available at the New York State Division of Criminal Justice Services website, http://www.criminaljustice.ny.gov/nsor/.

2-20. What are a school's responsibilities with regard to accessibility for persons with disabilities?

Under the Americans with Disabilities Act (ADA), schools must provide "reasonable accommodations" for persons with disabilities.

Facilities and programs must be accessible to students, staff, parents, and visitors. There must be plans for building accessibility regardless of whether a person with disabilities has been identified who needs to access the building. Each school building is required to conduct a self-evaluation of its accessibility including parking, access to an entrance, ability to move to programs in the building, and accessible bathrooms. Plans for new construction and renovation projects must include modifications to ensure accessibility in order to be approved by the State Education Department.

The building-level emergency response plan should include a list of students and staff who need assistance in an emergency because of permanent or temporary disability. A staff member will be assigned to each person listed and trained in emergency procedures. See question 2-22 for related information.

2-21. Who is responsible for students with disabilities in a fire drill?

The building-level emergency response plan should include a list of persons requiring assistance in an emergency. Each of these persons should be assigned a staff member who is responsible for their safe shelter or exit. Individuals located on the first floor should exit along the same routes as their classmates.

Because elevators may not be used in a fire, there must be a designated "area of refuge" on any floor not at ground level. Any student unable to navigate stairs must be taken by his/her caregiver to that location to await rescue. Communication systems are mandated for areas of refuge. Fire department officials should be made aware of the potential need for this type of rescue in each building.

Schools should not practice carrying students down stairways in fire drills. The area of refuge should be incorporated into the drills.

2-22. What is the New York State requirement for AEDs in schools? Who is responsible for maintaining the AED? Who must be certified in the operation of an AED device in local schools?

AEDs (automated external defibrillators) are required at on-site school-sponsored events and at athletic practices and events that are either on- or off-site; this does not include field trips. A written PAD (public access defibrillator) program, as well as a signed collaborative agreement with a physician or hospital that will serve as "the emergency health care provider," is required for each district. The PAD describes where the defibrillators will be located and who will be responsible for them; daily and monthly maintenance is required. The AEDs can only be used by a trained operator, and there must be at least one trained operator for an AED when there are school-sponsored or school-approved activities including extracurricular and competitive athletic events.

All main entrances are required to have a sign posted indicating the location of the AED in the building. It is helpful for staff to conduct drills at their sites and to review procedures. See Public Health Law 3000-b and Education Law 917 for more information.

2-23. What are the inspection requirements for school buildings?

There are three inspections that are required for student-occupied school buildings. (1) The asbestos triennial inspections must be conducted every three years by a certified asbestos inspector with six-month surveillances taking place during the intervening years. (2) Every 11 months, fire inspections are performed by a certified codes official. (3) The building condition survey (BCS), an in-depth inspection of the building components and systems, is completed every five years by a licensed architect or engineer.

A copy of the asbestos management plan must be maintained in each building and made available upon request. The building principal should also have copies of the fire and BCS inspections. Original copies of all inspections are maintained in a central district file.

2-24. What equipment requires a safety assessment?

Special inspections are required for bleachers, elevators, and gymnasium equipment. In addition, safety assessments may be conducted by insurance, risk management, and workers' compensation representatives. The liability associated with playgrounds makes it advisable to conduct thorough annual inspections with the insurance company representatives and periodic reviews of the playground maintenance and supervision procedures.

A security audit of each school building is required to be conducted and the date recorded in the building-level emergency response plan. See question 2-2 for more information.

2-25. What are the key components of the fire inspection that an administrator should be aware of throughout the school year?

An annual fire inspection must be completed of all buildings owned, operated, or leased by a district. The inspection must be completed by a certified code enforcement official who verifies that each building complies with Education Law 807a, the Commissioner's Regulations, and the New York State Uniform Fire Prevention and Building Code. The intent of the inspection is to protect life safety and safeguard the building against fire hazard.

Since inspections are only completed annually, it is the responsibility of the school administrator to ensure that fire safety regulations are followed throughout the year. Some of the most important regulation considerations are listed here: areas of egress such as rescue windows and exits are free of obstruction, operating freely, and well marked; fire alarms, extinguishers, and all other pieces of equipment are maintained according to code; extension cords are used properly; fire safety and evacuation plans are prepared; and storage and housekeeping are neatly maintained at a distance of at least 24" from the ceiling. See question 2-26 for regulations regarding artwork and holiday decorations.

2-26. How do fire regulations apply to student artwork and holiday decorations?

The New York State Education Fire and Life Safety Standards include specific requirements for schools to comply with Section 155.7 of the Regulations of the Commissioner of Education and the New York State Building Codes. Under these standards, student artwork, teaching materials, and decorations may not cover more than 20 percent of corridor wall space or hang from the ceiling. Classroom artwork and/or teaching materials may not cover more than 50 percent of each wall and must not impede safe exit from the classroom doorway and egress through hallways. Rescue windows in the classroom, as well as the areas in front of them, may not be blocked by projects, furniture, or other items. Curtains, drapes, and decorative materials hanging from walls or ceilings must be fire resistant. Any decorations hanging from the classroom ceiling must be at least 7' from the floor to the bottom of the hanging item.

See the Manual for New York State Public School Facility

Fire Safety Inspections at http://www.p12.nysed.gov/facplan/
documentsPUBLICFireSafetyManual.pdf for more information on
fire safety requirements.

2-27. What procedures should be followed in the event of a systems failure such as electrical, heat, water, and fire alarm systems?

In the event of a systems failure, the appropriate utility should
be contacted as soon as possible and a determination made about how
long it will take to repair the problem. For short-term outages, school
can remain in session if provisions are made to ensure health and safety.
For example, if the building is under a "boil water" order because of
a break in a water main, school may remain in session if provision
is made to shut off water fountains, provide potable water, and find
alternate means of food preparation.

A school may operate for short periods of time without electricity
if the emergency lighting is functioning and the temperature remains at
or above the required 65 degrees in classrooms (see question 2-33).

The State Education Department has recommended that fire
systems, including alarms, exit lights, and emergency lights, should be
maintained continuously during construction projects or provisions
made to provide equivalent safety. The local fire department should be
notified when a system is not operating as intended.

2-28. What procedures must be in place for electrically operated partition doors and curtains such as those in gymnasiums?

All electrically operated partition doors and curtains must be
equipped with safety features that stop the motion of the partition and
sense the presence of an individual in the stacking area. Two trained
persons are required to operate the partitions. No students may operate
key switches at any time.

Partitions that were not installed with this safety equipment
or retrofitted appropriately by 2002 must be taken out of service by
disabling them at the power source. Signs listing the appropriate safety
procedures must be posted at each key station. Any staff member who
will be expected to operate the partitions must be trained in their safe
operation.

2-29. What regulations govern swimming pools in schools?

Section 6 of Title 10 of New York State Public Health Law governs the operation of school swimming pools. A trained pool operator, familiar with the pool equipment and operations, is required to manage the chemicals and equipment necessary to maintain the pool in a safe and healthful manner.

Section 155.10 of Commissioner's Regulations requires that school swimming pools shall be supervised by a lifeguard possessing a current senior lifesaving certificate from an agency approved by the New York State Commissioner of Health.

Section 6-1.24 of Title 10 of New York State Public Health Law requires that bathing suits and towels supplied by the school must be washed with a detergent in hot water, rinsed, and thoroughly dried after each use.

2-30. What should a school do in the event of a hazardous chemical spill (e.g., mercury, science laboratory chemicals, cleaning products)?

In the event of a hazardous spill, the affected area should be evacuated immediately. Staff should consult the safety data sheet for containment and cleanup recommendations. Depending upon the level of hazard, it may be necessary to contact the local HAZMAT team or fire department for assistance.

A ban on the use or purchase of elemental mercury in schools went into effect in 2004. Any found in schools should be disposed of promptly. If a spill does occur, guidelines for cleanup of mercury spills and informational brochures for schools may be found at the New York State Department of Health website, https://www.health.ny.gov/environmental/chemicals/mercury/brochures/cleanup.htm.

2-31. What laws govern safety procedures in science laboratories of schools?

The OSHA Laboratory Safety Standard requires that schools appoint a chemical hygiene officer or chemical hygiene committee and develop a chemical hygiene plan to address safety in the science laboratory. Staff who use chemicals in the science lab must receive periodic laboratory safety training. Chemicals used in laboratory settings should be inventoried and carefully stored in accordance with accepted guidelines such as those available at the State Education

Department, http://www.emsc.nysed.gov/ciai/mst/pub/chemstorguid.
html.

These guidelines include details concerning Section 305
of Commissioner's Regulations, which govern safety in science
laboratories.

2-32. What regulations govern the use of pesticides on school property?

Commissioner's Regulation 155.4 requires that schools have
integrated pest management programs that use the least toxic approach
to controlling pests. Commissioner's Regulation 155.4 also provides
guidelines for notifying staff and parents when, how, and what
pesticides are used. With few exceptions, pesticides cannot be used
unless 48-hour advanced notification is provided. Under 155.24, every
district must appoint a pesticide representative who will implement the
notification program including issuing an annual written notification
to staff and parents about how to register for the 48-hour notification
list. The representative will also provide 48-hour notification prior
to a pesticide application, and distribute periodic summaries to staff
and parents of pesticide applications that have taken place. For more
information, see http://www.emsc.nysed.gov/facplan/HealthSafety.
htm.

In addition, Part 325 of Environmental Conservation Law
regulates the application of pesticides. Applications of pesticides of any
type, including ant and bee sprays, may be done by certified applicators
only. Postings must be displayed for 24 hours in accordance with the
law when pesticides are used, whether by school staff or by an outside
contractor.

Although pesticide use is allowed in school buildings, if the above
regulations are followed, the use of pesticides on school grounds is
prohibited. Information concerning pesticide exclusions and exceptions
as well as the use of emergency applications can be found online at
http://www.dec.ny.gov/docs/materials_minerals_pdf/guidancech85.
pdf.

2-33. What is the minimum operating temperature for school classrooms?

Section 602.4 of the Property Maintenance Code of New
York State requires that occupied school classrooms be maintained

at a minimum of 65 degrees from September 15 through May 31. Gymnasiums are not subject to this minimum due to the level of exercise.

2-34. What should a principal do if there is a question regarding the environment (e.g., air quality) of a school building?

If there is an immediate hazard (e.g., a toxic spill or carbon monoxide leak), the principal should evacuate the building and contact the appropriate authorities. Environmental concerns of a less urgent nature, when an evacuation is not necessary, can be addressed as recommended by the local health department, State Education Department, NYS Environmental Conservation Department, or other governing agency. The EPA Tools for Schools: Indoor Air Quality Action Kit contains guidelines for addressing IAQ issues using a school team approach. The kit is available at http://www.epa.gov/iaq/schools/actionkit.html.

Assistance with environmental concerns can also be found through BOCES Health and Safety/Risk Management programs.

2-35. Are there any regulations requiring the testing of drinking water in schools?

As of September 6, 2016, all schools are required to test potable water systems for lead contamination and take corrective actions. Public Health Law Subpart 64-4, Lead Testing in School Drinking Water, prohibits the of use of any potable water outlet(s) with lead concentrations over 15 ppb, and the outlet must be posted "Not for Drinking." After the outlet(s) has been remediated, and retesting has indicated levels below 15 ppb, use may be resumed. If needed, provide an adequate supply of potable water for drinking and cooking.

When testing results are received, notification needs to be made to the local health department within one (1) business day and in writing to students, staff, and parents/guardians within ten (10) business days. Results must be posted to the school's website within six (6) weeks and made available to the New York State Departments of Health and Education through the Department of Health's electronic reporting system.

Lead testing will be required again in 2020 and again every five (5) years following. NYS Facilities Planning has more information regarding sampling and notification of testing results to staff and students at

http://www.p12.nysed.gov/facplan/LeadTestinginSchoolDrinking
Water.html, or contact your BOCES Health and Safety/Risk
Management program for assistance.

2-36. Are there any regulations with regard to animals in the classroom?

Any warm-blooded animals, including gerbils, birds, cats,
dogs, and mice, may trigger asthma; therefore, the United States
Environmental Protection Agency discourages schools from having
pets in the classroom. Certain other animals, such as salamanders,
turtles, and iguanas, may carry salmonella and are not appropriate
for classroom settings. When children bring pets from home, the
vaccination status of the animal may be unknown. Normally well-
behaved pets may become excitable and bite or scratch when exposed
to groups of children.

There are also recommendations against the use of dead animals
(e.g., roadkills, wild game, deceased pets) for experimentation in the
science classroom. Only science specimens from approved suppliers
should be used.

Animal science, veterinarian, and/or pet grooming programs
that rely on animals brought in from home should have prior proof of
vaccinations.

2-37. What precautions should be taken in the event of a severe weather emergency such as a potential or actual thunderstorm?

In the event of a potential or actual thunderstorm, all outside
activities and indoor pool programs should be suspended until the threat has
passed. If thunder is heard, even in the distance, there is an immediate
potential for lightning strikes. It may be necessary to delay loading
or unloading buses and keeping student walkers at school until severe
storms have passed. In the event of high winds, students should be
moved away from windows and may be required to shelter in place

National Oceanic and Atmospheric Administration (NOAA)
weather radios and National Weather Service websites can help school
administrators monitor the path and severity of weather emergencies.

The building-level emergency response plan should be developed
using an all-hazards approach so that it can serve as a response guide
during weather emergencies.

For information specific to athletic events, schools should reference the NYSPHSAA Thunder and Lightning Policy at http://www.nysphsaa.org/portals/0/pdf/safety/ThunderLightningPolicy.pdf.

2-38. What procedures should be followed when considering the heat index and wind chill prior to outside activity?

Prior to any outside practice or athletic event, the heat index and wind chill should be evaluated, and the procedures provided by the New York State Public High School Athletic Association should be followed. The NYSPHSAA has approved procedures that include using the WeatherBug app (www.weatherbug.com) to obtain a current heat index and wind chill reading and a chart outlining the actions necessary given the conditions. Visit http://www.nysphsaa.org/ADs-Coaches/Safety-Research for the approved procedures.

2-39. What accommodations can be made for students or staff with specific health issues such as peanut or latex allergies?

Students with known allergies to bee stings, foods, latex, or other substances should have action plans developed by the school nurse in conjunction with the student's doctor and parents. Teachers, nurses, cafeteria staff, bus drivers, and other staff should be aware of any special procedures needed to protect the student. All children should be encouraged not to share or trade food.

Templates for action plans and resources on addressing student allergies can be found at the New York State Center for School Health (https://www.schoolhealthny.com/domain/85) and the American Academy of Allergy, Asthma, and Immunology (http://www.aaaai.org).

The Voluntary Guidelines for Managing Food Allergies in Schools and Early Care and Education Program (https://www.cdc.gov/healthyschools/foodallergies/pdf/13_243135_a_food_allergy_web_508.pdf), from the Centers for Disease Control and Prevention, recommend a comprehensive set of school district policies to manage allergies in school settings. The guidelines also recommend that the principal coordinate the implementation of a comprehensive food allergy management and prevention plan for the school.

2-40. What guidelines are available if a student is found to have head lice?

Any child may be infested with head lice. Since lice are transmitted by head-to-head contact, it is prudent for the school nurse to examine the student's head using a special light and/or comb before allowing the child to return to class. The school should be prepared to assist parents with strategies for preventing/treating head lice. Some schools institute a "no nit" policy that requires a student to be nit-free before returning to school. Such policies are not mandated in New York State.

Using pesticides to treat the classroom for lice is both unsafe and ineffective. Lice are transported by human contact; therefore, clothing should be separated in cubbies or lockers. Lice may survive up to 24 hours off the human host, so vacuuming of carpets and upholstered furniture is also recommended.

For more information and resources, visit the National Pediculosis Association at http://www.headlice.org/ and the New York State Center for School Health at https://www.schoolhealthny.com/Page/125.

2-41. What should be done if bedbugs are found at school?

Although an infestation of bedbugs at school is unlikely, it is possible for bedbugs to be carried to school and transferred from student to student. The New York State Center for School Health has guidance and sample letters for use regarding bedbugs at https://www.schoolhealthny.com/bedbugs.   Students should not be excluded from school nor should school be closed due to the presence of bedbugs.

When bedbugs are found or suspected in a school building, a licensed pest control professional should be called for assistance. If pesticides are required, all integrated pest management policies need to be followed. Bedbugs can live for up to a year and be difficult to eradicate so immediate action should be taken. More information regarding the use of pesticides on school property may be found in question 2-32.

2-42. What responsibility does the school district have to provide necessary medications to students?

A licensed prescriber's order and written parental permission are required for a school to administer any medications. Only medicine required by a student during the school day should be given. According to Section 6902 of Article 139 of NYS Education Law, a registered professional nurse (RN) or a licensed practical nurse (LPN) working under the supervision of an RN or another licensed provider according to Education Law, can administer prescription medications.

School nursing staff can administer nonpatient-specific medicines for the treatment of anaphylaxis (an allergic reaction that can be fatal within minutes; see questions 2-39 and 2-46 for more information). Under Section 916 of Education Law, students with asthma, diabetes, and possible severe allergic reactions may carry prescribed inhalers, insulin and related diabetes management supplies, and epinephrine auto-injectors for self-treatment with their doctor's written permission and the consent of their parents.

The school should develop specific procedures based upon the State Education Department's guidance, Guidelines for Medication in Schools. This resource as well as other assistance regarding medication management in schools can be found at https://www.schoolhealthny. com/Medication.

On field trips, at sports events, or during after-school activities, school staff should carry the self-directed student's medication so the student can take his/her own medication at the appropriate time. If the student is unable to self-medicate, the parent may attend the activity and administer the medication.

2-43. What responsibility does the school have to ensure student medications are kept in a safe place?

State Education Department guidelines recommend that students should not transport medicines to and from home. A second container prescribed by the physician should be secured in the nurse's office in a locked cabinet, drawer, or refrigerator. More information, including procedures for students who self-medicate, may be found in the guidelines referenced in question 2-44.

2-44. What steps should be taken to dispense medication if the school nurse is not available?

In the absence of the school nurse, only a physician or the parent can administer the medicine. Authorized staff can be trained to oversee a student's self-medication, but staff may not administer the medicine. Criteria for judging a student's ability to self-medicate are included in the guidelines referenced in question 2-43.

2-45. What choices does an administrator have if he/she does not have a nurse or an available nurse substitute? Who may give care to sick/injured students?

In the absence of a school nurse, anyone who is expected to care for sick or injured students should be included in the district's written exposure control plan and be provided training. Training should also be provided for the dispensing of medications. All staff should be encouraged and trained to use "universal precautions," which is an approach to infection control. Under universal precautions, blood and certain body fluids of all persons are considered potentially infectious for HIV, hepatitis B, and other bloodborne pathogens.

2-46. How should an administrator plan for an emergency that involves the need to use an EpiPen?

If a student with a known allergy has been prescribed an EpiPen by a licensed prescriber, a trained school employee may administer an EpiPen in a life-threatening anaphylactic incident if a nurse is not available. The school employee's actions are covered by the "Good Samaritan Law" according to the New York State Education Department's guidelines for use of EpiPens.

Education Law Section 921 also allows schools to have nonpatient-specific, onsite epinephrine auto-injectors (EAIs) for students or staff having anaphylactic emergencies that do not have a standing EAI order. In order to do so, Public Health Law 3000c must be followed. For further guidance, visit the New York State Center for School Health, https://www.schoolhealthny.com/ny.

2-47. Are schools required to have an opioid antagonist program?

Schools are not mandated but Education Law 922 gives them the option of having a nonpatient-specific opioid antagonist (naloxone) program. Due to the rise in opioid use, schools now have the ability to ensure that students and staff have access to an opioid antagonist (naloxone), which is a prescription medicine that is used to reverse an overdose by blocking heroin (or other opioids) in the brain for 30-90 minutes if suspected of having an opioid overdose. Schools that decide to participate must comply with Public Health Law 3309. Visit https://www.health.ny.gov/diseases/aids/general/opioid_overdose_prevention/schools.htm for resources and guidance in setting up an opioid overdose prevention program.

2-48. What are the required immunizations for students in grades K-12?

Public Health Law Section 2164(7) (a) requires that students be immunized against poliomyelitis, mumps, measles, diphtheria, rubella, varicella, hepatitis B, pertussis, tetanus, and, where applicable, Haemophilus influenzae type b (Hib). A chart of immunization requirements by grade level can be found at https://www.health.ny.gov/publications/2370.pdf.

2-49. May a parent refuse to have his/her child take a school physical or be immunized?

Section 904 of Education Law provides for student physicals for entry to school, participation in sports, and prior to entering first, third, fifth, seventh, and tenth grades. A parent may choose to have his/her child examined by a private physician and provide appropriate documentation, or the parent may refuse a physical or immunization for religious reasons. The parent must provide a written statement indicating that their religious beliefs prohibit these actions.

Students may not attend school for more than fourteen (14) days without proof of such immunizations unless the student is from out of state or another country and the time period is extended by the principal, according to Public Health Law 2164. A student may be exempted from immunizations for health reasons based upon written evidence from a physician. Procedures for religious exemptions are included in the law and in Commissioner's decisions such as *Appeal of D.L.*, 44 Ed Dept Rep 104, Decision No. 15,111. See question 2-48 for more information.

2-50. What pertinent information must be in the written statement from a parent declaring that his/her child will not be immunized due to religious reasons?

If a parent does not wish to have their child immunized due to religious reasons, he or she must submit a written and signed religious exemption form to the district. This form and guidance for administrators can be found at http://www.p12.nysed.gov/sss/schoolhealth/schoolhealthservices/fieldmemoreligiouseximmunprocedures.html. There is no specific information that needs to be included in the written statement; the statement needs only to establish the student's right to be exempt due to religious beliefs. School districts have the right to request additional information from the parents when making their decision.

2-51. What procedures should be followed if an employee or student is exposed to someone else's blood?

The OSHA Bloodborne Pathogens Standard requires that employers identify employees at risk of exposure to blood and include their job titles/tasks in the written exposure control plan (ECP). The ECP is updated annually and maintained in each school building. In the event of exposure to blood or other body fluids, the employee must receive a confidential evaluation by a licensed health care professional (HCP), as defined by OSHA. The HCP will indicate if a hepatitis B vaccination is required.

When a student is exposed to another student's blood, the parents of both individuals should be notified. The personal physicians may need to confer to determine appropriate treatments. Because of the confidential nature of the student's infectious status, the school will not be involved in the evaluation or subsequent treatments, if required.

All blood exposure incidents should be documented. The required form for staff exposures is included in the exposure control plan of the district.

Assistance with ECP concerns can also be found through BOCES Health and Safety/Risk Management programs. See also http://www.osha.gov/Publications/osha3186.pdf.

2-52. Who has a right to information about a student's HIV status?

New York State has very strict law with respect to the confidentiality of a person's HIV status. Confidentiality includes any information indicating that a person has had an HIV-related test, has HIV-related illness, and includes any information that could indicate a person has been potentially exposed to HIV. If a student, or the parent in the case of a minor, chooses to release HIV information, it must be done in written form. Any person in possession of this information may not share it with another person without further written consent.

Even nonspecific HIV information (e.g., information stating that there is an HIV-infected student in the building) cannot be shared with staff. Therefore, the building administrator should encourage staff to use "universal precautions," which is an approach to infection control. Under universal precautions, blood and certain body fluids of all persons are considered potentially infectious for HIV, hepatitis B, and other bloodborne pathogens.

2-53. Are there any regulations that stipulate the ratio of staff to students on a playground?

There is no mandate for a specific ratio of staff to students; however, one suggestion is that the supervision should be at the minimum consistent with that of the classroom. At least two monitors are recommended. If one is occupied by an injury or incident, the other is available to oversee the remaining children. If organized activities such as kickball are being conducted, one supervisor should be assigned to that activity. In addition, monitors should be equipped with two-way radios or cell phones for communication.

2-54. Should playground monitors administer first aid in the event of an emergency?

Most playground monitors are not trained in first aid and should not provide first aid in the event of an injury. Moving or treating the individual may result in further injury. The school nurse should be contacted immediately. Depending on the severity of the injury, she/he may need to treat the student at the site.

A playground monitor can assist by encouraging a child to lie still until the nurse arrives, keeping other students away from the incident, and supplying information about what contributed to the incident. If the monitor has been exposed to the student's blood, the district's procedures for blood incidents should be followed. See question 2-51.

2-55. Are there any regulations for schools that address noise levels in gymnasiums, cafeterias, shop areas, and during construction?

OSHA regulates noise levels for all workplaces on two bases: one for short-term exposures, the other for eight-hour time-weighted averages. The noise levels in gymnasiums and cafeterias do not reach the levels mandating hearing protection. Depending on what equipment is used, a shop might need to be evaluated for short-term exposures. Students and staff do not spend long periods of time exposed to high levels of noise where eight-hour averages would apply.

Noise levels in construction are regulated by Section 155.5 of Commissioner's Regulations. During construction and maintenance activities, noise levels above 60 dba in occupied spaces must be abated. The district should include provisions in the project bid specifications for scheduling certain work activities outside the regular school day.

During construction, the Health and Safety Committee is responsible for addressing complaints regarding excessive noise.

2-56. What regulations do schools have to follow regarding concussions?

Schools are required to have school coaches, physical education teachers, nurses, and certified athletic trainers complete a NYS Education Department-approved course on concussion management every two years. The State Education Department (http://www.nysphsaa.org/portals/0/pdf/safety/NYSED%20Guidelines%20for%20Concussion%20Management.pdf) and the Department of Health (https://www.health.ny.gov/prevention/injury_prevention/concussion.htm) websites contain information regarding traumatic brain injury, concussion signs and symptoms, and explanations of how such injuries can occur. These websites must be on any parent/guardian permission or consent form for participation in interscholastic sports.

Any student believed to have sustained a traumatic brain injury must be removed from athletic activities. The student must not return until they have been symptom free for at least 24 hours. The student must also have been evaluated by a physician, and must submit signed authorization permitting their return to interscholastic sports. The student also needs clearance from the district's medical director. For questions, contact the district's medical director. See also https://www.schoolhealthny.com/Page/115.

2-57. What are the responsibilities of a school in the event of a Department of Labor inspection?

The Public Employees Safety and Health (PESH) Bureau of the New York State Department of Labor enforces OSHA standards. A PESH inspector may visit the school without prior notification to conduct either a routine or complaint-based inspection. The inspector must allow the school time to assemble the appropriate parties for an opening conference before conducting the inspection. This should include union and administration representation as well as other knowledgeable participants such as the BOCES health and safety officer and the director of facilities or buildings and grounds. School representatives should accompany the inspector on the walkthrough of the building. The inspector will be looking at health and safety violations that affect staff, not students. Subsequent to the inspection, the district will receive a formal citation listing any violations of OSHA regulations. The district will have time to comply without a fine being imposed.

If the inspection is complaint based, the name of the complainant will not be provided to the district. All responses should be completed without discriminating against any district employee.

Section 3
Parent/Guardian – School Connections

3-1. What rights do parents have to remove their children from academic intervention services (AIS), and could they remove their student from academic intervention services (AIS) against the wishes of the school?

The New York State Education Department has stated that each district and school has responsibility for the placement of students in educational programs during the regular school day. Commissioner's decision No. 12,887 clarified, "Education Law 1709(3) authorizes a board of education to regulate the admission of pupils and their transfer from one class or department to another. Consistent with that authority is the power to place students."

Academic intervention services (AIS) provide instruction that supplements the general curriculum, and assist students in meeting the state learning standards according to Section 100.1(g) of Commissioner's Regulations. Districts must develop a policy for providing AIS services that includes a description of which student performance measures and associated scores will be utilized to determine eligibility. The policy must be posted on the district website or distributed to parents in writing (Commissioner's Regulations 100.2 (ee) (2) (d)). Commissioner's Regulation 100.2 (ee) also states that academic intervention services are provided following a two-step identification process. The required description of the services must also include the criteria for ending services.

The State Education Department has addressed the question of what a district's responsibility is when a parent objects to having a child receive AIS:

> The district should, in a timely manner, listen to parental concerns, share evidence of the student's need for academic intervention services, and work with the parent(s) to assure the provision of appropriate academic intervention services.
>
> Placement in educational programs during the regular school day, however, remains the responsibility of the district and school (see http://www.p12.nysed.gov/part100/pages/AISQAweb.pdf).

If parents do not want their students to participate in AIS programs, they should submit the request in writing to the appropriate school official declining such services. After receipt, this request should be placed in the student's file. The written request to decline services does not abrogate the responsibility of the district to continue to work with students who might benefit from AIS.

3-2.   Does a parent have the right to refuse to have their student sit for a state exam?

The state indicates:

> All students are expected to participate in State tests as part of the core academic program. Absences from all or part of the required academic program should be managed in accordance with the attendance policies of the district. For accountability and other statewide purposes, students who do not participate in an assessment are reported to the state as "not tested." Schools do not have an obligation to provide an alternative location or activities for individual students while the tests are being administered. (http://usny.nysed. gov/docs/common-core-assessment-faq.pdf)

The state has also stated:

> With the exception of certain areas in which parental consent is required, such as Committee on Special Education (CSE) evaluations for students with disabilities and certain federally-funded surveys and analyses specified under the federal Protection of Pupil Rights Amendment (see 20 U.S.C. 1232h), there is no provision in statute or regulation allowing parents to opt their children out of State tests. The failure to comply with the requirements provided above will have a negative impact on a school or school district's accountability, as all schools are required to have a 95 percent participation rate in State testing. (http://www.p12.nysed. gov/assessment/ei/2013/student-participation.pdf).

What school districts should do when students opt out of tests remains a matter of local policy (https://saanys.org/new-york-state-education-department/state-testing-and-parentstudent-opt-out/). See also Commissioner's decision No. 16,787.

3-3. How is the educational responsibility determined for a homeless student?

Education Law 3209, which addresses homeless students, gives the right of choosing the school district for the student to a "designator." A designator is either the parent, the homeless child if there is no parent or someone in parental relation, or the director of a residential program for runaway and homeless youth (in consultation with the homeless child) that has authorization from New York State. The designator may choose the school district of origin, the school district of current location, or a school district participating in a regional plan that provides for education of homeless children and has been approved by the Commissioner. See also Commissioner's Regulation 100.2 (x).

The amended McKinney-Vento Act requires that the designated local education agency (LEA) must determine if the designated school is in the best interests of the homeless child. See the Field Memorandum from SED at http://nysteachs.org/media/NYSFieldMemo_ESSA_10_2016.pdf. The memorandum addressed 16 areas of change that relate to homeless students. See also question 8-18 about the McKinney-Vento Homeless Assistance Act and student transportation.

3-4. What determines student residency? What process should the administrator follow to determine student residency? What are acceptable forms of proof of residency?

A board of education, or its designee, determines eligibility of students to attend its public schools (Commissioner's Regulation 100.2 (y) (1)). Commissioner's decision No. 17,000 stated:

> "Residence" for purposes of Education Law §3202 is established by one's physical presence as an inhabitant within the district and intent to reside in the district (Longwood Cent. School Dist. v. Springs Union Free School Dist., 1 NY3d 385; Appeal of Naab, 48 Ed Dept Rep 484, Decision No. 15,924).

The Commissioner has held that a child's residence is presumed to be that of his or her parents. However, a student can rebut this presumption by declaring himself or herself to be an emancipated minor. In order to be considered emancipated, a student must be beyond compulsory education age, live separately and apart from parents without parental custody or control, not receive any financial support from parents, and have no intent to return home. See *Appeal of Caban*, 35 Ed Dept Rep 532, Decision No. 13,622.

Students may also be deemed as homeless. School districts must be compliant with changes to the McKinney-Vento Homeless Act as a result of the passage of the Every Student Succeeds Act (ESSA). See question 3-3.

The Commissioner has provided clarification about joint custody and residency. Commissioner's decision No. 16,684 ruled, "In cases where parents have joint custody, the child's time is 'essentially divided' between two households, and both parents assume responsibility for the child. The decision regarding the child's residency lies ultimately with the family." The same decision also noted that "when parents claim joint custody but do not produce proof of the child's time being divided between both households, residency is to be determined by the traditional tests of physical presence in the district and intent to remain there."

For guidance about students who are not citizens of the United States, see http://www.p12.nysed.gov/sss/pps/residency/studentregistrationguidance082610.pdf.

3-5.   What rights do parents have to visit and to observe their children in school? What rights do parents have to eat lunch with their children in school?

Education Law 1709 gives the authority to boards of education to establish rules and regulations with regard to order and discipline in schools. Education Law 2801 also requires that a code of conduct be adopted that governs the conduct of visitors, among others, in order to "assure safety and security of students and school personnel."

As an example, the Commissioner upheld an elementary principal's decision to have parents remain in a foyer area and not allow them to escort their children to classrooms in the morning (*Appeal of Havens*, 42 Ed Dept Rep 13, Decision No. 14,758). The Commissioner has also upheld a board of education policy that required advance permission from the building principal for classroom visits. In that decision, the Commissioner also considered whether the district had acted arbitrarily or capriciously in that instance and concluded that there was a valid concern by the district that gave a reasonable basis for the decision (*Appeal of Canazon*, 33 Ed Dept Rep 124, Decision No.

12,997).

It is important to have a policy or language in the code of conduct for visitors to schools and classrooms. The policy should state that permission from the principal in advance is required prior to visits. Elementary principals should consider a policy concerning parents having lunch with students if this situation is not addressed in any other policy. Such a policy should be one that the school can reasonably and equitably administer. Any requests to visit classrooms or go to lunch with students should go through the principal. A decision should be made based on a rationale that is not arbitrary or capricious, with consideration to safety, security, and/or any disruptions to the educational program.

3-6. What steps should be taken if a parent goes to a classroom to confront a teacher without stopping at the office to follow sign-in procedures?

There are a number of steps that can be taken to communicate appropriate procedures with a parent. The administrator should consider the facts of the circumstances and whether similar behavior had taken place in the past. The goal should be to have an effective relationship between the parent and the school. Possible steps include meeting with the parent, giving written notice about the procedures, putting in writing steps that the district would take if the situation reoccurred, and limiting access to the school without specific authorization in advance from the principal. It should be noted in the district's code of conduct that a violation could result in the activation of a school lockdown, especially when numerous attempts have been made with a particular parent regarding the appropriate procedures for accessing teachers during the school day. See question 3-5 for additional information.

3-7. What rights do parents have to take their children out of school? May a school district restrict the number of times a parent may ask to have his/her child released early from school?

Education Law 3210 holds that a school district may presume that either parent of the student has the right to obtain the release of his/her child from school unless the school has been provided with a legally binding document to the contrary. For example, there may be a custody agreement that restricts circumstances under which a student may be released from school.

Commissioner's Regulation 104.1 (i) requires that a district adopt a comprehensive attendance policy. The regulation requires that the policy include a description of the intervention strategies to address identified patterns of unexcused pupil absence, tardiness, or early departure. The attendance policy should define "release" as an absence for an appointment or some other short-term situation as opposed to being taken out of school indefinitely.

The comprehensive attendance policy must also include a description of incentives to encourage attendance according to Commissioner's Regulation 104.1 (i). School administrators recognize that students may need to be released to their parents/guardians for a variety of reasons. However, continually having a child released from school may have an adverse impact on a child's educational development. District policies should encourage parents to schedule appointments and other activities during after-school hours or during vacation periods with the understanding that some circumstances may prevent this from occurring.

3-8. What role do foster parents play in the education of their student as it relates to residency and tuition? Does this relationship change when the student is in a group home?

Foster parents play an extremely important role in the education of children placed in their care. When a child is placed in the care of foster parents by social services and the placement is not in the district where the child previously resided, the child's previous district is responsible for the payment of any tuition incurred.

When a child is placed in a group home and this is the only residence of the child, the group home is considered the residence of the child, and the school district in which the group home is located is responsible for providing the education for this child. However, if the group home is not the only residence of the child, then the school district may require the payment of tuition for the child's education. See Section 3202 (4)(b) and (c) of New York State Education Law for more information.

Also, additional information regarding foster parents may be found in the *New York State Foster Parent Manual* at http://ocfs.state. ny.us/main/publications/Pub5011.pdf.

The State Education Department and the New York State

Office of Children and Family Services (OCFS) have agreed that there should be clear procedures about transportation to the school of origin for students in foster care and a designated point of contact in the school district to work with the local child welfare agency. For more information, see http://www.p12.nysed.gov/sss/documents/FosterCareMemo12-2-16_FINAL.pdf.

3-9. Under what conditions may a school release a student to a noncustodial parent?

The parent may indicate, at the time of enrollment of a minor, a list of those people to whom the parent's child may be released. A minor may not be released to someone who has not been indicated by the parent except by the principal, or the principal's designee, in an emergency. In an emergency, the parents must be contacted and agree to the release of the student. The principal or the designee has sole discretion in this case and must verify the facts of an emergency.

Education Law 3210 gives guidance and states: "No civil or criminal liability shall arise or attach to any school district or employee thereof for any act or omission to act as a result of, or in connection with, the duties or activities authorized or directed by this paragraph [of Education Law 3210]." The procedures of the law do not apply to releasing a student under the protective custody provisions of Social Services Law and the Family Court Act. For more information about attendance laws including education law, see http://www.p12.nysed.gov/sss/lawsregs/.

3-10. Does a noncustodial parent have the right to pick a child up from school if he/she is not listed on the release form?

A noncustodial parent may not have the right to pick a child up from school if he/she is not listed on the release form. School administrators must be cognizant of any court documents concerning noncustodial parents and any limitations that are indicated in these papers. Education Law 3210 clearly states, "If such person is identified as a person not included on such list, such minor may not be released except in the event of an emergency as determined in the sole discretion of the principal of the school, or his designee, provided that the person or persons in parental relation to the minor have been contacted and have agreed to such release."

3-11. What rights does a biological parent have when a child does not reside with the parent or the parent does not have custody of the child? What serves as proper documentation to determine biological parents?

The school should presume that both parents have the same rights unless there is a certified document from a court such as a divorce decree or a custody order. That document should define the arrangements for custody. It may also define conditions for communication from school to parent and the release of a student from school. The principal should review the copy and consult with the district's counsel if there are any questions or language that is not clear.

The arrangements for custody can raise questions of residency if the parents live in different school districts. The Commissioner's decisions for these situations have been consistently clear: when a court awards custody to one parent, the child's residence is presumed to be with that parent. When joint custody has been granted and the time is "essentially divided" between the two residences, the parents may designate one residence for educational purposes. However, if the parents do not provide proof that time is equally divided between the two residences, residency is determined by physical presence in the district and the intent to remain in the district (*Appeal of Seger*, 42 Ed Dept Rep 266, Decision No. 14,849).

In addition, Education Law 3210 holds that a school may presume that either parent has the authority to have his/her child released from school unless there is a certified copy of a legally binding order from a court to the contrary. If there is a certified document from a court that addresses custody, the document will provide the custodial arrangements for each child.

Documentation for biological parents should at the very least include the original birth certificate indicating the names of both parents. In some cases, the name of the mother will be the only parent indicated. When children are adopted, birth certificates are amended to indicate the adoptive parents.

3-12. What rights do stepparents have?

According to Education Law 3212, the definition of "person in parental relation" includes "stepfather" and "stepmother." Also, according to the Family Educational Rights and Privacy Act, 20 U.S.C. 1232g, and 34 CFR Part 99 (FERPA), a stepparent who lives with the natural parent and is involved on a day-to-day basis with their child has the same rights as the natural parent, especially if the other natural parent is not involved on a day-to-day basis. If a stepparent is not involved on a day-to-day basis with the natural parent and the child, then the stepparent does not have any rights under FERPA. Questions about the role of a stepparent should be determined on a case-by-case basis when the natural parent is not going to be involved in decision making concerning the child. It is helpful to have a consistent practice of requiring documentation in situations in which natural parents have delegated decision-making authority to stepparents, such as when a natural parent may be unavailable. For more information regarding the topic, consult https://nces.ed.gov/pubs97/p97527/exh_5_1.asp.

3-13. What rights do grandparents have?

The roles and rights of grandparents must be clarified on a case-by-case basis. Parents can designate grandparents to provide temporary care and custody, such as after-school supervision, or in the absence of parents. Grandparents may also become legal guardians and, in those cases, court documents will exist to verify the relationship. Part 200.1 (ii) of Commissioner's Regulations acknowledges that a grandparent may be designated to serve in the place of a birth parent. It is important to be clear about the relationship of a child with both parents and grandparents in cases where there are questions about residency.

3-14. If a parent is incarcerated, what is acceptable documentation of temporary guardianship? May family members sign a "consent to test" if no legal guardian has been appointed?

When a parent is incarcerated, the other parent is probably serving as the legal guardian of their children. In many cases, however, grandparents and other family members assume the role of legal guardian. In all cases, the best possible documentation is a court order providing temporary guardianship.

With regard to a "consent to test," if a family member is providing day-to-day care for the child and the child is living with that family member, it would seem logical that the family member could sign this form. However, the best way to resolve this problem is by having the family member seek and obtain temporary guardianship through the local family court. For more information, see http://ocfs.ny.gov/main/publications/Pub5120.pdf.

3-15. What are the requirements for the school in providing duplicate copies of reports and records to the noncustodial parent?

Duplicate copies should be provided to both the custodial and noncustodial parents unless there is a court order or mutual written agreement in writing from both the custodial and the noncustodial parents to do otherwise.

3-16. What responsibilities does an administrator have with regard to custodial rights, visitation, orders of protection, and sharing such information with staff?

The school should presume that both parents have the same rights unless there is a certified document from a court such as a divorce decree or a custody order. That document should define the arrangements for custody and visitation. The principal should review the court document with the counsel for the district if there are any questions about it. Administrative staff, appropriate pupil personnel staff, and any other staff who would be in a position to release students should be aware of such information. Sharing such information must be in accordance with FERPA policies (see question 3-17). For more information, see questions 3-9, 3-10, 3-11, 3-12, 3-13, 3-14, and 3-15. Information about an order of protection is found in question 1-34.

When a parent/guardian is registering child/children for school, proof of custody should be provided to the school administrator. For more information, see www.p12.nysed.gov/sss/documents/EnrollmentBrochure_English.pdf.

3-17. What are the responsibilities of a building administrator under the laws regarding release of information for HIPAA and FERPA?

The Health Insurance Portability and Accountability Act (HIPAA) of 1996 is not as restrictive as the Family Educational Rights and Privacy Act (FERPA) for the privacy of student records. Compliance with FERPA, the federal law that protects the privacy of student records, ensures compliance with HIPAA since all educational records of students fall under the protection of FERPA. Administrators should follow FERPA and the district policy for access to student records with respect to requests for health records of students. See also questions 1-36 and 1-37, along with websites http://www.p12.nysed. gov/sss/schoolhealth/ and https://www2.ed.gov/policy/gen/guid/fpco/ doc/ferpa-hipaa-guidance.pdf.

3-18. What information may be released regarding requests from the military services?

The names, addresses, and telephone numbers of secondary students must be provided to military recruiters unless parents have "opted out" of providing such information. According to FERPA, schools must provide notice to parents annually that directory information, such as a student's name, address, telephone number, date and place of birth, honors and awards, and dates of attendance, can be released publicly unless parents request that the information not be released without prior consent. Schools must also notify parents that the directory information of names, addresses, and telephone numbers will be released to military recruiters unless parents request in writing not to release the information. Schools may use one notice for both directory information and information requested by military recruiters. For more information, see Policy Guidance at http://www2.ed.gov/ policy/gen/guid/fpco/hottopics/ht-10-09-02a.html.

3-19. What rights do social service agencies have to come into school and interview students? Does the student's age make a difference? When should parents be contacted and involved? Who should meet with representatives of Child Protective Services?

Regulatory changes were enacted in 2016 that addressed interviews of children in schools by child protective workers. School districts are required to provide access to records relevant to the investigation of suspected abuse and maltreatment. School districts must also provide:

> Access to any child named as a victim in a report of suspected abuse or maltreatment or any sibling or other child residing in the same home as the named victim. This includes conducting an interview of a child or children without a court order or the consent of the parent, guardian or other person legally responsible for

the child or children. (https://bit.ly/2Mn7muc)

Notably, under these new regulations neither parental consent nor a court order is required for CPS to have access to students in school. In addition, a school district may allow a staff member to accompany the child during the interview with the CPS worker.

Most schools have well-established procedures for coordination with local departments of social services in order to serve the best interests of children and protect the educational process. The administrator should check district policy, or encourage a policy to be developed if it does not exist, that outlines procedures for any interviews requested by social service agencies, including contacting (or not) parents. That policy should also contain the school's thoughtful approach to which school personnel should be present during interviews. Support staff who are likely to be involved, depending on their roles within the district, might include social workers, counselors, nurses, and administrative staff.

A local department of social services is required to initiate an investigation within 24 hours of a report to the New York State Central Registrar of Child Abuse and Maltreatment. The investigation will likely include the school. The local department should have established procedures that have been developed in consultation with schools for investigating such reports. The Child Protective Services unit has responsibility for contacting parents about a report that has been made to the registrar. The policy of a school should describe under what circumstances the school would also communicate with the parent about a report.

There are reasons for an interview of a child to take place in a school. There may be imminent danger to the health and safety of the child that would necessitate immediate contact with a child. The social services agency may have the consent of the parent to interview a student in school. The school may have filed the child abuse report that required the child to be interviewed. Section 421 of Social Services Law states that the child, where possible and appropriate, should be interviewed without the subject of the report present. There is also the infrequent possibility that a court order for an investigation may require an interview at the school site.

See also question 1-38, which relates to interviews by police.

3-20. What identification is needed from the CPS worker(s) involved? What are the questions a principal should ask to verify the ID?

The school administrator has the right to ask the CPS representative for identification and may make a photocopy of the worker's identification badge or other documentation that is provided.

Schools and local social service agencies should have an established understanding about verifying the credentials of social service department officials. Guidance from SED notes that school administrators may be asked to provide photographic employment identification or an alternate form of government-issued photographic identification but may not be asked for or required to provide any other information or documentation as a condition of having access to a child or children (http://www.p12.nysed.gov/sss/documents/regchangescpsinterviewsofchildreninschools.pdf).

The regulations also indicate that the district may request compliance by the CPS representatives with reasonable policies or procedures of the school unless those policies and procedures are contrary to the requirement to give access to the child or children.

Investigations into Article 23-B of Education Law, which applies to child abuse in an educational setting by employees or volunteers, are the responsibility of law enforcement agencies and may require their presence in schools. The administrator should also note whether the request is related to work of the Committee on Preschool Special Education (CPSE) since an agency responsible for the preschool child can have a representative on the committee.

3-21. If an outside agency uses a school building to counsel students, what responsibility does it have to share information with the school district?

The school district should approve any arrangement with an outside agency. This practice will ensure that all understandings about communication are discussed in advance. Agencies should be licensed, such as by the New York State Office of Alcoholism and Substance Abuse Services (OASAS). Credentialed, certified, or licensed staff should be used by the agency so that services are consistent with legal, ethical, and professional standards that ensure confidentiality and appropriate communication. The agreement with the agency should also specify compliance with education law and school policies.

The position statement of the National Association of Social Workers (https://bit.ly/2lCnnB2) is that social workers are "not bound to keep information confidential when clients discuss intent to harm themselves or someone else." For additional information about practice guidelines for maintaining confidentiality for social workers from the SED Office of Professions, see http://www.op.nysed.gov/prof/sw/swconfidential.htm.

The position of the New York Association of School Psychologists is "school psychologists respect the confidentiality of information obtained during their professional work. Information is revealed only with the informed consent of the child, or the child's parent or legal guardian, except in those situations in which failure to release information would result in clear danger to the child or others." See the New York Association of School Psychologists Ethics and Professional Standards Manual (2004) (http://www.nyasp.org/pdf/NYASP%20Ethics%20Manual%202004.pdf).

In a related case that should be noted, the Commissioner has stated, "No decision of the courts or the Commissioner of Education has granted privileged status to communications between a student and school personnel" (*Appeal of the Board of Education of the City School District of New York*, 31 Ed Dept Rep 378, Decision No. 12,673). Although the case applies to school personnel, it addresses the notion of confidentiality that should be clarified with any outside group that uses school facilities.

3-22. What is required in order to release information through the mail, phone, fax, email, etc. to another agency or to an attorney representing a family?

All requests for information concerning an individual student should be given to the person in charge of student records. Release of any information in response to those requests must comply with FERPA (see questions 1-4 and 3-17). In general, this will mean that the request must come from the parent or the student who is eligible to authorize a release. However, there may be a request for information about other students by an attorney representing a family. In those cases, it is a good practice to review such requests with the counsel for the district, since those requests should come through a court-approved process. It is also helpful to clarify exactly what information an attorney is seeking in order to supply only that which is sought since there may be many records for the student.

3-23. Should parents be allowed to visit a school or a class prior to enrollment?

Parents should feel welcome at schools. Since families may be relocating and considering several schools as part of their move, it is important for parents to visit a school and have the opportunity to learn about its programs. It helps with the selection process and builds community support when parents have a better understanding of the educational opportunities offered by a school.

Many schools provide opportunities for parents who already live in a district to visit schools before their children begin a particular program. For example, there may be a program before the start of a school year for parents of prospective kindergartners. The program typically includes a tour, an educational information session, and an opportunity for questions and answers. A parent may visit a special education classroom prior to a meeting of the Committee on Special Education that will be considering the appropriate program for the parent's child.

It is important for an administrator to welcome prospective parents and to provide an opportunity for them to visit the school. The opportunity to visit a classroom should be consistent with school policy and have the cooperation of the teacher. An educator should accompany the parent on any visit in order to explain activities and to answer questions.

3-24. What are the rules for outside groups using school facilities?

A board of education policy should describe criteria and procedures for outside groups that ask to use school facilities. The policy should include insurance requirements that are reviewed on a regular basis with the insurance carrier for the district. Advance notice should be required for requests so that they will be processed in a timely manner. The policy should clarify any priorities for building use. School groups should have first priority when scheduling facilities.

The request form for groups using school facilities should include requirements for adequate supervision of children and the responsibility to maintain care of the facility. Outside groups should be required to comply with all New York State laws and local policies with regard to security and safety. If a swimming pool or kitchen is being used, the group must comply with relevant Department of Health and safety guidelines.

There may be a fee structure if the use incurs extra costs to the school. A board of education may allow use of buildings as a contingent expense if there is no expense to the taxpayers or the extra costs are paid in advance. Education Law 414 requires that any commercial organizations that charge fees must use the proceeds for educational or charitable purposes, but not for activities of a "society, association or organization of a religious sect or denomination."

Outside groups should be aware that automated external defibrillators (AEDs) are available in each school building (see question 2-22). Although public schools are required to have personnel certified in the use of AEDs available at all school-sponsored activities, public school districts are exempt from providing this service for extracurricular activities not sponsored by the school. See New York State Education Law Section 917 (2) and 8NYCRR Sections 136.4 (c)(d).

See question 1-51 for information about student groups and sale of commercial products using school facilities.

3-25. What rights do parents have to select their child's teacher, courses, and school of attendance? What rights do parents have with regard to retention? How should an administrator handle these requests?

Education Law 1709 gives boards of education the authority "to prescribe the course of study for students by which students shall be graded and classified and to regulate the admission of pupils and their transfer from one class or department to another as their scholarship warrants. Consistent with that authority, boards have the power to place students in particular classes" (*Appeal of Dawn H.*, 39 Ed Dept Rep 635, Decision No. 14,336).

The Commissioner has also applied Education Law 1709 to decisions about retention. For example, in *Appeal of Face*, 31 Ed Dept Rep ___, Decision No. 12,547, regarding an appeal of a decision to retain a student, he noted, "In the absence of a showing that a determination with respect to a student placement is arbitrary, capricious, or unreasonable, the Commissioner of Education will not substitute his judgment for that of local authorities."

Education Law 1709 also gives the authority to boards of

education "to manage and to administer the affairs of a school district, including the assignment of pupils to schools therein." Education Law 2503 also authorizes boards to "determine the school where each pupil shall attend" (*Appeal of Johnson*, 37 Ed Dept Rep 465, Decision No. 13,906).

For situations regarding promotion and retention, the administrator should check board of education policy. A district policy can provide support to the principal and staff with guidance to follow in making a decision to promote or to retain. The administrator should also have an established process to receive requests by parents, to consider those requests, and to discuss with them the basis for a decision for promotion or retaining. There should be a rationale with research-based criteria for decision making so that the decision by the district or administrator is not an arbitrary or capricious one.

The No Child Left Behind Act provided school choice options. See http://www.p12.nysed.gov/accountability/T1/fieldmemos/SchoolChoiceDataCollectionFM.pdf.

3-26. What rights does a parent have who has a conflict with a teacher's expectations and requirements? What if a parent wants his/her child to be transferred to another teacher's class?

The Commissioner has noted that the Supreme Court has confirmed that school authorities have wide discretion in regulating matters of curriculum. In addition, he noted that he will not substitute his judgment in a curriculum matter for that of a board of education unless he found evidence that the board had acted in an arbitrary, capricious, or unreasonable manner. In the same case, a factor cited in his decision was that students did not have any prior knowledge of teachers' expectations in a summer reading program (*Appeal of Lease*, 39 Ed Dept Rep 215, Decision No. 14,219).

The Commissioner has ruled that local school authorities have considerable discretion concerning grading policies and practices and, absent a finding that such policies and practices are arbitrary or unreasonable, they will not be set aside (*Appeal of R. W.*, 40 Ed Dept Rep 671, Decision No. 14,580). The Commissioner has also ruled, "It is well settled that decisions regarding student grading rest initially with the classroom teacher and ultimately with the board of education" (*Appeal of Mee Jo*, 44 Ed Dept Rep 198, Decision No. 15,147).

Administrators should have a process that encourages discussion of parent concerns about expectations and requirements with the teacher first. It is advisable for administrators to review some of the Commissioner's rulings concerning grading with their faculties. A periodic legal briefing by an attorney is also helpful so that faculty members have the benefit of some legal perspective when developing grading standards. It is also helpful to review individual grading requirements and practices with teachers and to discuss the requirements with them so that any potential problem issues can be avoided. Grading criteria and expectations of the teachers should be communicated clearly and in advance to students.

The district should have a policy for requests to change teachers. If a parent requests that their child is transferred to another teacher's class, the principal should investigate the reasons for the request and gather relevant information from all teachers and service providers who work with the student. In addition to gathering information, there should be a process to meet with the parents and the teacher. There should also be criteria for making the decision to ensure that the decision is in the best interests of the student. Decision No. 13,063 ruled that "Education Law 1709(33) authorizes a board of education to manage and administer the affairs of the school district, including the assignment of pupils to schools therein" (*Appeal of Joannides*, 32 Ed Dept Rep 278; Matter of Older, et al. v. Board of Ed., 27 NY2d 333). The decision noted that the district's policy in this case regarding intradistrict transfers authorized such transfers upon evidence that it is in the best interests of the child or children involved.

3-27. Do parents have a right to appeal a disciplinary consequence? What information does an administrator need to justify a consequence?

Parents have a right to appeal a disciplinary consequence. The Commissioner has also held that there is nothing in Education Law 3214 that prevents a district from having a policy that has an appeals process within the district for administrative remedies to disciplinary decisions. The process of appeal must be consistent with Education Law 310, which gives rights to have a decision ultimately appealed to the Commissioner (*Appeal of Amara S.*, 39 Ed Dept Rep 90, Decision No. 14,182).

Education Law 3214 requires that a suspension in excess of five days be appealed to a board of education before it is appealed to the

Commissioner. Education Law 3214 does not prevent suspensions of five days or less from being appealed directly to the Commissioner without appealing to a board of education.

It is advisable to have a board of education policy with a defined process for decisions to be appealed since questions are best addressed at the level of day-to-day interaction with students. A process will also allow issues to be considered at the building and district levels rather than being referred directly to a board of education or the Commissioner without such consideration. A sound administrative decision, based on policies and facts, will stand up to the process.

To justify a consequence, the administrator needs to have evidence that the student participated in the objectionable conduct. The Commissioner has held that a decision to discipline a student must be based on "competent and substantial evidence" that the student participated in the conduct that was charged. Any investigation conducted by a school administrator must be fully and thoroughly documented to withstand scrutiny prior to the imposition of any disciplinary action (see question 1-24). There will be situations in which the evidence must be questioned, so it is a good idea to review the matter with counsel for the district in those situations.

3-28. Do parents have a right to interview the other student(s) in a disciplinary matter?

Education Law 3214 (3) (b) gives parents the right, with suspensions being considered for five days or less, to an informal conference with the principal. The parent has the authority to ask questions of the complaining witnesses at that meeting. Both the principal and the complaining witnesses must be present (*Appeal of Deborah P.*, 39 Ed Dept Rep 433, Decision No. 14,279).

In certain circumstances where the complaining witness is a student, the school administrator conducting the informal conference may request that the parent of this student also be present. Education Law 3214 does not address the parental right to demand that a parent of the complaining witness be present at conferences regarding disciplinary actions that call for suspensions of five days or less. It may be prudent, however, if the complaining witness is a student, that parents of the student be contacted by the administrator indicating that their child may be asked to give testimony at an informal conference and that they be present during that informal conference.

The procedures of Education Law 3214 (3) (c) for suspensions that may be for longer than five days give the right to a pupil, who may have an attorney, to question witnesses against the pupil.

The parent, in other cases that are not governed by statutes, would not have the right to interview the complaining witness. The administrator, in view of the circumstances of the case, could give permission, but there should be clear guidelines for conduct of the meeting and communication with the parents of any students who would be questioned.

3-29. Do parents have a right to demand that no staff member, including an administrator, question or discipline their child unless they are present?

The Commissioner has held that "there is no legal requirement that a parent be contacted or present during an administrative investigation of an incident involving student conduct. Education Law 3214 requires only that, for suspensions of five days or less, parents be provided an opportunity for an informal conference with the principal" (*Appeal of Phyllis and Marc B.*, 38 Ed Dept Rep 301, Decision No. 14,039).

Under FERPA, only school officials with legitimate educational interests can have access to a student's educational records. The nature of the information would determine which staff members should be aware of the information. For example, an order of protection that affects a student may require that anyone in a supervisory position with the student be aware of such order. Any questions about sharing an order of protection should be clarified with the court through the school's attorney. See question 1-37 for more information about FERPA.

3-30. When addressing the issue of effective parent communication, what is an appropriate building- and district-level chain of command?

Most school districts have an established chain of command or process for parents to follow to resolve a school problem that affects their child. This chain usually begins with the teacher. It may include a counselor or social worker. If the matter is not resolved at that level, an appeal might be made to the supervisor of the teacher, counselor, or social worker. The next step involves the building administrator.

After the building administrator, the process moves to a district level, depending on the size of the district, and ultimately the superintendent. After the superintendent, an appeal could go to the board of education and to the State Education Department for a Commissioner's ruling.

It has been helpful for districts to publish this process and encourage parents to follow it. Most problems are best solved at the level that has day-to-day interaction with the child. If there is no board of education policy to address the communication process or process for appeal, it will be helpful for the district to adopt one.

3-31. Is there a recommended policy for working with the media?

A school administrator should become familiar with all district policies and guidelines for communicating with media. The administrator should also understand any guidelines or procedures involving the superintendent's office and/or the public relations office in a large district.

It is important to establish an effective working relationship with the media. The relationship should be built upon open, honest, and accurate communication. There are times when the administrator may not be able to give all of the information that is requested by the media. For example, an administrator is not able to release student information that would be in violation of FERPA (see questions 1-4, 1-37, 3-17, and 6-24). It is also helpful, when responding to questions about controversial issues, to ask the reporter questions in order to understand the intent of the story. If an administrator cannot speak to a reporter when the reporter calls, it supports an effective working relationship to know the reporter's deadline and return the call before the deadline. If the media intends to report a story, it is important to have the school's position included in the article. Be succinct; use facts and try to avoid conjecture. Every school administrator must be careful not to make any casual or "off the record" comments to the media. This includes parents or members of the community who work for the media. It is valuable to reach out to the media when there are newsworthy stories in the school. The administrator should also anticipate when there is going to be a call from the media, such as a call seeking a local comment on a national educational story, and should be prepared with some brief talking points.

3-32. Who determines when you talk to media and what is said?

This determination is a local school district decision. The district may want to ensure that statements made by district personnel are consistent for district and general educational matters. The school administrator should be familiar with district policies and guidelines for communicating with media. The administrator should also understand any guidelines or procedures from the superintendent's office or from the public relations office in a large district. There may be cases when there is a designated spokesperson, such as in a crisis situation. The administrator should know whether any local contracts with bargaining units have language that pertains to communication with the public (see also question 3-31).

3-33. How should an administrator positively promote programs?

It is helpful to develop a plan in collaboration with parents, staff, and students that identifies the points to be emphasized about the school and the ways in which the information will be communicated. Parents and staff should be included in drafting the plan since many people will obtain information about the schools and form perceptions about them from the people who work in schools and the parents.

The plan should consider use of social media, consistent with the district's policies and philosophy about social media and communication, to engage its community. For more information and examples, see "Social Media Use by School Districts," (Senger, 2013) at https://www.nspra.org/files/docs/SENGER_Social_Media_Schools-web.pdf.

Examples of electronic communication include the swift and efficient communication of urgent information through texts and emails. School forms needed by parents can be easily downloaded from websites and printed at their homes. Posting photos and performance data on websites helps promote programs and extracurricular activities.

In addition, it is helpful for school leaders to develop and maintain strong and active relationships with parents, staff, and students. "A Practical Guide to Promoting America's Public Schools" (Learning First Alliance, 2005) offers steps to deal with seven areas for public communication that include values, school discipline, academics, benefits of public education, public education, accountability, and parent involvement. The steps indicate how these areas can be applied to local schools. For more information, see https://www.masb.org/Portals/0/Advocacy_and_Legislation/practical guide.pdf. See also question 5-36.

3-34. How should an administrator respond to negative publicity?

If there is an opportunity before a negative circumstance is publicly reported, then the administrator should develop talking points to address the issue. If time is needed to develop the talking points, the administrator should find out if there is a media deadline and then contact the media before the deadline. The talking points should be accurate and based on the facts. They should also indicate actions that will be taken to address the situation. The administrator should make sure that the superintendent is aware that there is going to be a story reported by the media.

If the story has already been reported, then there are several steps that an administrator can take to respond. The response should be reasoned and thoughtful. It is helpful to consider how the uninformed public might interpret the story. Staff and parents should be informed concerning the facts of the situation. These can be communicated in writing, at faculty meetings, and at PTA meetings. If corrective action is required, the steps should be indicated. In a case such as weak test results or issues related to safety or security, emphasize the serious approach that the district takes to such matters. Call attention to the many planning efforts that the district uses to improve in these areas. It may be useful to indicate that the district will be reviewing the particular situation, taking appropriate steps and adjusting plans and policies. Appropriate reporting on the progress of the actions will support the credibility of the district. If the matter has involved law enforcement personnel, the district should coordinate responses with the law enforcement agency to ensure accurate information for the public.

3-35. Can a parent who is a registered sex offender come into school for a parent-teacher conference?

There are a number of factors that need to be taken into consideration if a student's parent is a registered sex offender. School administrators should consult local law enforcement and legal counsel regarding actions/policies pertaining to sex offenders' access to school campus and events.

The Commissioner has determined that when a level one offender has met the terms of the probation or conditional discharge, prohibition from entering school may not be appropriate (*Appeal of K.M.*, 55 Ed Dept Rep, Decision No. 16,796). That decision notes that the provisions of Penal Law Section 65.10(4-a) concern circumstances under which sex offenders are prohibited and can be prohibited from entering onto or being on school grounds.

3-36. What is the purpose of a parent-teacher conference? What support can the principal provide for teachers to enhance the effectiveness of the conferences?

The parent-teacher conference provides an opportunity for the parent and the teacher to discuss a student's performance in school in addition to ways to enhance that performance. The discussion should include academic data as well as social and behavioral observations.

To enhance parent-teacher conferences, the principal should seek teacher input about best practices for covering key points, discussing critical data, creating a welcoming atmosphere, and avoiding common pitfalls. This information can be used to create a template/guidance document to share through professional development at a faculty meeting.

For additional information about parent-teacher conferences and the roles of principals, teachers, and parents before, during, and after the conferences, see the Parent Teacher Conference Tip Sheets from the Global Family Research Project at https://www.globalfrp.org/Articles/Parent-TeacherConference-Tip-Sheets-For-Principals-Teachers-and-Parents.

3-37. What is suggested if there is a language barrier between school personnel and parents when English is not the primary language of the parents?

The first step for school leaders is to learn as much as possible about the parents' culture. Reaching out to community organizations that provide assistance to non-English-speaking populations is a good place to start. This can help prevent uncomfortable moments. For example, making eye contact and shaking hands may not be acceptable in some cultures. Also, there may be religious or cultural traditions that impact school attendance or participation in school-sponsored programs/events. Professional development should be provided for any staff members who will be working with English language learners. Local support may be available through the Regional Bilingual Education Resource Network (RBERN) of SED. See http://www.nysed.gov/bilingual-ed/schools/regional-supportrberns.

If the parents do not have a friend or relative who speaks English, the school enrollment process may be overwhelming. Other local options to consider for finding an interpreter who can assist are churches, refugee centers, language professors from a nearby college/university, and bilingual high school students.

3-38. What steps can the principal take to make sure that information is getting to the parents/legal guardians? When students are moving between households and their contact information keeps changing, how does the principal ensure that records are kept up to date?

When a student is registered, it is important to find out the name of one person whom the parent/legal guardian maintains contact with at all times. That individual may be a relative who does not live locally. It is likely that person will still hear from the parent/guardian in the event that phone numbers on record at school are no longer in service and/or the family has changed residence. That person may be able to assist the school with new contact information or share with the parent/guardian that school personnel are having difficulty reaching them.

Letters sent via registered mail require a signature. This provides proof that the parent/guardian has received the communication. If the letter cannot be delivered, that is also documented. Letters sent via regular mail service may or may not be returned to the school.

Section 4
Curriculum and Instruction

4-1. What are the New York State Learning Standards and Common Core Learning Standards?

The learning standards are defined in Commissioner's Regulation 100.1(t) as "the knowledge, skills and understandings that individuals can and do habitually demonstrate over time as a consequence of instruction and experience." The learning standards are divided into seven curriculum areas that include English language arts; mathematics, science, and technology; social studies; languages other than English; the arts; health, physical education, and family and consumer science; and career development and occupational studies. There are core curricula for the learning standards that give greater specificity with key ideas and performance indicators. They provide a foundation for the state assessments. For more information, see http://www.p12.nysed.gov/ciai/cores.html.

The Regents have approved Common Core Learning Standards for English language arts and literacy, as well as mathematics. In addition, the Regents have approved a set of prekindergarten standards that align with the learning and common core standards. See http://www.p12.nysed.gov/ciai/common_core_standards for more information about these standards. For additional information and curriculum resources, see EngageNY and https://www.engageny.org/common-core-curriculum-assessments.

The Regents have also approved a K-12 social studies framework that integrates the existing New York State Learning Standards for Social Studies and the New York State Common Core Standards for Literacy and Writing into a single, three-part document. It is intended to serve as a guide for local districts in developing their social studies curricula.

The framework includes the college, career, and civic life (C3) framework for state standards in social studies (National Council of Social Studies, 2013) and the New York State K-12 Social Studies Framework. Both emphasize the foundation of literacy through an integration of the common core learning standards and through unique disciplinary literacies of social studies in civics, economics, geography, and history.

The framework includes the inquiry arc. The inquiry arc provides an overall approach to increasing rigor by developing questions and planning inquiries, applying disciplinary concepts and tools, evaluating sources, and using evidence to communicate conclusions and take informed action. For additional information, see http://www.p12.nysed.gov/ciai/socst/frameworkhome.html and https://www.engageny.org/resource/new-york-state-k-12-social-studies-framework. New York State P-12 learning standards for science became effective on July 1, 2017. Additional information about the NYS P-12 science standards can be found at http://www.p12.nysed.gov/ciai/mst/sci/nyssls.html. These state standards are based on the foundation of the National Research Council's *A Framework for K-12 Science Education: Practices, Crosscutting Concepts, and Core Ideas*; and the next generation science standards. The standards are more process based than content based. Their focus is on the application of science, infusing the engineering design process, using scientific methods, and solving problems with real-life application.

4-2. What are the main features of the Every Student Succeeds Act (ESSA), which replaced No Child Left Behind (NCLB)?

The Every Student Succeeds Act was signed into law by President Barack Obama on December 10, 2015, and it reauthorized the 1965 Elementary and Secondary Education Act. ESSA requires states to have an accountability system based upon multiple measures. States are required to adopt challenging academic standards in mathematics, language arts, and science. Standards must be aligned to college and career/technical standards. States are not required to adopt the common core learning standards.

Students must be assessed in English language arts and mathematics once each year during grades 3-8 and once in high school. Students must be assessed in science once during elementary school, once in middle school, and once in high school. Assessments must be aligned to the state's challenging academic standards.

Additional resources and information can be found at http://www.p12.nysed.gov/accountability/essa.html.

4-3. How should an administrator evaluate curriculum?

Curriculum evaluation is best carried out using a comprehensive systems approach. The administrator should set up procedures to review the written curriculum, the taught curriculum, and the tested curriculum.

The administrator should strive for a school culture that values and supports continuous improvement and collaboration. Teachers and administrators working in teams to establish goals and analyze results produce superior gains. The administrator ensures that resources and professional development are ongoing, timely, and targeted to specific teacher needs. Celebrate successes and collaborate to close gaps in curriculum and content (*Curriculum Handbook*, ASCD, 2004).

Effective administrators routinely and systematically review and renew curriculum documents. These documents often include a prioritized essential curriculum adopted by the board of education expected for all classrooms, curriculum maps, key vocabulary lists, and common assessments. They ensure that the curriculum is aligned with the goals of the school and the district.

To evaluate the taught curriculum, administrators must make formal and informal visits to the classroom. Administrators can ask for examples of student work and student performance results as other ways to evaluate curriculum.

As discussed in question 4-6, close support and monitoring of the team learning process is a proven means for ensuring consistency in not only what curriculum is taught, but more importantly, the extent to which the curriculum is learned.

This question addresses evaluation of curriculum. See questions 6-1 through 6-6 for more information about teacher evaluations.

4-4.   What is curriculum mapping?

Curriculum mapping is the process for collecting, reviewing, modifying, and publishing the actual curriculum of the school. Curriculum maps can be simple or elaborate. Most curriculum maps contain information about the content of a particular class or subject, the timeframe and pacing of instruction, and how the learning will be assessed. Curriculum maps can help a school district provide common curriculum across different teachers and schools. An analysis of curriculum maps can help identify content gaps.

Research has shown that a "guaranteed and viable curriculum" is provided by effective schools and is one of the most important things that a school can do to raise student achievement by allowing students to learn material covered in the time allotted in any classroom to which they are assigned (*What Works in Schools: Translating Research into Action* by Robert Marzano, ASCD, 2003). Curriculum mapping assists in meeting this objective by calling upon teachers to collaboratively answer the question, What do we want students to know and be able to do at the end of this lesson, unit, or course?

Schools can choose to keep the maps an internal document; more commonly, they are published in newsletters or on a website. Curriculum maps can help families keep in touch with schools and what children are learning. For more information on curriculum mapping, see *An Educational Leader's Guide to Curriculum Mapping* by Janet Hale and Richard Dunlap, Corwin Press, 2010.

4-5. Can an administrator mandate that a teacher or group of teachers use a specific instructional approach?

Education Law 1709 empowers a board of education with authority to determine courses of study, instructional programs, and curriculum content. A specific instructional approach is often part of an approved course of study or curriculum content. The administrator, acting for the board of education, has the authority to require a specific instructional approach as part of the approved curriculum. For example, some reading programs are scripted concerning how a particular skill is taught, leaving little discretion to the teachers. The administrator should also refer to district policy. Many school policies address teaching methods. The Annual Professional Performance Review (APPR) may address instructional strategy and methods issues through the observation component of the evaluation process. The administrator should also check negotiated agreements and contracts for language on instructional approaches.

An administrator, acting as a supervisor, has an obligation to evaluate the effectiveness of teaching strategies and methods (see questions 6-1 and 6-2 for related information). The administrator, deeming such practices ineffective, may restrict some practices, or mandate others. For example, an administrator may require increased student engagement in the classroom and mandate the use of instructional strategies that promote student engagement. The APPR process provides an evaluative opportunity, using the state-approved rubric with the teacher observation category consistent with the locally negotiated contract. See also questions 6-1, 6-2, and 6-5.

Note that Education Law 3012-d and sections 30-2.14 and 30-3.17 of the rules of the Board of Regents establish transition scores and ratings for teachers and building principals for the 2015-2016 through 2018-2019 school years as the state transitions to new state assessments aligned to higher learning standards and a revised state-approved growth model. For additional information, refer to EngageNY (https://www.engageny.org/resource/appr-3012-d).

4-6. How does an administrator ensure consistency in the classroom with regard to delivery of core content?

Consistency can best be achieved through collaboration and accountability. Administrators must provide teachers with clear expectations about curriculum and the opportunity to work together. Many schools have success with mapping the curriculum, which details content, pacing, and assessment. Looking at common assessment data is another way to ensure consistency of content. The most common approach is to require common assessments, such as end-of-course examinations, portfolios, or other products. Consistency can also be reinforced through the teacher evaluation process. For more information, see *What Works in Schools: Translating Research into Action* by Robert Marzano, ASCD, 2003.

Professional learning communities represent an effective means for achieving higher quality teaching and learning on a more consistent basis throughout a school. They require teachers to engage in a team learning process. Several characteristics of learning communities support consistency in the delivery of content within a school. These include a shared mission, beliefs, goals, and collective learning. The collaborative work of teams can support consistency by:

1. Identifying essential outcomes for each course or grade level by asking and answering the question, What do we want students to know and be able to do?
2. Developing common, comprehensive assessments to measure the essential learning outcome and asking the question, How will we know if they are learning?
3. Identifying proficiency levels that all students should achieve on those assessments by asking the question, What are our expectations for "quality" work?
4. Reviewing results from assessments, identifying problem areas, and developing plans for addressing those areas by

asking and answering the question, How do we respond to those students who are not learning or who have mastered the content?

By continuously supporting and monitoring teachers as they engage in the team learning process, an administrator ensures consistency with regard to delivery of the core content. For more information on professional learning communities, see *Learning by Doing: A Handbook for Professional Learning Communities at Work* by Dufour, DuFour, Eaker, & Many, 2006, and the website, http://www.allthingsplc.info/.

4-7.   What steps should an administrator take to use performance-based data to affect classroom instruction?

It is very important for administrators to make data available to teachers in a clear, timely manner in order for the data to impact classroom instruction. Administrators should work with teachers to focus on a few, rather than many, core areas of importance. See that teachers focus planning, instruction, and assessments in these areas. Formative (assessment for learning) and summative (assessment of learning) measures should be utilized. There is an abundance of evidence citing the impact of formative assessments on student learning and achievement. Michael Fullan (2005) notes in his book, *Leadership and Sustainability*, that "'assessment for learning' has become a high yield tool for school improvement and student learning" (p. 23).

Administrators should provide teachers the support, direction, resources, time, and training to engage in the team learning process outlined in question 4-6, and should then regularly monitor the results of the common formative assessments. Regularly monitoring, analyzing, and immediately responding to common formative assessment results allow teachers and administrators to:

- Target specific areas for improvement in essential instructional areas.
- Provide frequent opportunities to celebrate measurable progress and results.
- Create an internal sense of urgency necessary for instructional improvement and innovation.

4-8.   What are the required assessments that are administered

to students in New York State?

The required assessments for students in grades 9-12 are noted in the diploma credential chart referenced in question 4-15 (http://www.p12.nysed.gov/ciai/gradreq/Documents/Current DiplomaCredentialSummary.pdf). This diploma credential chart outlines the multiple pathways available for students to earn a Regents diploma, a Regents diploma with honors, or a Regents diploma with advanced designation.

Students in grades 3-8 must take English language arts and mathematics tests annually at each grade level. Students must take science exams in grades 4 and 8. For more information, see http://www.p12.nysed.gov/assessment/ei/eigen.html.

4-9. What important steps must an administrator keep in mind when administering Regents exams?

Administrators should have the latest version of the test manual for school administrators for Regents examinations. An online version is available from the SED website through the Office of State Assessment at http://www.p12.nysed.gov/assessment/sam/secondary/hssam-update.html.

Good planning is essential to effective administration of Regents exams. The best way to administer Regents exams is to schedule a series of meetings, or tasks, for the administration team. Tasks can be divided into general categories such as planning and conducting exams.

Planning:
1. Develop safety plans that include procedures for low-level bomb threats and power outages.
2. Establish the location of exam sites, including adequate space and staff for students with special needs. Consider lighting and climate control.
3. Ensure security for ordering and storing exams and exam material, including special exams. All requests for exam materials must be made using the online request system.
4. Develop an examination proctor and assignment schedule. Publish the schedule in advance of the exam. Assign trusted and experienced staff as head proctors.
5. Develop and publish a plan for inclement weather.

Conducting Exams:
1. Inspect the exam site each day.
2. Follow procedures for students entering and exiting the exam site.
3. Check the SED website for updates and corrections.
4. Visit all exam sites. Proctors should arrive on time, and be active and attentive to the students. Hats, books, and electronic devices should be stored away from students.

It is important for administrators to read carefully the most recent Administrator's Manual for Regents examinations and memoranda from the State Education Department Office of Assessment Policy, Development and Administration for specific directions on ordering, administering, scoring, and storing Regents examinations.

4-10. Can course credit be granted for passing a Regents exam even if the student failed the course?

Section 100.5 (a)(5)(v) of the Commissioner's Regulations does not permit schools to give a unit of credit for passing a Regents exam unless the student has passed the course or has met the requirements of Section 100.1 (b) for credit by an examination. Section 100.1 (b) requires that a student must score 85 or better on the exam and successfully complete a special project or oral examination. An administrator should ensure that there is a policy in place to describe procedures to be used for a request to receive credit by examination. Please note that there is a laboratory requirement that must be met before admission to any Regents exam in science.

4-11. What are the requirements for academic intervention services (AIS) in New York State?

Academic intervention services assist students who are at risk of not achieving the state learning standards. These services are intended to assist students who are at risk of not achieving state standards for English language arts and mathematics in grades K-12, and social studies and science in grades 3-12 (Commissioner's Regulation 100.2 (ee)).

AIS includes two components. The first is additional instruction that supplements the regular classroom instruction provided by the general curriculum. The second is student support services including guidance, counseling, attendance, support, and instruction in study skills. Both components are needed to address barriers to improved academic performance (Commissioner's Regulation 100.1 (g)).

Students eligible for AIS are:

- Those who score below the designated performance levels on elementary, intermediate, and commencement-level state assessments in English language arts, mathematics, social studies, and science.
- Those at risk of not meeting state standards as indicated through district-adopted procedures, including K-3 students who lack reading readiness.

Commissioner's Regulations for AIS include a number of requirements. A board of education must adopt a description of services with procedures for determining student eligibility and criteria for ending services for a student. The description of services must be reviewed on the basis of student performance every two years. Personnel providing services must be qualified and appropriately certified. See Commissioner's Regulation 100.2 (ee) (1) (2) (3) for requirements for different grade levels.

There must be parental notification prior to providing any AIS services, regardless of whether the services occur before, during, or after the school day. Parental notification must include notice of starting services, a summary of the services to be provided, the reason for the services, and the consequences of not meeting expected performance levels. There must also be parental notification when services will be ended. There must be ongoing communication with parents that includes opportunity to consult with the professional staff providing the services, and quarterly reports on the student's progress. Parents shall also be provided with information on ways to work with their child to improve achievement; monitor their child's progress; and work with educators to improve their child's achievement" (see Commissioner's Regulation 100.2 (ee)(6)(iii)(c)).

Commissioner's Regulations 100.1 and 100.2 provide the regulatory foundation for these services. For more information, see also http://www.p12.nysed.gov/part100/pages/AISQAweb.pdf.

Current regulations allow an RtI program to be provided in place of AIS if the RtI program meets state requirements and is available at grade levels and subject areas for which students are eligible for AIS, and if all students who are eligible for AIS are provided AIS if they are not enrolled in RtI. See also 4-14. (https://www.regents.nysed.gov/common/regents/files/P-12%20-%20Academic%20Intervention%20Services.pdf).

See question 3-1 about parental requests to remove students from AIS.

4-12. What is the most effective way to provide AIS services to students?

The most effective way of providing AIS services is during the school day as much as practical. Academic intervention services are designed to help students meet learning standards in major academic areas. These services are a state mandate. Services may be provided before, during, and in extended academic time beyond the regular school day. Services may also occur during summer. Schools typically provide most of their services during the school day.

Building administrators should review carefully the regulations and ways that services can be offered. For example, one of the practices that a number of districts use includes extending the school day. The State Education Department also allows evening, weekend, and summer sessions. Administrators should review the effectiveness of each service as related to improving student achievement.

A student cannot eliminate instruction in another area to meet the AIS mandate except in certain areas in grades 7 and 8. Commissioner's Regulation 100.4 (c) (5) states:

> Academic intervention services shall be provided in a manner that does not diminish instructional time to a degree that may prevent a student from achieving the State learning standards in any area required for graduation or from meeting local standards for promotion. A principal shall consider a student's abilities, skills and interests in determining the subjects for which the unit of study requirements may be reduced.

AIS should not be perceived as punitive. For more information, see question 4-11.

4-13. What constitutes an effective AIS program?

An effective AIS program provides individualized instruction based on students' learning needs and styles, along with frequent diagnostic progress monitoring. The administrator ensures an effective AIS program by fully implementing the requirements, including but not limited to: defining and describing the services, determining eligibility for services, parent notification, and monitoring progress.

In English language arts in grades K-2, schools will provide AIS when students lack reading readiness or are at risk of not achieving state performance levels in English language arts and math.

AIS will be provided to students in grades 3-8 when they score below the state-designated performance level on one or more of the state elementary assessments and are at risk of not achieving learning standards as determined by the district's adopted procedures.

Required AIS services will be provided to students in grades 9-12 when they score below the state-designated performance level on one or more of the state intermediate assessments or are at risk of not achieving learning standards as determined by the district's adopted procedures.

For additional information on specific requirements for academic intervention services, see Commissioner's Regulation 100.2 (ee) at http://www.p12.nysed.gov/part100/pages/1002.html.

Effective AIS curricula address the barriers to improved academic performance. A system to assess the specific barriers must consider academic and nonacademic factors from multiple sources. Common barriers to academic success include language issues (limited English proficiency), mobility issues, and family issues.

4-14. What is response to intervention (RtI)?

Commissioner's Regulation 100.2(ii) defines RtI as a school district's process to determine if a student responds to scientific, research-based instruction. The New York State Response to Intervention Technical Assistance Center describes RtI as follows:

> Response to Intervention or RtI can be defined as a school-wide, multi-tiered prevention framework that provides supplemental, needs-specific intervention to students with learning problems, most notably in the area of reading. Key components of an RtI framework involve: (1) data driven assessment and problem-solving and tiered supports. Data driven assessment and problem-solving occur at all

levels of the framework and includes universal screening
to determine risk status and progress monitoring to
determine student response to supplemental intervention.
Tiered support or intervention increases in intensity based
on student needs and progress. RtI operates within a
collaborative context that includes educators and families
working together to promote academic student success. (See
https://nysrti.org/.)

RtI is not a "wait to fail" model; it is intended to give help
promptly in the general education setting. The elements of RtI are
referenced in Part 100 of Commissioner's Regulations as part of the
process for prereferral interventions for general education students
experiencing academic and behavioral challenges. (See Commissioner's
Regulation 100.2 (ii)). RtI is also included in the Individuals with
Disabilities Education Improvement Act (IDEA) for use in identifying
learning disabilities.

All school districts must have an RtI program in place as part of
the process to determine if a student in grades K-4 is a student with a
learning disability in the area of reading. See Commissioner's Regulation
200.4 (j). See also https://nysrti.org/files/documents/resources/general/
implementation_of_response-to-intervention-programs.pdf.

The New York State Education Department has also established a
general policy framework for RtI in the regulations for districts that wish
to adopt an RtI model for implementing schoolwide approaches and
prereferral interventions to remediate a student's academic performance
or behavioral functioning prior to referral for special education. See
guidance from SED at https://nysrti.org/files/documents/resources/
general/nysed_rti_guidance_document.pdf.

4-15. What are the requirements for graduation in New York State?

The graduation requirements are described in Section 100.5 of
the Commissioner's Regulations. For specific information about these
requirements, see the following webpages at SED.

http://www.p12.nysed.gov/part100/pages/1005.html and
http://www.p12.nysed.gov/ciai/gradreq/intro.html.

A detailed chart outlining diploma requirements for
grade 9 students first entering high school in 2016 is available at

http://www.p12.nysed.gov/ciai/gradreq/DocumentsCurrent DiplomaRequirements.pdf. Students entering grade 9 in the 2008-2015 school years will need 22 units of credit to receive a Regents, Advanced Regents, or local high school diploma. There are multiple pathways, endorsements, and appeals that are outlined on a detailed chart available at http://www.p12.nysed.gov/ciai/gradreq/Previous%20 version%20of%20GradReq/GradReq2008_2015June2016.pdf.

Credit and assessment requirements for Regents, Advanced Regents, and local diplomas, as well as requirements for a Career Development and Occupational Studies (CDOS) Commencement Credential and a Skills Achievement Commencement Credential, are outlined in a diploma/credential chart available at http://www.p12.nysed. gov/ciai/gradreq/Documents/CurrentDiplomaCredentialSummary. pdf.

Students identified with disabilities through the Committee on Special Education have safety net options available as outlined in a memo that can be found at http://www.p12.nysed.gov/specialed/ publications/safetynetcompensatoryoption.html.

There is an option for students with disabilities to earn a local diploma through a superintendent's determination. For students with disabilities, otherwise eligible to graduate in June 2016 and thereafter, a school superintendent (or the principal of a registered nonpublic school or charter school, as applicable) has the responsibility to determine if a student with a disability has otherwise met the standards for graduation with a local diploma when such student has not been successful, because of his/her disability, at demonstrating his/her proficiency on the Regents examinations required for graduation. Additional information about this determination can be found at http://www.p12.nysed.gov/ specialed/publications/safetynetcompensatoryoption.html. See 7-44 and 7-47.

Commissioner's Regulation 100.5 (b)(7)(ii) describes how a Regents diploma or Advanced Regents diploma may be awarded with honors. A student must achieve an average of 90 for all Regents exams that were taken for the student's diploma. The regulation explains how to make this determination if a student substitutes no more than two alternate assessments.

The Regents also approved an appeals process in which students who score within five points of 65 (60-64) and have achieved the state learning standards would be eligible to appeal if they met certain criteria. See Commissioner's Regulation 100.5 (d) (7) and an SED memo outlining the requirements for an appeal at http://www.p12. nysed.gov/ciai/memos/expanded-appeal-memo-4-20-16.pdf.

4-16. What roles do the teacher contract, state law, and Commissioner's Regulations have in the creation of a master schedule?

The local teachers' contract will outline negotiated agreements with regard to class and duty assignments of teachers. Commissioner's Regulation 100.2 (i) states, "The number of daily periods of classroom instruction for a teacher should not exceed five. A school requiring of any teacher more than six teaching periods a day, or a daily teaching load of more than 150 pupils, should be able to justify the deviation from this policy." The Commissioner has explained that the intent of this regulation is to provide quality instruction for students and that each case must be evaluated as to whether a particular assignment does not allow effective teaching in a way that "diminishes quality instruction" for students. In one case, which involved a physical education teacher, the Commissioner noted that he would consider aspects of a teacher's load to include time for grading and reviewing student work, preparation time, number of students, and number of classes per day. He added that in a previous case he had determined that a physical education teaching load of 9-11 classes per day and 189-232 students did not unduly impair the teacher's ability to teach (*Appeal of Kleinman*, 34 Ed Dept Rep 1, Decision No. 13,212). See also *Appeal of Kellee Koenig*, 50 Ed Dept Rep, Decision No. 16,145.

The building administrator should review contractual language for assignments to ensure compliance. When there are deviations from the Commissioner's Regulation such as for physical education, special education, art, music, and other special areas, there should be consideration of the aspects that would affect the assignment and delivery of instruction. If there are questions, a labor relations specialist should be consulted.

4-17. What is the role of the principal in creating the master schedule?

Although the role varies depending on the level and size of the school, the principal is responsible for the master schedule. A successful master schedule is crucial to support effective curriculum and instruction. The master schedule is a plan to allocate the resources of time, classroom space, and teaching assignment. The administrator makes decisions about class size, teacher assignment, and room utilization. Limitations on teacher's workload, planning time requirements, and class size constraints, are frequently included as a provision in collective bargaining agreements. The administrator should also be familiar with all local requirements and Commissioner's Regulations (see question 4-16).

The principal generally uses computer tools and staff assistance to develop the master schedule. Most schools use some form of master schedule software. In schools with no assistant principal and/or counselor, the principal often has direct and sole responsibility to develop the schedule. In larger schools, the responsibility of developing the master schedule is often shared or delegated.

The administrator should establish goals and objectives for the master schedule. Top priorities include honoring course requests for students and balancing class size.

In addition to goals and objectives for the master schedule, the master schedule should support the vision of the school and be part of a continuous improvement process. An effective administrator is familiar with various scheduling strategies and scenarios.

Schools and communities grapple with several issues relating to scheduling of instructional time, expanded learning time, and school calendars. Research about these issues can be found at the National Center on Time and Learning (http://www.timeandlearning.org/).

The administrator should retain copies of master schedules for reference or questions about them in the future.

4-18. What is block scheduling?

A block schedule organizes time into longer class periods than traditional schedules. There are several variations of a block schedule. The two most common types of block schedule are the alternate day (i.e., A/B schedule) and the semester model (i.e., 4x4 schedule). A third option, the trimester plan, allows students to take two or three courses over 60 days to earn six to nine credits per year.

In the alternate day schedule, classes are approximately twice as long as in a traditional schedule, but they meet on alternate days. In a 4x4 schedule, class length is twice the length of a class in a traditional schedule, and classes meet each day but only for one semester.

There are several reported advantages to block scheduling. Instructional time has fewer interruptions because classes are longer. More time works well for lessons aimed at student engagement and deeper understanding. Fewer class changes generally improve the orderliness of the school. Schools report a decrease in discipline referrals. Advantages for students include more focused study, especially in the 4x4 or semestered models. Block scheduling often allows a student to advance his or her course of study by taking more than one course in a given subject in a year's time.

Critics of block scheduling argue that longer periods of time do not necessarily result in more engaging classrooms. In 4x4 models students often have gaps in the study of a particular subject. For example, a student may study a foreign language in the first semester of one school year, and not study the next course in the sequence until the second semester of the next school year. Critics also point out that there is no definitive research that proves that block scheduling leads to improved student achievement.

See question 4-16 for more information about the use of time in school. Additional resources and research regarding block scheduling may be found at http://www.nea.org/tools/16816.htm.

4-19. What is independent study? When may it be used? How does it relate to online learning and blended courses?

Commissioner's Regulation 100.5 (d) (9) states that,

> Students enrolled in a school district, a charter school, or a registered nonpublic school may earn a maximum of three units of elective credit toward a Regents diploma through independent study, pursuant to the following:
>
> i.   a school district or a registered nonpublic school shall, and a charter school may, provide its students with an opportunity to earn such credit through independent study;
>
> ii   in the case of a school district or a registered nonpublic school, the students participation in independent study shall be approved by a school-based panel consisting of, at a minimum, the principal, a teacher in the subject area for which independent study credit is sought, and a guidance director or other administrator. The panel shall approve the student's participation in independent study based on

the following criteria:

a. the student has demonstrated readiness and has a high likelihood of success (may be indicated by a given grade point average in general or in the given subject area, as determined by the school district or registered nonpublic school) in each subject in which he or she seeks to undertake independent study; and

b. the student has accumulated the expected number of units of credit for the student's grade level; and

c. the student has passed the appropriate number of Regents examinations or other assessments required for graduation, for the student's grade level.

iii. The principal, after consultation with relevant faculty, shall award credit to the student for successful completion of the independent study and demonstrated mastery of the learning outcomes for the subject.

iv. For purposes of this paragraph, independent study shall be: academically rigorous and aligned to the New York State commencement-level learning standards;

a. overseen by a teacher knowledgeable and experienced in the subject area of the independent study;

b. based on a syllabus on file for each independent study; and

c. of comparable scope and quality to classroom work that would have been done at the school district, charter school, or registered nonpublic school awarding the credit.

v. For purposes of this paragraph, credit for independent study may be awarded for elective courses only, and shall not be awarded for courses required for the Regents diploma as specified in subparagraph (iv) of paragraph (7) of subdivision (b) of this section.

The New York State Education Department allows the principal to award transfer credit for independent study that, upon review, is determined to be consistent with the state's commencement-level standards and comparable to the work that would have been done in the principal's school. The State Education Department says that the principal should consult with "relevant faculty" in making this decision.

For more information, see http://www.p12.nysed.gov/part100/pages/1005.html.

To receive credit, the student must earn an 85 percent or its equivalent on a New York State-approved exam according to the Commissioner's Regulations and must pass an oral exam or complete a project to demonstrate proficiency normally developed in the course, but not measured on the exam. The superintendent, or designee, must decide whether the student's past academic performance indicates that the student will benefit from this option.

A student may receive credit for participation in a school's major performing organization for the unit of credit in art and/or music or the unit of credit in visual arts and/or music such as band, chorus, orchestra, dance, or theatre. The state has indicated that this should apply only to groups that are a regular part of the school program rather than one that operates in a limited capacity and does not meet the time requirement for one unit of credit. A student may also receive similar credit for participation in exceptional situations for out-of-school art or music activity. The appropriate department chair, if there is one, and the principal must grant approval, and the participation must be consistent with goals and objectives of the school's music program. The arts supervisor, the appropriate arts teacher, and the principal must approve a course outline in advance that is consistent with the state standards and the goals and objectives of the school music program. See Commissioner's Regulations 100.5 (d) (2) (i) (a) and 100.5 (d) (2) (i) (b) and http://www.p12.nysed.gov/ciai/arts/pub/artsum.pdf.

Commissioner's Regulation 135.4 (c) (2) (ii) (c) permits students in grades 10-12 to receive credit in physical education for participation in out-of-school activities approved by the physical education staff and school administration or extraclassroom programs for students "who have demonstrated acceptable levels of physical fitness, physical skills, and knowledge of physical education activities." In those cases a time requirement must be met that is comparable to the requirements of the Commissioner's Regulations. A student may also receive credit for participation in an equivalent program approved by the Commissioner.

School districts seeking to expand offerings for students should also develop procedures and guidelines for virtual independent learning opportunities. Commissioner's Regulation 100.5 (d) (10) addresses requirements for online and blended courses that are aligned with the New York State Learning Standards (see question 4-1). Instruction must be provided under the direction of a certified teacher from the district where the student is enrolled or from BOCES. Blended courses take place through a combination of classroom-based and digital or Internet-connected media.

In addition, Commissioner's Regulation 100.5 (d) (8) describes requirements for programs that are offered for making up incomplete or failed course credit. These programs may include online study that is comparable in scope and quality to regular classroom instruction, that provides for documentation of satisfactory student achievement, and that provides regular and substantial interaction between student and teacher. The programs also include repeating an entire course, taking the course again as part of a summer school program, receiving intensive instruction in the deficiency areas of the course, and online study. Students must demonstrate mastery of the learning outcomes for the subject including passing any required Regents examinations or other assessment required for graduation. See http://www.p12.nysed.gov/part100/pages/1005.html#makeupcredit.

An administrator should ensure that policies with criteria for each of these situations exist and are publicized. They should require advance approval so that all conditions and expectations, especially for projects, are clear.

4-20. What are local college partnerships? How does a school district enter into such a partnership?

Local college partnerships are arrangements between a school and a local college. The arrangements may provide staff development opportunities for faculty members and/or learning opportunities for students.

These learning opportunities are sometimes called articulation agreements. The agreements define the circumstances under which a student may receive college credit for a high school course. The partnerships are common in career and technical education programs that provide a coordinated curriculum starting in high school and concluding with a two- or four-year college degree. BOCES may enter into agreements for career and technical education students. The agreements can support a smooth transition from high school to college for students.

In all cases, the agreement should be kept on file by the school district and signed by the appropriate college and school officials. The agreements should be reauthorized on a regular basis. Boards of

education should approve the agreements or provide a board policy
that outlines the criteria for approval by a school representative.

4-21. Can students be separated by gender for instruction?

Title IX regulations prevent educational activities or programs
from being offered separately on the basis of sex in a district that
receives federal funding. Title IX protects any person from sex-based
discrimination, regardless of their real or perceived sex. Female, male,
transgender, and gender-nonconforming students, faculty, and staff are
protected from any sex-based discrimination, harassment, or violence
(https://www2.ed.gov/about/offices/list/ocr/lgbt.html).   See   also
https://www2.ed.gov/about/offices/list/ocr/frontpage/faq/sex.html.

However, the regulations allow the following: Students may be
grouped separately within physical education classes or activities for
wrestling, boxing, rugby, ice hockey, football, basketball, and other
sports or activities that involve bodily contact. Those parts of classes
at the elementary or secondary level that deal exclusively with human
sexuality may be conducted separately for males and females. There
can be requirements based on vocal range or quality that may result
in a chorus or choruses with one sex or predominantly one sex. For
more information, see 34 C.F.R. parts 106.34 and 106.41 of federal
regulations.

4-22. What are required health education topics? How should sex education be taught at the high school level? Can you separate boys and girls for instruction? Who delivers instruction in sex education?

*A Guidance Document for Achieving the New York State Standards
in Health Education* (November, 2005) is available from the New York
State Education Department resources at http://www.p12.nysed.gov/
ciai/health/.

This document focuses on best practices for health education
and includes standards, skills, functional knowledge, resources, and
definitions for health educators. The guidance emphasizes that health
education, including sexual risk, family life/sexual health, and HIV/
AIDS knowledge, should be delivered by a qualified and skilled health
educator.

See question 4-21 for grouping of students according to gender.
A school district should consider this question in the larger context of

the comprehensive health program, age-appropriate instruction, and the best ways to support learning by students.

Each school district is required to update its health education curriculum to include the most up-to-date, age-appropriate information available regarding the misuse and abuse of alcohol, tobacco, and other drugs including, but not limited to, heroin and opioids (http://www.p12.nysed.gov/sss/documents/FinalNYSEDHeroin-OpioidsInstructionalResourcePacket6.16docx.pdf). Resources can be found at https://on.ny.gov/2yKeqio. The curriculum must include information regarding drugs and other substances that are more prevalent among school-aged youth.

Commissioner's Regulations 100.2 (c) (11) require that students in senior high school be provided instruction in hands-only cardiopulmonary resuscitation and the use of an automated external defibrillator at least once before graduation.

Sex education should be taught in every high school as part of a comprehensive health education program. It should be the culmination of a program designed K-12, and taught by certified health educators. Sex education should be considerate of the culture and expectations of a community, but the program needs to be realistic regarding the necessity for educators to provide young adults with the information and resources they need to make healthy decisions.

Commissioner's Regulation 135.3 requires that instruction about AIDS be provided at both elementary and secondary levels. The regulation also states that the instruction be age-appropriate and consistent with community values.

4-23. What steps must a district take to offer a summer school program?

See Section 110 of Commissioner's Regulations for summer school requirements. A district must file the Application for Approval of Summer Driver Education by June 1 with the State Education Department.

There are some general requirements for summer schools. Summer programs must be offered in facilities approved by the Commissioner of Education and must have a certified principal at each school where a summer program is operated. Teachers must be certified for the courses they teach. There must be 20 hours of instruction during the months of July and August, exclusive of registration and administration of final examinations. Elementary schools must have at least one hour of daily instruction, but not more than five hours daily. Secondary schools must have at least one hour of daily instructional sessions, but not more than five and one-half hours daily. Regents examinations must be administered in accordance with the Commissioner's Regulations.

The State Education Department has a webpage for summer school programs: http://www.p12.nysed.gov/sss/summerschool/. The Handbook for Summer School Administrators and Principals, which includes many of the requirements, may be accessed there. Administrators should review carefully the requirements concerning course credit, entrance to Regents examinations, and residency within the district.

4-24. What is home schooling?

Home schooling is instruction provided at home for students of compulsory education age. Students who are being home schooled are not attending a public or nonpublic school. Students with disabilities who are in home instruction programs are eligible to receive special education services from their school district, according to Education Law 3602-c (http://www.p12.nysed.gov/sss/homeinstruction/homeinstructionguidance708.html).

The following site also contains important information about the home instruction of children who wish to seek entrance to college and more information and answers to questions about home schooling: http://www.p12.nysed.gov/sss/homeinstruction.

In addition, the State Education Department states:

> Commissioner's Regulation (CR) 135.4 (c) (7) directs that a participant in interscholastic sports must be enrolled in the public school; CR 135.1 directs that a participant in intramurals must be enrolled in the public school; however, children educated other than at the public school may participate in school-sponsored club activities. It is recommended that each board of education establish a policy to this effect. (http://www.p12.nysed.gov/sss/homeinstruction/homeschoolingqanda.html#General).

4-25. What are the district's responsibilities both for a request to home school a student and for the annual assessment of the student?

Part 100.10 of the Commissioner's Regulations requires that parents must provide an annual written notice by July 1 to the superintendent of their intent to home school their child. An exception exists in the case of a family moving into the district after the start of the school year. In that case, written notice must be provided within 14 days of beginning home instruction for their child. A district must respond to the parents within 10 days of the receipt of the notice of intent. That response must include a copy of Part 100.10 of the Commissioner's Regulations and a form on which to submit an individualized home instruction plan (IHIP) for each child of compulsory education age who will be educated at home.

Parents must file an annual assessment at the time of the fourth quarterly report. Commissioner Regulations require that a commercially published norm-referenced test approved by the State Education Department or an alternative form of evaluation (a written narrative for grades 1-3 and every other year for grades 4-8) be used to determine student progress. The superintendent must consent to the administration of the approved norm-referenced test, including the site location, the test administrator, and the test scorer, if the test is not to be taken at the public school or a registered nonpublic school. The parents are responsible for any costs to administer the test at a location other than the public school. In the case of the alternative form of evaluation, the superintendent must consent to the certified teacher, peer review panel, or other person chosen by the parent to interview the student, review the student's work, and prepare the written narrative.

A home schooled program may be placed on probation for up to two years if the composite score on the norm-referenced test is below the 33rd percentile, the student's academic growth is less than one year, or the alternate evaluator does not certify that the student has made adequate academic progress. When a program is placed on probation, the parents are required to submit a plan of remediation to address the areas of deficiency for the child. The district can require changes before accepting the remediation plan. The child must attain 75 percent of the objectives in the remediation plan at the end of any semester during the probation period or 100 percent of the objectives after two years. In those cases, the superintendent must provide notice to the parents, and the board of education reviews compliance of the program with the Commissioner's Regulations.

The superintendent may require one or more home visits during the period of probation if the superintendent has a reasonable basis to believe that the home instruction program is not in compliance with the Commissioner's Regulations (Part 100.10 of the Commissioner's Regulations).

The "Home Instruction Questions and Answers" from the State Education Department include the following:

> If phone calls or letters do not elicit the information, the district should notify parents by registered mail that the evaluation is due and set a reasonable date for its submission. If the information is not forthcoming, the district is without evidence that instruction has been taking place. In that case, the district would be obligated to report the case to the central registry as a case of suspected educational neglect. (http://www.p12.nysed.gov/sss/homeinstruction/homeschoolingqanda.html#Evaluation).

Homebound and hospital instruction resulting from injury or illness that is physical or emotional has a different set of regulations and laws than home schooling for its administration. Please see http://www.p12.nysed.gov/sss/lawsregs/#HomeHospitalInstruction.

4-26. What are the required parameters for teaching character education in schools? How do these requirements relate to parental values and religious teachings?

Education Law 801-a requires instruction in civility, citizenship and character education. It is important to note that character education initiatives should be embedded into the core curriculum of the school and should be further fostered through well-defined activities, programs, and events. The school culture should reflect and emulate strong character and cultural aspects as a part of everyday school and community life.

Learning standard 2 for health, physical education, and family and consumer sciences applies to the instruction of character education since students are expected to learn personally and socially responsible behavior while engaged in physical activity.

Social studies standard 5 notes that students will identify, respect, and model core civic values such as justice, honesty, self-discipline, due process, equality, majority rule with respect for minority rights, and respect for self, others, and property.

It is important for the administrator to ensure that local curriculum efforts are connected with New York State standards or curriculum that has been approved by the board of education following a review process. These assurances provide a basis for response to any parent concerns about character education. Schools should adopt programs for character education that are connected with New York State standards and that have the involvement of teachers and parents in recommending the programs to a board of education.

4-27. What are the requirements for teaching technology skills to students in New York State?

Each student must take a unit of study in technology education by the end of grade 8 that is designed for the student to meet the state learning standards. Commissioner's Regulation 100.4 (a) (1) for grades 5-8 states:

> Technology education means a program of instruction designed to assist all students in meeting State intermediate standards for technology. Technology education uses concepts of science, mathematics, social science, and language arts in a hands-on, systems-based approach to problem solving that guides students in the understanding, design and development of systems, devices and products to serve human needs and wants.

Students must have the opportunity to start an approved career and technical education sequence in grade 9 (Commissioner's Regulation 100.2 (h)). See also question 4-15 about graduation requirements. In pre-K through grade 4, Commissioner's Regulation 100.3 (b) requires schools to provide instruction that is designed for students to meet the elementary learning standards in math, science, and technology.

Technology education should also be integrated into the regular school curriculum through well-articulated activities and opportunities that expose children to a cadre of tools and experiences. Problem-based and project-based experiences should foster technological literacy through well-defined guided practices. The administrator should ensure that all reviews of curriculum consider the integration of technology education.

4-28. What is an acceptable computer use policy and how does this affect Internet or email use in schools?

The following information is from the New York State Education Department:

> An AUP serves as the guideline for the use of Internet, web-based products, and computer access provided by school districts. The AUP is a written agreement outlining the terms and conditions for the use of technology-based devices maintained by schools and may include provisions related to personal technology-based devices used during school hours on school property. (p. 46) (http://www.p12.nysed.gov/dignityact/documents/ FINALDignityForAllStudentsActGuidanceDec2017.pdf).

Each district should develop its own policy, approved by a board of education, for acceptable use of computers, social media (e.g., Facebook, Twitter), networks, Internet access, and other information technology equipment. The policy should be developed collaboratively with staff, parents, and students so that local issues are discussed and greater understanding is gained of the importance of the policy. SED also strongly suggests that administrators consult their school attorney with specific questions or concerns related to Internet safety and AUP (*The New York State Dignity For All Students Act: A Resource and Promising Practices Guide for School Administrators and Faculty*). For example, staff should be informed that professional email and texts are subject to FOIL. See question 6-30.

The policy should include, but not be limited to, a statement of educational philosophy for the role of technology and Internet use, educational purposes for the use of technology, a code of conduct, definitions of acceptable and unacceptable use of electronic resources, and descriptions of consequences for policy violations. The policy should be connected to the code of conduct (see questions 1-1 and 1-17). It should be flexible to address the many unanticipated situations that an administrator faces. The policy should educate students about the risks of disclosing personal information and discourage them from doing so. It should protect the district from liability for inappropriate use.

The administrator should make sure that the policy is clearly explained to all students and educators each year. Parents should be aware of the policy. Displaying the policy on the website for a school district and posting the policy in public areas, such as computer labs, can provide a helpful reference for staff, students, and parents.

4-29. What is alternative education? How does a school district develop a program? Who is eligible to attend? Where should a program be housed?

The State Education Department defines "alternative education" as any nontraditional environment that offers an elementary, middle, or high school curriculum that is comprehensive. Students are able to master learning standards and earn high school diplomas in the program. The program is learning centered with multiple learning opportunities and frequent feedback to students about their learning progress. There are also creative uses of community resources to support youth development.

Alternative education also includes programs operated by local school districts, Boards of Cooperative Educational Services (BOCES), and the Office of Children and Family Services that prepare students under 21 years of age to pass the General Educational Development (GED) tests and receive a New York State High School Equivalency (HSE) diploma (http://www.p12.nysed. gov/sss/ssae/AltEd/AlternativeEducationMakingDifference.html).

In "Alternative Education: Making a Difference," the NYSED Student Support Services identifies the following specific practices that distinguish the more successful and well-organized programs:

- A flexible education program allows comprehensive student development and serves the academic, social, and personal needs of the learner.
- The student/teacher ratio fosters a learner-centered school climate geared to individual ability.
- Mastery of learning standards and completion of diploma requirements occur because of innovative curricula and varied teaching methodologies that use external resources, experiential learning, and technology.
- Ongoing review and evaluation of performance by teachers,

students, parents, and the community result in continuous program improvement and distinction.

- The school/program governance policy demonstrates democratic principles and empowerment to all and results in a clearly defined program with measurable goals and objectives developed in conjunction with students, staff, and community members.

- Participant involvement in all aspects of the educational process results in enhanced self-concept, desire for learning, and the development of critical thinking, problem solving, and communication skills.

- Recruitment strategies and professional development opportunities for teachers and administrators stress varied leadership, instruction, and assessment techniques, and result in a highly qualified teaching force and supportive and proactive leadership.

- A working relationship is maintained with conventional schools/programs to create a collaborative environment that fosters the exchange of practices, strategies, and resources and the integration of optional alternative education approaches throughout the system (http://www.p12.nysed. gov/sss/ssae/AltEd/AlternativeEducationMakingDifference. html).

Many alternative education programs are located at sites separate from the traditional school programs in order to support a nontraditional approach that has a different philosophy from the traditional program. The program also may be separated within a building from a traditional program.

The size of a district and numbers of potential students are factors in deciding whether a district will start its own program or work cooperatively with other districts to begin a program through BOCES. It is helpful for districts that are interested in a program to gather information from the State Education Department and to contact BOCES and districts that have successfully implemented a program. Important considerations are program and budget planning.

4-30. What are the regulations regarding curriculum for an alternative education program? How are students identified?

The curriculum must include the New York State Learning Standards and the opportunity to earn a high school diploma (see question 4-29).

An alternative education program should have specific criteria for students' entrance into a program. These criteria should reflect the philosophy of the program (see question 4-29) and should be reviewed periodically so that student needs are met.

4-31. What funding alternatives are available for alternative education programs?

School districts that send students to a BOCES-sponsored program may be eligible for BOCES aid toward the costs of student participation. The district may also choose to use budget funding for alternative education that will save expenses in another part of the budget resulting from student participation in the alternative education and not in the general education programs. There may be aid available for an incarcerated youth program that a district may use for alternative education in that setting.

4-32. What types of records must be kept for a student placed outside the district?

The school district has the responsibility for the educational records of all students who are located on campus or off campus. There should be a clear system to ensure accountability for the records of a student who is placed in an off-campus program. The educational records of a student who is placed in a career and technical program for part of a day will likely have records in the guidance office of the home school. Students who are placed in an off-campus special education program should have the records located with the CSE chair or the principal of the district school of residence for the child. Educational records for students in off-campus programs should be maintained in a manner consistent with local district practice and procedures for all students in the district. There should be communication with the administrators of off-campus programs so that copies of educational records are provided to the home district. A consistent location on campus will ensure that records are not lost if a placement changes or location of a program is moved.

4-33. What are the guidelines for English Language Learner (ELL) students?

The purpose of Part 154 of the Commissioner's Regulations is to establish standards for school district pupils with limited English proficiency to assure that they are provided opportunities to achieve the same educational goals and standards as the general education students. ELL students must be given equal access to all school programs and services offered to their age and grade-mate peers. The guidelines for the development and implementation of programs for ELL students are found in Education Law 3204 and Parts 117 and 154 of the Commissioner's Regulations. See http://www.nysed.gov/program-offices/office-bilingual-education-and-world-languages-obewl/ for more information.

4-34. What is the district's responsibility to educate students who are English Language Learners?

The board of education of each district must develop a written policy that describes education programs provided by the district for limited English proficient students. Part 117 of Commissioner's Regulations requires that all students who enter a New York State school for the first time, or reenter without documentation that the student had been screened, must be screened to determine if they qualify for services. Parents are required to fill out a home language questionnaire (HLQ) at the time of enrollment. A student whose parent indicates that a language other than English is spoken in the home must be assessed to determine their level of English language proficiency. An informal interview with the student provides a preliminary indication of the student's level of English proficiency. If the student speaks no English, the student is designated as ELL and must be placed in either an English as a New Language (ENL) or bilingual program. If the student requires further testing, the New York State Identification Test for English Language Learners (NYSITELL) is administered to determine if ELL services must be provided. If the student qualifies, the NYSITELL will provide the level of services that the district is required to provide. Students must be identified and placed in an appropriate ELL program within 10 school days of enrollment.

A student who is receiving ENL services must be tested annually in May with the New York State English as a Second Language Achievement Test (NYSESLAT) to measure progress and determine if the student still qualifies for services and, if so, what level of service.

There are two types of approved program models for ELLs in New York school districts (http://www.nysed.gov/common/nysed/files/programs/bilingual-ed/guideforparentsofellsinnysenglish.pdf):

Bilingual Education (BE) Program

Commissioner's Regulation 154-2.2 (b) states:

Bilingual education program shall mean a research-based program comprised of three components:
(1) a language arts instruction component, including home language arts and English language arts;
(2) an English as a new language component; and
(3) a bilingual content area instructional component (including all bilingual content areas, i.e., math, science, and social studies depending on the bilingual education program model and the student's level of English language development, but must at a minimum include at least two bilingual core content areas (i.e., math, science, and social studies).

English as a New Language (ENL) Program

Commissioner's Regulation 154-2.2 (h) explains:

English as a new language program shall mean a research-based program comprised of two components: a content area instructional component in English (including all core content, i.e., English language arts, math, science, or social studies) with home language supports and appropriate scaffolds, and an English language development component (stand-alone and/or integrated English as a new language).

See http://www.nysed.gov/bilingual-ed/schools/program-options-english-languagelearnersmulti lingual-learners.

Commissioner's Regulation 154-2.3 (d) (2) also states:

Each school district in which the sum of each school's

annual estimate of enrollment of English language learners equals 20 or more English language learners of the same grade level, all of whom have the same home language that is other than English, shall provide a sufficient number of bilingual education programs in the district in the following school year, such that there are bilingual education programs available in the district for at least 70 percent of the estimated English language learner students who share the same home language other than English and grade level districtwide.

For more information about screening, program placement, and parental notification, see http://www.nysed.gov/common/nysed/files/bilingual/ellidchartguidance7.1.15.pdf.

Commissioner's Regulation requires that districts and BOCES provide professional development to teachers, level three teaching assistants, and administrators that address the needs of ELLs. Administrators should check the policies of the board of education and the services of the ENL Regional Bilingual Education Resource Network (RBERN). There are eight centers located throughout the state that provide resources, staff development, and technical assistance to improve instructional programs and practices relating to ELL students. (See http://www.nysed.gov/bilingual-ed/schools/regional-supportrberns.)

For additional information, see the blueprint for ELL/MLL Success: http://www.nysed.gov/common/nysed/files/programs/bilingual-ed/nysblueprintforellsuccess.2016.pdf.

4-35. What are the classroom teacher's responsibilities regarding ELL students?

The administrator should be aware that Commissioner's Regulation 154.-2.3 (k) requires that school districts must provide in-service training to all personnel providing instruction or other services to ELL or ENL students.

Classroom teachers should communicate frequently with the ENL teacher. The ENL teacher should provide the classroom teacher with strategies and techniques to utilize in the regular classroom to assist the ELL student.

The   teacher   should   review   the   information   at http://www.nysed.gov/bilingual-ed/schools/program-options-english-language-learnersmultilingual-learners. This site has information about assessments, ELL/MLL educator resources, students with interrupted learning/inconsistent learning experiences (SIFE), and parent engagement.

4-36. What is the proper procedure for approving textbooks? How does one evaluate a textbook?

Education Laws 701(1) and 1709(4) authorize boards of education to designate and approve textbooks for use in schools. These laws do not describe procedures for how to make textbook recommendations. In New York State, textbook adoption is a local decision. Important considerations for process include a team of educators, including reading teachers, who evaluate potential textbooks according to the same set of criteria and make recommendations for adoption. The criteria might include but are not limited to: readability, content alignment with state standards, assessment strategies, accommodations for students with special needs, learning strategies, diversity issues, and any considerations of bias. Textbook materials should be reviewed on a scheduled basis to ensure that standards and content included in the materials are current.

While a district may wish to consult with its legal counsel, education laws that apply to traditional textbooks would apply to online or e-textbooks since they are part of a course of study and are an electronic form of textbook.

There are Commissioner's decisions that describe the authority of a board of education in this area. For example, see *Appeal of Smith*, 34 Ed Dept Rep 346, Decision No. 13,335 and *Appeal of Munch*, 47 Ed Dept Rep 199, Decision No. 15,667.

4-37. Do students have a right to receive homework assignments before going on a vacation while school is in session?

There is no legal basis for a student to receive homework assignments before being absent from school for the purposes of going on a vacation. A vacation may be regarded as an absence from school authorized by a legal guardian that is not related to an academic purpose. The administrator should ensure that there is a policy that addresses whether homework assignments should be given out in advance of student absences. The policy should be consistent with the comprehensive attendance policy and grading policies. It is important to establish consistency for this practice within a school in order to avoid similar situations that are handled differently in different classes. It is also important to communicate the practice to parents in advance of any requests.

It should be noted that the Commissioner has stated that "a teacher must be given some latitude to determine how to teach a lesson" and indicated that there is a burden of proof for parents or student to show that teaching methods are arbitrary or capricious (*Appeal of Mee Jo*, 44 Ed Dept Rep 198, Decision No. 15,147) and "barring a showing that a grade determination is arbitrary, capricious, or unreasonable, it will not be set aside (*Appeal of Carangelo*, 49 Ed Dept Rep 217, Decision No. 16,006).

Section 5
Athletics

5-1. Who is responsible for hiring coaches in New York State? What process must be used to hire coaches?

Section 135.4(c)(7) of Commissioner's Regulations authorizes boards of education to appoint coaches for interscholastic teams. The statute does not mandate a process for recommending candidates.

A school district should have a written policy that outlines the process to follow when recommending a candidate. This procedure should be similar to the process used when selecting candidates for teaching positions. The policy may include, but not be limited to, the following steps:

- A procedure should be established for advertising the coaching vacancy. Many teacher contracts require that a vacancy be posted internally for a period of time. Advertisements may be put in newspapers and on appropriate websites.
- A committee may be formed to screen applications and conduct interviews. This committee may consist of an administrator, the athletic director, the head coach of the program, and any other person or persons the district may want to include.
- Reference checks should be completed.
- A recommendation should be made first to the superintendent and then to the board of education.

5-2. What coaching qualifications are required in New York State?

The Commissioner of Education defines coaching qualifications. Section 135.4(c)(7) of Commissioner's Regulations outlines the requirements to be a coach in New York State. The statute requires different qualifications for physical education teachers, certified teachers, and noncertified teachers who coach.

Physical education teachers must:
- possess a New York State provisional or permanent

certificate to teach physical education;

- complete an appropriate first aid course prior to the start of the season;
- possess adult CPR certification, and
- complete biennially, a course approved by SED, related to recognizing the symptoms of mild traumatic brain injuries.

Other certified teachers must:

- possess a New York State provisional or permanent teaching certificate;
- complete an appropriate first aid course prior to the start of the season;
- possess adult CPR certification;
- on a biennial basis, complete a course of instruction relating to mild traumatic brain injuries;
- complete an approved course on Philosophy, Principles, and Organization of Athletics in Education within two years of the date of employment and;
- complete approved courses on Health Sciences Applied to Coaching and Theory and Techniques of coaching (specific to the sport coached) within five years of the date of employment.

All courses must be completed within five years of the initial appointment unless an extension has been approved by the State Education Department.

A certified teacher does not need to apply for a temporary coaching license. It is the responsibility of the school district to monitor and require certified teachers to meet all requirements to coach.

A certified teacher coaching in a New York State school district prior to September 1, 1974 qualifies for a grandfather clause and need not meet all of the requirements outlined above. This teacher may be appointed to coach any sport in that district after completing first aid and adult CPR courses prior to the start of the season.

A nonteacher coach must:

- complete an approved first aid course prior to the start of the season;

- possess adult CPR certification;
- show evidence of completion of a child abuse workshop and violence abuse prevention workshop;
- obtain a current temporary coaching license from the Board of Cooperative Educational Services (BOCES) (reissued each year);
- complete or be enrolled in an approved course on Philosophy, Principals and Organization of Athletics in Education before the start of the second season; and
- complete or be enrolled in approved courses on Health Sciences Applied to Coaching and Theory and Techniques of coaching (specific to the sport coached) within five years of the date of employment.

New York State regulations require that there must be no certified teachers available with appropriate experience and qualifications to coach if a person without a teaching certificate is employed.

Nonteacher coaches may receive a three-year renewable professional coaching certificate if they have:
- met the fingerprinting requirement;
- completed appropriate first aid courses and have CPR certification;
- completed the child abuse and violence prevention workshops,
- completed at least three years of coaching in a particular sport;
- completed all three course requirements needed to maintain a temporary coaching license;
- received a satisfactory evaluation by either the principal or the director of physical education and athletics for each year coached.

For more information about guidelines for coaching, refer to the New York State Education Department website at http://www.p12.nysed.gov/ciai/pe/toolkitdocs/coachingguidelines_07_09.pdf.

For more information about completing the three required coaching courses through an alternative pathway, see http://www.p12.nysed.gov/ciai/pe/documents/Coaching-Course-

NFHSSecond-PathwayGuideline-1-6-17-FDraft.pdf.

5-3.   Do coaches receive tenure?

Section 135 of Commissioner's Regulations and the Education Law regarding tenure has no reference to tenure for coaches. Therefore, there is no tenure for coaches in New York State. Coaches serve at the discretion of the board of education and may be removed at any time.

There is no due process and/or just cause when it comes to coaches retaining their positions unless there are such procedures in a local negotiated agreement. The Commissioner has ruled in one case that an assistant coaching assignment had been in the "nature of at-will employment for each individual season." Further, he noted that the tenure statutes did not have application. (*Appeal of Hendrickson*, 36 Ed Dept Rep 128, Decision No. 13,678).

5-4.   Is there a requirement for school districts to evaluate coaches?

Section 135.4 of Commissioner's Regulations does not require districts to evaluate all coaches with the exception of a coach who has a professional coaching certificate. A district that employs an individual as a coach with a professional coaching certificate must ensure that the principal or athletic director conducts an evaluation during each year that the nonteacher coach is employed.

It is recommended that the athletic director/administrator use some evaluative tool at the end of each season to give constructive feedback to coaches. The evaluation process gives the athletic director and the coach an opportunity to communicate regarding the recently completed season and to set goals for the future.

5-5.   How does the building administrator communicate expectations to coaches?

The building administrator has numerous means to communicate with coaches. He/she may use written or electronic communication, meet individually with coaches, or meet in groups. Perhaps the best avenue to use is to meet with all of the coaches of a particular season at the coaches' pre-season meeting. Most school districts mandate these meetings, which give the administrator a chance to talk about expectations with all coaches and obtain feedback on concerns they may have. Also, many districts now have postseason meetings where the administrator may again communicate with coaches.

5-6. What is the role of the administrator with regard to coaches who do not follow district policy or are accused of improper conduct?

First it must be determined that the policy was not followed or that the improper conduct actually occurred. The administrator conducting the investigation must recognize that the burden of proof rests with the administration to prove that the conduct took place. Care should be taken to ensure that confidentiality, access to information, ethical considerations relative to questioning others and acquiring information, and due process issues are resolved.

A key to successful problem solving is to be aware of problems and to confront them early. Effective communication between the building administrator and the athletic administrator is important in identifying any problems and agreeing on a course of action that will solve the problems.

The administrator and/or athletic administrator should consider what actions will lead to the targeted level of improvement and implement the agreed-upon plan. The administrator and/or the athletic director should confer with the coach regarding the problem and finalize a plan for improvement. The situation must be closely monitored to determine if the agreed-upon solution is implemented and whether the problem has been solved.

If this process is followed and the coach does not work with the building administrator and athletic administrator to solve the problem, it may then be necessary to recommend to the superintendent that the coach be removed or not rehired the following year.

When a coach is accused of physical contact with a student, the administrator must conduct an immediate investigation. If it is determined that the accusation is valid, the administrator should review the matter with school counsel and make a recommendation to the superintendent for appropriate action. If it is an allegation that child abuse in an educational setting occurred, reporting requirements according to Article 23-B of Education Law must be followed.

See also question 5-3 and question 6-16.

5-7. What are the eligibility requirements for students to compete in interscholastic athletics?

Section 135.4(c)(7)(ii)(b)(2) of Commissioner's Regulations states:

> A pupil shall be eligible for interschool competition in a sport during a semester, providing that he is a bona fide student, enrolled during the first 15 school days of such semester, is registered in the equivalent of three regular courses, is meeting the physical education requirement and has been in regular attendance 80 percent of the school time, bona fide absence caused by personal illness excepted.

When a student enters grade 9, that student is eligible for interscholastic competition during four consecutive seasons of any sport until the student's nineteenth birthday. If the student turns 19 on or after July 1, the student may continue to participate in all sports during that school year.

If an athlete misses a season and the chief school officer presents sufficient evidence that the failure to enter competition during one or more seasons was "caused by illness, accident, or similar circumstances beyond the control of the student, such pupil eligibility shall be extended accordingly in that sport" (Commissioner's Regulations Section 135.4(c)(7)(ii)(b)(1)).

If an athlete misses a season and the chief school officer presents sufficient evidence that the failure to enter competition one or more seasons was "caused by such pupil enrollment in a national or international student exchange program, that as a result of such enrollment the pupil will be required to attend school for one or more additional semesters in order to graduate, and that the pupil did not enter competition in any sport while enrolled in such program, such pupil's eligibility will be extended accordingly in such sport" (Commissioner's Regulations Section 135.4(c)(7)(ii)(b)(1)).

These exceptions in Commissioner's Regulations do not include references to students who have participated in four consecutive seasons and repeat a grade during those four seasons. Therefore, the regulations have been interpreted to mean that a student who takes more than four years to complete graduation requirements is not eligible to participate in interscholastic athletics beyond four seasons.

Students in grades 7 and 8 may be eligible to participate in an interscholastic sport for a fifth and/or a sixth year if they have been approved through the Selection/Classification program of the State Education Department. This program has been designed to assess a student's physical maturation, physical fitness, and skills so that a student may be placed at a level of competition that will result in success. A board of education must adopt a policy to provide this opportunity, and administrators should ensure that such a policy is in place.

Section 135.4(7)(c)(ii) of Commissioner's Regulations outlines eligibility requirements for athletics in grades 7-12. The procedures and forms necessary for an athletic director to administer the athletic placement process (APP) may be found on the State Education Department's website at http://www.p12.nysed.gov/ciai/pe/toolkitdocs/AthleticPlacementProcessJuly2016.pdf. See also question 5-11 that addresses eligibility for foreign exchange students.

5-8. What are the high school standards for interscholastic athletics?

Section 135.4(c)(7) of Commissioner's Regulations states that sports standards for all sports between schools shall be in compliance with guidelines established by the Commissioner. The New York State Public High School Athletic Association (NYSPHSAA) (www.nysphsaa.org/handbook) publishes the high school standards for interscholastic sports in its handbook. The sports standards are listed in a chart that cites all sports that are played in New York State high schools. The standards include the number of practices needed prior to the first scrimmage, the number of practices prior to the first contest, the team and individual maximum number of contests, the minimum time between contests, the individual limitations per day, and the ruling body for each sport. Following the chart, there is a description of other pertinent information regarding each sport.

All principals should be knowledgeable in regard to the NYSPHSAA Handbook. This is an important reference for questions regarding athletics.

5-9. What are the standards for "modified" interscholastic athletics?

Interscholastic sports competition for students in grades 7, 8, and 9 is covered by modified rules of the NYSPHSAA. The modified standards for interscholastic athletics are published in the NYSPHSAA

Handbook. The standards include the number of practices needed prior to the first scrimmage, the number of practices prior to the first contest, the team and individual maximum number of contests, the minimum time between contests, the individual limitations per day, and the ruling body for each sport. The modified standards also include time and distance limits for trips. The descriptions for each sport explain the special rules that modified programs in New York State must follow.

Principals of middle and junior high schools should be familiar with the modified standards in the NYSPHSAA Handbook (www. nysphsaa.org/resources/handbook) and should understand that the purpose of modified sports, according to the NYSPHSAA, is to give younger athletes a chance to participate and improve their skills.

5-10. What is the transfer rule for students moving from one school district to another?

The transfer rule is found in rule #30 of the bylaws and eligibility standards of the NYSPHSAA (www.nysphsaa.org/resources/handbook).

This rule states that "a student in grades 9-12 who transfers, with a corresponding change in residence of his/her parents shall become eligible after starting regular attendance in the second school." A critical element of this rule is that the parents of the student must change their residence from one school district to another.

It is important that the administrator be familiar with the transfer rule as well as district policies and educational statutes for residency when registering new students who have played interscholastic sports in other school districts. The administrator should ensure that there is a procedure for reviewing all transfer students who participate in the interscholastic athletic program.   See question 3-4 for more information about student residency.

5-11. What are the eligibility requirements for foreign exchange students to participate in interscholastic athletics?

According to the bylaws and eligibility standards of the NYSPHSAA, a foreign exchange student is eligible for one year of participation in interscholastic sports provided the student:

- Has not graduated from the secondary school system in the student's home country,

- Is in the U.S. through an established student exchange program (i.e., accepted for listing by the Council of Standards for International Educational Travel),
- Has not participated in an organized sports program that was equivalent to or on a higher level than the U.S. high school programs, and
- Was not encouraged to be an exchange student for athletic purposes.

For further clarification, administrators should check the Handbook of the New York State Public High School Athletic Association, Inc. (www.nysphsaa.org/resources/handbook).

5-12. What are the rules of the National Eligibility Center for students wishing to compete in Division I or II of the NCAA?

Rules regarding students who wish to compete in an NCAA Division I or II athletic program in college are administered by the National Collegiate Athletic Association (NCAA). The NCAA annually publishes a Guide for the College-Bound Student-Athlete, available online. This guide outlines Division I and Division II academic eligibility requirements, has several question-and-answer sections, high school core course requirements, test score requirements, and directions for the student to register with the clearinghouse. Students register through the NCAA website, www.ncaaeligibilitycenter.net.

Each year a high school must ensure that its list of NCAA-approved core courses is accurate and up to date. This process allows the high school to inform the NCAA Eligibility Center about new courses, changes in course titles, and courses that have been eliminated. The center may request more information about some courses prior to deciding if a course qualifies as a core course. Incorrect information on this list of core courses could prevent a student from being eligible to participate in athletics in college, and in turn jeopardize financial aid. The high school principal must approve the core course information presented to the NCAA.

As an administrator, some familiarity with the NCAA Eligibility Center is important when communicating with athletes about going to college. Building administrators in particular should be familiar with the types of courses taught in their school that do not qualify as NCAA core courses.

All high school counselors should have the NCAA guides and

be familiar with advising student athletes about eligibility for college athletics and registering with the clearinghouse.

5-13. What are the requirements regarding equity between male and female athletic teams?

Title IX, which prohibits sexual discrimination in any activity or program receiving federal funds, guides school districts as they develop athletic programs. In 1996, the U.S. Department of Education clarified the policy used to determine if discrimination exists for students of either sex in opportunities to participate in athletics. The Department of Education notes that this policy, while designed for intercollegiate athletics, often applies to elementary and secondary programs. The policy includes a three-part test in order to determine whether a school district is in violation of Title IX. To be in compliance, a school district must comply with only one of the following three parts from the Clarification of Intercollegiate Athletics Policy Guidance: The Three-Part Test:

- Whether interscholastic level participation opportunities for male and female students are provided in numbers substantially proportionate to their respective enrollments; or
- Where the numbers of one sex have been and are underrepresented among interscholastic athletes, whether the institution can show a history and continuing practice of program expansion that is demonstrably responsive to the developing interests and abilities of the members of that sex; or
- Where the members of one sex are underrepresented among interscholastic athletes and the institution cannot show a history and continuing practice of program expansion as described above, whether the district can demonstrate that the interests and abilities of the members of that sex have been fully and effectively accommodated by the present program. (Office for Civil Rights, U.S. Department of Education, 1996)

Male and female students must be given equal opportunities to participate in interscholastic competition, either on separate teams or in mixed competition. Students may not be excluded from athletic teams by reason of their sex, except according to Section 135.4(c)(7)(ii)(c) of Commissioner's Regulations. If there are separate teams for males and females in a sport, the superintendent may permit females to participate on a team organized for males, but males may not participate on teams organized for females. However, when separate competition is not provided for males and females in a specific sport, the superintendent may restrict males from participation on teams organized for females if such participation would have "an adverse impact on the opportunity" for females to participate. This regulation also describes the sports in which there may be mixed competition upon a review panel's finding that the student is fit to play.

Whenever a school district has questions regarding Title IX or gender equity in athletics, it is always wise to consult with the school attorney, the local section athletic office or the NYSPHSAA. This topic is one that may be very complicated, and legal opinions are frequently based on case law.

5-14. Are there guidelines for participation in interscholastic activities by transgender students?

The New York State Public High School Athletic Association provides guidelines and procedures. The New York State Public High School Athletic Association Transgender Guidelines state:

> The New York State Education Department and NYSPHSAA recognize the value of participation in interscholastic sports for all student athletes. The NYSPHSAA is committed to providing all students with the opportunity to participate in NYSPHSAA activities in a manner consistent with their gender identity and the New York State Commissioner of Education's Regulations. The Dignity for All Students Act (DASA) prohibits discrimination and/or harassment of students on school property or at school functions by students or employees. The prohibition against discrimination includes discrimination based on a student's actual or perceived sex and gender. Gender includes a person's actual or perceived sex as well as gender identity and expression. (p. 25 of the ByLaws and Eligibility Standards of the NYSPHSAA, http://www.nysphsaa. org/Portals/0/PDF/Handbook/2016-17%20Handbook/ ByLaws%20and%20Eligibility%20Standards.pdf)

In addition, SED has issued Guidance to School Districts for Creating a Safe and Supportive School Environment for Transgender and Gender Nonconforming Students. See http://www.p12.nysed.gov/dignityact/documents/Transg_GNCGuidanceFINAL.pdf.

5-15. Can an athletic code of conduct be more restrictive than a school's code of conduct?

An athletic code of conduct should be consistent with a school's code of conduct. (See question 1-1 about codes of conduct.)

5-16. What are appropriate discipline measures when a student violates the rules in an athletic code of conduct? What rights do students and parents have when rules are violated? What right of appeal do students and parents have regarding proposed punishments?

Many school districts choose to have an athletic code of conduct that outlines athletic sanctions for student athletes when general school rules are broken. It is recommended that all athletic codes of conduct become part of board of education policy so that an administrator is not acting alone when determining punishments for rule violations.

The primary discipline measure that athletic codes of conduct have in common is some form of suspension from participation in athletics. The determination of the severity of the suspension rests with the school district. In New York State, student athletes are entitled to "minimal due process." The student athlete must be told of the offense with which he/she is charged and allowed the opportunity to respond to the charges. The Commissioner has ruled that procedures governing "the suspension of extracurricular privileges need only be fair and give students and parents an opportunity to discuss the conduct being reviewed with the person or body authorized to impose the discipline" (*Appeal of N.C.*, 42 Ed Dept Rep 19, Decision No. 14,794).

It is advisable to have a board of education policy with a defined process by which decisions may be appealed since questions are best addressed at the level that has day-to-day interaction with the student. A process of appeal will allow any issues to be considered at the building and district levels rather than being referred directly to a board of education or the Commissioner. This process means that any requests that go to a board of education would be referred to the appropriate party before being considered at the board level. A sound administrative decision, based on policies and facts, will stand up to such process.

To justify a consequence, the administrator needs to have evidence that the student participated in the objectionable conduct. The Commissioner has held that a decision to discipline a student must be based on "competent and substantial evidence" that the student participated in the conduct that was charged (see question 1-24). There will be situations in which the evidence must be questioned, so it is advisable to review the matter with counsel for the district if conclusiveness of the evidence is in doubt.

The following procedures will help in cases that involve violations of athletic rules:
- A written athletic code of conduct should be adopted.
- Each athlete and each parent should be required to sign a statement acknowledging receipt of the rules.
- A school official should be charged with the investigation of alleged rule violations.
- A hearing should take place to consider a potential rule violation. The student athlete and the parent should have an opportunity to respond to the charges.
- A written decision should be generated outlining the appeals process if the student athlete or parent does not agree with the determination of the consequence. This appeals process should have a time frame for appeal, and outline who will hear the appeal.

5-17. What are the positives and negatives of an academic eligibility process? What are the details of an eligibility process that does not discriminate against the student who struggles academically?

Education Law or state statutes do not mandate academic eligibility policies. Such a policy is up to the discretion of the local school district. The proponents of an athletic eligibility policy stress the important connection between academics and athletics. This argument holds that if the athlete is truly a student athlete, the student must maintain a certain grade point average in order to participate in athletics. Thus, if the student wants to be an athlete, the student will study harder and maintain the grades necessary to participate.

The negatives of an academic eligibility policy begin with the sometimes cumbersome logistics of gathering academic records and maintaining the paperwork necessary to determine students who are eligible and those who are not. A school district must decide who keeps such records and make this task a part of the job description. This task will require additional time of the staff member. Nonsupporters of academic eligibility policies emphasize that such policies, even when working properly, only help a very small number of students. This argument asks the question, Is the time and energy put into this program worth what little benefit is derived by the students? Many school districts have found that some of their most academically successful students are athletes. Many students have to work harder in order to manage their time more effectively to succeed academically. Some eligibility policies bring concerns that pressures are imposed on teachers with regard to grading for individual students who might be negatively affected by the policy.

It is difficult to have an academic eligibility policy that does not discriminate against the student who struggles academically. Schools aim for policies that support academic improvement and keep students in activities that offer supportive adults and meaningful participation. Good integration of athletics with academics is seen in a study hall for all athletes directly after school. School may end at a certain time, but practice may not start for 30-45 minutes after school. Athletes can go to a specific location to complete homework or study. All athletes are treated equally and have time to concentrate on academics. Another such program is one that does not hold a student out of athletic contests if grades go down, but mandates an extra study period after school or in the evenings until grades improve for that student.

If a school is considering an academic eligibility policy, other districts where established and effective athletic eligibility programs exist should be consulted. The issue should be studied by consulting districts that do have an eligibility policy and districts that do not. Questions that should be asked include the following:

- Did the district evaluate the program to determine its effectiveness and, if so, how was the evaluation conducted?
- Has student participation in athletics been affected?
- Does the district also have a similar academic eligibility program for extracurricular activities other than sports?
- How does the district manage the necessary communication between teachers and coaches, and was extra help hired to do so?

- Are there any computer software programs available that make this process manageable?
- Does the academic eligibility policy include attendance?
- Does the policy address only varsity levels or does it extend to junior varsity and modified teams?

5-18. How does the building administrator communicate expectations to student athletes and parents?

The best way for a building administrator to communicate expectations to student athletes and their parents is through written and verbal communication. The administrator may prepare a letter to go home to all athletes on school teams. The administrator may also meet with each team and their parents to discuss expectations of student athletes.

Some of the points addressed in this communication would include the responsibilities and expectations for players, eligibility rules, and athletic code guidelines. It is also helpful to post the athletic code of conduct, which communicates expectations, on the website for the school district.

5-19. How should the athletic director communicate to coaches the rules and regulations regarding interscholastic sports?

The coach should receive information through a preseason coaches' meeting. This meeting gives the athletic administrator the opportunity to review such items as goals for the year. Other topics may include, but not be limited to: first aid/CPR requirements, AED training, concussion management protocol, eligibility rules, game schedules, facility schedules, coaches' responsibilities, selection process for teams, athletic physicals, injuries, and the preseason parent meeting.

5-20. How should the coach communicate rules to athletes and parents?

Teams and student athletes should receive an overview of rules through a meeting with the coach prior to the first day of the season. This meeting gives the coach the opportunity to meet the athletes, review physical exam requirements, fill out necessary paperwork, distribute practice schedules, review eligibility rules, and discuss the criteria for making the team.

It is an effective practice for the coach to have a parent meeting after the team has been selected. The parent meeting gives the coach an opportunity to address a number of topics that include expectations of players and parents, player participation in contests, player conditioning, transportation requirements, eligibility rules, and communicating with the coach.

It is also helpful to post the athletic code of conduct, which communicates expectations, on the website for the school district. This three-part process should ensure that athletes, parents, and coaches receive the same information and should support consistent communication.

5-21. What are the rules regarding daily school attendance and participation in athletics?

The Commissioner has ruled, in a case that involved athletic eligibility and attendance, that "a board of education has very broad authority to establish reasonable standards of conduct for participation in extracurricular activities, and unless it is shown that the board has abused its discretion, its policy will be upheld" (*Appeal of Bonacasa*, 41 Ed Dept Rep, Decision No. 14,670).

All school districts must adopt a comprehensive attendance policy according to Section 104.1(i) of Commissioner's Regulations. This policy must include incentives and identify any disciplinary sanctions to be used for student attendance. This provides the opportunity to develop and include a policy for attendance and athletic participation.

It is a common expectation among schools that an athlete must be in attendance during the school day in order to participate in practices and contests that day. School districts decide the number of hours a student must be present in order to be eligible to practice or play in a contest scheduled that day. School districts establish a time of day when a student must arrive at school in order to be eligible. Schools must also include requirements for Friday attendance in order for a student to participate in a practice or contest during the weekend. For example, school districts may require a student to be in attendance by a certain time on Friday. Some school districts include a statement that permits students to play on the weekend with a doctor's note or demonstrated recovery from illness and the approval of school administration.

It is recommended that school districts adopt board policy that addresses these points. Such policies establish that school comes first, and a student athlete must attend school or be ineligible to participate in the athletic program.

See questions 1-39 and 1-40 for more information about comprehensive attendance policies. See question 5-7 for information about attendance and eligibility.

5-22. Should a school district establish a vacation policy for interscholastic athletic team members during times of school vacations?

A dilemma for many school districts occurs when a sports season overlaps a school vacation when families want to travel. It is a larger problem at the varsity level where win-loss records are important for league and sectional seeding.

It is important to have a policy that ensures consistency among different varsity sports. There are at least three ways a policy can approach this issue: (1) A policy may mandate that parents have the right to take their student athlete on vacation with no consequences upon the student's return. (2) A consequence such as the "benching" of a student for the number of contests that are missed may be allowed. (3) No contests are allowed during all or some specified vacation periods. The need for consistency and early communication about the policy to parents is important. The policy should be adopted by the board of education and reflect the interests of the school district and community.

5-23. What role does the school district have in supervising athletic contests and after-school activities?

The building administrator and the athletic administrator should work together to develop a supervision plan for athletic activities that has the best interests of the spectator and the athlete in mind. Some considerations that should be in the plan include the number of supervisory and police personnel for events, an evacuation plan, the number of custodial personnel for events, code of conduct rules, and the designated event supervisor.

When dealing with athletic contests that may draw large crowds or have anticipated crowd management concerns, a school district should have security personnel present such as district employees and/ or police officers.

See question 1-44 for information about the responsibilities of schools for school events.

5-24. What rights does a school district have to discipline parents who misbehave at school athletic events?

The code of conduct governs the behavior of visitors on school property. For related information, see questions 1-1 and 3-5.

The Commissioner has upheld the right of school districts to deny the access of parents to school property and exclude them from athletic events (*Appeal of Mayer*, 39 Ed Dept Rep 195, Decision No. 14,212). In that case, the parent did not demonstrate the right of access to school property. In another matter, the Commissioner found that a district did not act arbitrarily or capriciously by denying access to particular activities based upon related events (*Appeal of Anonymous*, 44 Ed Dept Rep 260, Decision No. 15,167).

Additionally, the Commissioner (*Appeal of Anonymous*, 48 Ed Dept Rep, Decision No. 15,855 has explained that in cases of inappropriate behavior on school grounds and/or the harassment of school students and/or employees, "school district officials are encouraged to seek the assistance of law enforcement and/or the courts where necessary to ensure the safety of students, staff and/or school property."

School districts should let parents know about the behavior they expect at contests and practices. Many districts require that coaches have a parent meeting before the first contest of the season. This is an excellent opportunity to communicate behavior expectations to parents. Announcements at each sporting event as to the expectation for good sportsmanship from the audience are also helpful.

5-25. What are the legal requirements that a school district must follow when a parent or nonparent gives an athlete a ride home after an away contest?

Many times, after an athletic contest, a coach is faced with a request by parents to transport home their children and maybe other children. When a school district transports students to a school-sponsored athletic event, it must transport those student athletes back to the point of departure or to the appropriate school. A parent or guardian may provide the school district with written notice, consistent with district policy, authorizing an alternate form of transportation home for the student athlete. It is recommended that the school district have a policy to ensure that coaches will handle this situation consistently.

The law also states that when "intervening circumstances make transportation of the student back to the point of departure or an appropriate school impractical," a school representative must stay with the student until the student has been delivered to the parent or the parents have been contacted and informed about the intervening circumstances.

Specific language, common to all school districts in New York State and depending on the size or the type of the district, is found in Education Laws 1604(41), 1709(41), 1804(11), 1903(2), 1950(19), 2503(20), 2554(27), and 2590-e (10).

5-26. How should an administrator respond to parent complaints regarding a coach, team rules, and playing time?

The administrator should listen to complaints and always communicate with the athletic administrator regarding such calls so that they may work together to respond to parent concerns. It is helpful to have an established procedure for dealing with concerns in order to achieve a constructive approach to addressing them. It may be helpful to publicize and communicate the process. The procedure should begin with the coach and, if the problem is not resolved, move to the athletic administrator before going to the building administrator.

Proactive communication with parents gives coaches and athletic administrators the opportunity to let parents know how to express their concerns. One vehicle for this communication is the preseason parent meeting. The coach should hold this meeting after the team has been selected. At this meeting the coach has the opportunity to talk about team information (see question 5-20) and at the same time let parents know how and when to communicate with the coach regarding questions. See also questions 5-18 and 5-19.

5-27. What if a parent requests that their child play at a higher level of competition?

It remains the responsibility of coaches to select teams and to conduct tryouts according to the athletic policies of the school district. It should be noted that according to the New York State Athletic Placement Process (APP) for Interschool Athletic Programs, effective in fall 2015, a student, teacher, coach, or parent may make a request to the director of physical education/athletics for a student to go through the Athletic Placement Process. The procedure is used to determine whether a student, who is not 15 prior to September 1 and is in grade 7 or 8, can play safely on a high school team. A board of education must have a policy to permit participation in the Athletic Placement Process (see also question 5-7). Details of this process may be found at http://www.p12.nysed.gov/ciai/pe/documents/AthleticPlacementProcess2-11-15Revised.pdf.

5-28. What provisions should be in place for medical emergencies at athletic events?

Someone with emergency training must be present at all athletic events. Education Law 3001-b and Part 135.5 of Commissioner's Regulations mandate that all coaches in New York State, prior to each sport season, provide valid evidence that they have current first aid and adult CPR certification as offered in a course of study by the American National Red Cross or meet other requirements, including course work for concussion management, certified by the Commissioner.

Section 917 of Education Law authorizes the use of automated external defibrillators (AEDs) in school districts. All school districts in New York State must provide and maintain at least one on-site AED. School districts must ensure the presence of one staff member who is trained in the use of an AED at all school-approved and school-sponsored events. Many school districts have chosen to mandate that coaches receive annual training in the use of AEDs. See question 2-22 for more information.

In addition to the coaches' training to meet emergencies, many school districts in New York State employ athletic trainers. Section 135.4 of Commissioner's Regulations establishes basic qualifications and the scope of duties and responsibilities of athletic trainers who may be employed by boards of education. Trainers work with injured athletes daily and attend contests in order to treat medical emergencies.

Some school districts employ physicians or emergency medical technicians (EMTs) who may be asked to attend athletic events that have greater risk of injuries, such as football and ice hockey games. Finally, the increased use of cell phones at the site of activities has provided quick access to emergency services that are needed following an injury.

5-29. What are the guidelines for a student athlete who sustains a concussion while playing interscholastic sports?

The Guidelines for Concussion Management in the School Setting (NYSED, 2015) state:

When developing concussion management plans, districts will promote an environment where reporting signs and symptoms of a concussion is required and important. Students should be seen by their primary medical provider for diagnosis, who then may choose to refer the student to a specialist as needed. If the student does not have a primary medical provider, district health personnel may assist families in finding one by providing information on local clinics and/or providers along with information on public health insurance. Additionally, districts should be cognizant of the various constraints that many students' families face. Although districts may assist parents/guardians with finding an appropriate medical provider, they should not require students to see a district-chosen provider for a fee in order to be cleared to return to athletic activities. Per this law, any evaluation and clearance authorizing a student to return to athletic activities must be performed, written, and signed by a licensed physician. Such written clearance must be sent to the school for review by the district medical director and is to be kept in the student's cumulative health record. (p. i)

The guidelines further note:

Local boards of education are strongly advised to develop a written concussion management policy. This policy should reference the district's protocols, written collaboratively with the district medical director to give direction to staff involved in the identification of a potential concussion. These policies and protocols assist a student who will return to school and need accommodations after being diagnosed with a concussion. Policies should provide clear protocols, but permit accommodations for individual student needs, as determined by the student's medical provider and/or district medical director.

The New York State Education Department (NYSED) and the New York State Department of Health (DOH) recommend the following be included in a district's policy on concussion management:

- A commitment to implement strategies that reduce the risk of head injuries in the school setting and during district sponsored events. A specific list of preventative strategies should be included in a guidance document appended to the board policy.

- A procedure and treatment plan, developed by the district medical director and other licensed health professionals employed by the district, to be utilized by district staff who may respond to a person with a head injury. The procedure and treatment plan should be appended to the board policy.
- A procedure to ensure that school nurses, certified athletic trainers, physical education teachers, and coaches have completed the NYSED-approved, required training course. Additionally, the policy should address the education needs of teachers and other appropriate staff, students, and parents guardians, as needed.
- A procedure for a coordinated communication plan among appropriate staff to ensure that private provider orders for post-concussion management are implemented and followed.
- A procedure for periodic review of the concussion management policy. (p. 2)

For more information, see the guidelines at http://www. nysphsaa.org/portals/0/pdf/safety/NYSED%20Guidelines%20 for%20Concussion%20Management.pdf.

5-30. What are the medical requirements for students who wish to participate in interscholastic athletics?

The Commissioner of Education mandates that any student who participates in interschool competitions shall receive an adequate physical examination and health history update and may not practice or participate without the approval of the school medical officer. The results of the physical are valid for 12 months through the last day of the month in which the physical was conducted. If the physical exam expires during a sport season, the athlete may complete the season as long as the health history update was completed prior to the start of the season (Bylaws and Eligibility Standards, #10 Health Examination, www.nysphsaa.org/resources/handbook).

5-31. What guidelines are appropriate for injured athletes who seek medical treatment from a doctor?

"Any pupil, whose safe participation is in question as a result of a health history interview, or injury, or prolonged absence, must be requalified by the school physician prior to participation" (Bylaws and Eligibility Standards, #10 Health Examination, www.nysphsaa. org/handbook). Many school districts interpret this to mean that if an athlete seeks medical attention from a doctor due to a possible injury, he/she will not be allowed to participate in interschool athletics until the school receives clearance from the attending doctor. The school medical officer may also examine the athlete to determine if he/she may resume interschool athletics.

5-32. What programs should be in place to address the issue of hazing?

Hazing should be included in the board-adopted code of conduct and should be clearly defined. It is also worthwhile to have a separate policy that addresses the steps the district will take to make sure that hazing activities do not take place. The building administrator should ensure that a program is in place to prevent hazing in all extracurricular activities.

For athletic teams, the athletic administrator should remind all coaches about the ban on hazing at the preseason coaches' meeting. Coaches are in the best position to educate students and take steps to ensure that hazing does not take place among team members. Administrators should ensure that coaches take part in staff development programs that address hazing prevention. It is important for students to be involved in the discussion about hazing and the development of policy. Also, the coach should warn all athletes about hazing at the first team meeting. Should a hazing incident take place, it should be addressed quickly in the manner outlined in the district code of conduct.

The Commissioner has stated, "School officials must take any type of hazing seriously and act to eliminate the practice." (*Appeal of J.W.*, 44 Ed Dept Rep 443, Decision No. 15,225). For more information, contact the school district's insurance carrier or see http://www.stophazing.org.

5-33. How should an administrator resolve conflicts among team members, between different teams, or between team members and coaches?

When a conflict exists among team members, the coach should be the first person to address the issue. When the conflict exists between teams or between a team and their coach, the athletic administrator will need to be involved. The athletic administrator should meet individually and/or as a group with the coach(es) and team(s) to determine the cause and extent of the problem and to formulate a strategy to resolve the issues. By following this approach, students will be involved in the problem-solving format and they will be more likely to participate in the solutions. In situations like this, it is a good idea for the athletic administrator to inform the building administrator of the issues, since students and/or parents may contact the building administrator.

5-34. What is an appropriate media policy for the athletic department?

Since athletic activities receive a great deal of press coverage, it is important that school district athletic departments have a procedure/policy for dealing with the media. In most cases, media communication about athletic matters should originate from the athletic administrator. However, since much communication involves reporting scores and making comments to a reporter after a contest, most districts delegate this to the coaches. It is important that the athletic administrator work with the coaches at the preseason meeting on how to communicate with the press in a constructive manner.

Use of social media for communication about school athletic activities should be consistent with the district's policies about communication, the use of social media, and acceptable use policies for technology and media.

5-35. Is competitive cheerleading an interscholastic sport?

The Board of Regents has recognized competitive cheerleading as an interscholastic sport. The SED has defined cheerleading and requires that a coach be certified according to Commissioner's Regulations. In addition, APP and mixed competition guidelines apply to the sport.

Schools could offer cheerleading as an interscholastic activity or as a traditional cheerleading squad, which would not compete and follow the rules and regulations of SED or the NYSPHSAA.

For information from SED, see http://www.p12.nysed.gov/ciai/pe/toolkitdocs/Comp_Cheer_FAQ_Dec2014.docx.

For information about competitive cheerleading and high school sports standards, see http://www.nysphsaa.org/Portals/0/PDF/Handbook/2016-17%20Handbook/Sports%20Standards_1.pdf.

5-36. What resources are available to provide administrators information about laws, rules, and policies regarding athletics at the state and national levels?

There are a number of helpful resources available to administrators concerning interscholastic athletics.

- Physical education information at NYSED (see www.p12.nysed.gov/ciai/pe)
- Part 135 (Health, Physical Education and Recreation) of Commissioner's Regulations (see http://www.p12.nysed.gov/ciai/pe/documents/CR135.4-Current%20through%20August%2015%202015.pdf)
- The Handbook of the NYSPHSAA (see http://www.section2athletics.org/handbooks)
- The New York State Athletic Administrators Association (http://www.nysaaa.org)
- The National Collegiate Athletic Association (www.ncaaclearinghouse.net)
- The handbooks of the athletic sections of the NYSPHSAA
- National Federation of State High School Associations. (www.nfhs.org)
- New York State Association of Independent Schools Athletic Association (http://www.nysais.org)
- Public Schools Athletic League of the City of New York (http://www.psal.org)

Section 6A
Faculty/Staff Supervision and Evaluation

6-1. What is the purpose of a formal teacher evaluation and end-of-year summative evaluation?

The term "evaluation" in the field of education refers to the process in which an administrator determines the degree of a teacher's competency. When a teacher is evaluated formally throughout a school year, the evaluator can provide feedback related to improvements, effectiveness of current techniques and strategies used by the teacher, changes that are needed, and/or the areas of teaching in need of improvement.

The purpose of formal teacher evaluation is to provide feedback to individual teachers concerning the effectiveness of their teaching skills. It is also information that must be used in determining the teacher's effectiveness rating for the subcomponent section called "teacher observation" of the New York State Annual Professional Performance Review (Education Law 3012-d) (see question 6-2).

"Summative evaluation" refers to a summary evaluation that is used to help make a personnel decision such as a recommendation for granting tenure, continuing employment, or not granting tenure.

6-2. What is the comprehensive teacher and principal evaluation law in New York?

New York State Education Law 3012-d, enacted in April 2015, replaced Education Law 3012-c. Both of these laws required public school districts in New York State to have an Annual Professional Performance Review plan that met certain criteria. The plan required negotiation with the teachers' and principals' local associations.

Under Education Law 3012-d, the number of areas to be negotiated was greatly diminished. There are now only two components that make up a teacher's effectiveness rating: teacher observation and student performance.

The teacher observation component consists of a minimum of two observations. All observations are conducted using one of several state-approved rubrics. The building principal is required to conduct at least one of the observations but one observation is also required from an "independent evaluator." An independent evaluator is anyone from outside the district or an administrator from within the district who does not work in that particular building (works in a building with a different BEDS code). The independent evaluator's score is defined in the school district's local plan but may not be worth more than 20 percent of a teacher's overall rating in this component (there is a waiver for districts that can prove hardship). There is an option to negotiate for a "peer observation." There are further limitations on the extent to which these observations can be included in the teacher's rating for this component. All evaluators are required to be trained as a lead evaluator.

The student performance category was originally intended to require that all classes that ended in a state-required exam, including grade the 3-8 math and ELA assessments, would utilize the students' success on these assessments as a means of deriving an effectiveness rating in this category. However, in May 2016 the Board of Regents placed a moratorium on the use of grades 3-8 ELA and math scores to derive effectiveness ratings for teachers. This moratorium is scheduled to last through the 2018-2019 school year. However, student performance on Regents examinations and grades 4 and 8 science assessments is not covered under this moratorium. Additionally, districts may send in local exams for review and approval by the New York State Education Department as a means of gaining additional data to complete this component of the Annual Professional Performance Review.

Effectiveness ratings from the two components are then combined on the matrix below to determine the teacher's effectiveness rating (highly effective, effective, developing, and ineffective):

Figure 1. Teacher's Effectiveness Rating

		Observation			
		Highly Effective (H)	Effective (E)	Developing (D)	Ineffective (I)
Student Performance	Highly Effective (H)	H	H	E	D
	Effective (E)	H	E	E	D
	Developing (D)	E	E	D	I
	Ineffective (I)	D*	D*	I	I

Figure 1. The teacher's effectiveness rating is based on observation and student performance. **If a teacher is rated "ineffective" on the student performance category and a state-designed supplemental assessment was included as an optional subcomponent of the student performance category, the teacher can be rated no higher than "ineffective" overall. From Guidance on Education Law 3012-d and Subpart 30-3 of the Commissioner's Regulations at https://www.engageny.org/resource/guidance-on-new-york-s-annual-professional-performance-review-law-and-regulations.

For the purposes of implementing Education Law 3012-d, it is important to know and follow the locally approved APPR plan.

More detail regarding Education Law 3012-d can be found at https://www.engageny.org/resource/appr-3012-d.

6-3. What are the teacher's rights and responsibilities regarding observations?

Teacher rights and responsibilities are described in most local collective bargaining agreements between teachers' associations and superintendents of schools.

Employees are expected to be treated fairly and without discrimination, prejudice, or harassment as outlined in various federal and state statutes. These include state and federal laws that prohibit discrimination against employees on the basis of age, race, color, national origin, sex, sexual orientation, religion, creed, or marital status (Title VII of the Civil Rights Act of 1964; Title IX of the Education Amendments of 1972; Human Rights Law; New York State Human Rights Law). Age discrimination is prohibited by the Age Discrimination in Employment Act (ADEA).

Title VII prohibits discrimination in employment on the basis of pregnancy and protects the right to reinstatement of women on leave for reasons related to pregnancy.

Title IX prohibits sexual discrimination in education programs.

The New York State Human Rights Law provides for equal protection of law for all persons within the state.

Under Education Law 3012-d, teachers have rights to appeal their overall rating but there are limitations on the grounds they can use to launch the appeal.

6-4. What are the recommended procedures for observing teachers?

It is important to follow any contractually agreed-upon procedures in completing observations. All observations for the purposes of APPR must be conducted using the district-approved teacher practice rubric.

Administrators should observe professional courtesies that include (1) an agreed-upon time and day of a formal classroom observation, (2) an understanding that the purpose of the observation is to improve instruction and student learning, and (3) an understanding that the process is intended to be constructive. The use of a preobservation conference, observation, and postobservation conference design is a professionally acceptable framework to follow. At a preobservation conference it is considered good practice to discuss the objective(s) of the lesson. During this discussion the administrator and teacher clarify what the students will know, what they will be able to do, or what other attributes will they acquire if the lesson is successful. Background information about the lesson expectations, teacher strategies and techniques to be used in the lesson, student learning styles, and other related issues often are part of that discussion.

Frequency and duration of observations used for APPR purposes are determined locally according to Subpart 30-3.34 of the Rules of the Board of Regents. It is useful to have a mix of announced and unannounced observations in order to get an accurate view of what the classroom looks like from day to day. Expectations for unannounced observations are different from those for an announced observation. The observer may be entering in the middle of a lesson rather than watching the lesson from beginning to end.

During the formal observation the observer should be as nonintrusive as possible. The observer should present a positive and supportive posture toward the teacher and students. Note taking and other observation instruments can serve as the basis for postobservation conference discussion.

The postobservation conference is a conversation between the teacher and the administrator to reflect on the success of the lesson relative to intended student learning. The discussion should focus on teacher behaviors that made the lesson successful, teacher behaviors that hindered the success of the lesson, and the ability of the teacher to engage all learners. Often this conference serves as a time to reinforce teacher behaviors, address those that are barriers to student success, and enhance those that need refinement. Both parties should believe that the exchange has been helpful and constructive.

6-5   What are some best practices for teacher evaluation?

Frequently the format, composition, and procedures to be followed in a formal evaluation of teachers are contained in the collective bargaining agreement between the teachers' association and the superintendent of schools. This document sometimes references the instrument to be used, the type of evaluations to be conducted, and the time of year and frequency of formal evaluations. Additionally, each school building often has an established tradition that informally defines the cultural ground rules for evaluation of teachers. Approved APPR plans now define the rubric that may be used to judge teacher performance on an observation.

Often the frequency of a formal observation is defined in the labor agreement based on the tenure status and experience of the teacher to be observed. As a general practice, nontenured teachers receive more formal observations per year than do tenured teachers. However, administrators must make professional judgments relative to the need for teachers whose performance is unacceptable to incur more frequent formal evaluations (see also question 6-7).

Subpart 30-3.34 of the Regents rules requires a minimum of two observations of each teacher per year. Through a district's negotiations, there may be more than this minimum requirement. Additionally, the law limits the type of information that may be used to evaluate the teacher observation. Education Law 3012-d does not allow teacher portfolios of student work not measured by the approved rubric, parent or student surveys, or professional goal setting as evidence of teacher effectiveness. It also does not allow artifacts from the classroom that would usually be shared in a pre- or postconference as evidence that standards on the rubric have been met; only "observable" evidence may be used.

6-6. May teachers refute any information on their formal evaluation?

Yes, teachers have the right to provide a rebuttal statement that must be appended to the evaluation record. There is no formal timeline in the law that limits a teacher's right to add a statement or comment on his/her evaluation. Once the teacher writes a rebuttal and signs the evaluation, both will become part of his/her personnel file for the remainder of his/her career. Sometimes a principal may not care for what the individual writes in his/her rebuttal but there is no formal recourse for this situation.

If a teacher refuses to sign the evaluation entirely, it is recommended that the district's attorney or labor relations specialist be contacted for guidance in these rare circumstances.

Additionally, each district's APPR plan must include a locally negotiated appeals process for the annual performance evaluation. The appeal applies only to the teacher's final effectiveness rating, and not to observations conducted throughout the school year.

6-7.   What are teacher improvement plans (TIPs)?

A teacher improvement plan documents specific performance deficiencies of a teacher, states specific expected changes, establishes resources for support, and sets a timeline for improvement. It is suggested that these plans be reviewed by the district's labor relations expert and/or the school attorney to ensure their legal quality.

Part 30-3.11 of the Regents rules explains that a teacher receiving an "ineffective" or "developing" rating on the annual professional performance review must have a teacher improvement plan, which is to be developed by either the superintendent or his/her designee. More times than not this will mean that the building principal will be responsible for writing the teacher improvement plan. The Commissioner's Regulation states that a plan must be in place by October 1 of the school year following the school year of the review or "as soon as practicable thereafter."

It is important to note that teacher improvement plans have been a common tool to help teachers improve prior to the implementation of the Annual Professional Performance Review laws. Additionally, TIP plans are not considered a disciplinary action. TIP plans usually include:

1.   The determined area of needed improvement,
2.   The steps the teacher is asked to take to improve in this area,
3.   The steps the district is willing to take to help that teacher improve,
4.   Frequency of meetings to check progress,
5.   The manner in which the improvement will be assessed, and
6.   A timeline showing the end date of the plan when evaluation of improvement will be completed.

See NYCRR-NY 30-3.11 for more information.

6-8.   If a teacher, teaching assistant, or teacher's aide has a student with an IEP or 504 plan, what should the principal look for when evaluating that person?

The administrator should expect compliance with the IEP/504

plan, to the best of the educator's ability within the scope of the position or job description in the school. Any professional shortcoming should be addressed in order to enable the staff member to comply with the plan. It is expected that the skills, knowledge, and attributes of every member of the instructional team will be brought to bear in the best interests of the student and in compliance with all applicable laws, regulations, and policies.

6-9. What is a 3020-a procedure?

The procedure for removing or disciplining tenured teachers is described in Education Law 3020-a. Usually the superintendent files written charges, and the board of education votes to prefer charges against the teacher. The teacher is notified of the charges and is entitled to request a hearing regarding the charges (Education Law 3020-a (2) (a)(c); Section 82-1.3(b) of Commissioner's Regulations). A prehearing conference must be held (Education Law 3020-a (3)(c) (ii); Part 82-1.6(e) of Commissioner's Regulations).

The 3020-a hearing is usually conducted before a hearing officer who determines the guilt or innocence of the teacher and imposes a penalty if the teacher is found guilty. However, when the charges against the teacher concern pedagogical incompetence or issues involving pedagogical judgment, the teacher may choose either a single hearing officer or a three-member panel, often called a 3020-a panel (Education Law 3020-a (2)(c); Parts 82-1.3(d) and 82-1.4 of Commissioner's Regulations).

A teacher's resignation after the conclusion of a hearing but prior to the hearing officer's decision does not preclude a school district from continuing the disciplinary proceedings and placing a record of the final determination in the teacher's personnel file.

If acquitted, the teacher must be restored to his or her teaching position with full pay for the period of suspension without pay, and the charges must be removed from the teacher's personnel record. If the hearing officer finds that any charges filed against the teacher were frivolous, a board of education is ordered to reimburse the State Education Department for all or a portion of the costs of the hearing and to reimburse the teacher for all or a portion of the reasonable costs incurred in defending the charges (Education Law 3020-a (4)(b)(c)).

6-10. How does Education Law 3020-b address APPR?

Education Law 3020-b allows for schools to use a streamlined process for removal of teachers if they have received two or more years of "ineffective" ratings on their Annual Professional Performance Review. The law states that if the teacher has received two consecutive years of ineffective ratings, the district "may" bring 3020-b charges of incompetence against him/her. If the teacher receives three years of "ineffective" ratings, the district is required to ("shall") bring 3020-b charges of incompetence.

6-11. What are the possible results of a 3020-a procedure?

See question 6-9 for more information with regard to acquittal. Penalties may include suspensions, loss of pay, termination, or any combination. A hearing officer in a proceeding according to Section 3020-a of New York State Education Law will consider efforts to correct the teacher's behavior when determining the results of the charges. Such efforts frequently include remediation, peer intervention, participation in an employee assistance program, recommendations for improvement of performance, guidance, clearly articulated expectations, and encouragement (Education Law 3020-a (4)(a)).

6-12. At what point does an administrator proceed with charges according to Section 3020-a of Education Law after working with a tenured teacher to facilitate change both instructionally and interpersonally?

Technically an administrator does not formally "proceed" with a 3020-a proceeding. The superintendent, with authorization of the board of education, guides the process. It is the superintendent of schools who must prefer charges in the form of a recommendation to the board of education. The history of evaluations and counseling memos from building administrators are factors in the superintendent's decision. The superintendent must be willing to proceed after efforts such as counseling, remediation, peer intervention, and other programs have not changed the teacher's behavior and all other remedies and alternatives have been exhausted. There may be circumstances in which immediate steps must be taken to remove a teacher from the classroom. It should also be noted that 3020-a proceedings are time consuming, costly and potentially disruptive.

See question 6-10 about the requirements of Education Law 3020-b with regard to "ineffective" ratings on an APPR for two consecutive or three consecutive years.

6-13. When supervising nontenured teachers, what documentation should be used to support nonrecommendation for tenure? What timelines should be followed?

There are internal guidelines established by the school districts as administrative regulations or practices, and there may be contractual obligations in the collective bargaining agreement between the teachers' association and the superintendent of schools.

Regardless of where official guidance may be found, some basic parameters offer practical assistance. Documentation is the key to a nonrecommendation of tenure. The record should include:

- Formal written observations and evaluations of the teacher. These should include all information related to the meetings between the supervisor and the teacher in preparation for, and subsequent to, the formal observations. Notes of these meetings should also be included in this documentation. The teacher's strengths, weaknesses, or identified areas of growth or improvement must be clearly stated in unbiased terms. Evidence of unsatisfactory teacher performance may include comments by the supervisor or data gleaned from formal observations.

- Any minutes of meetings about mentoring or counseling sessions with the teacher, especially those that emphasize strategies agreed upon by the teacher and supervisor for improvement of teaching performance. In the absence of agreed-upon strategies for improvement, suggestions for improvement by the supervisor should exist in writing to the teacher. All suggestions for improvement must be free of bias, clear, unambiguous, fair, and substantiated by observations or data provided by a supervisor.

- Any teacher improvement plans that were developed as the result of an "ineffective" or "developing" rating according to the comprehensive teacher evaluation system (APPR). The improvement plan should be delivered in compliance with the time constraints of the APPR process. Under Education Law 3012-d, probationary teachers who receive an "ineffective" rating in their last year of probation are not allowed to be granted tenure (but may be eligible for an extension of their probation). Additionally, probationary teachers must receive an "effective" or "highly effective" rating in three years of their four-year probationary period to be considered for tenure.

- Timeline records related to any improvement plan for the teacher and meetings that involved the teacher. Communications to the teacher or the appropriate parties relative to the attempt to improve teacher performance should be part of the documentation.
- Any minutes of meetings that involved the supervisor, the teacher, and union representatives related to the need for improved teacher performance and strategies for improvement. Communications related to these minutes are also used to support documentation.

The assistance of a labor relations specialist or personnel administrator should ensure that the documentation is appropriate and useful. If the principal has a question about what documentation may or may not be used, the principal should consult with the labor relations specialist or school attorney. As a practical matter, the role of the principal is paramount in any successful disciplinary action against a teacher.

6-14. When should nontenured teachers be informed that they will not be recommended for tenure?

Education Laws 2509(1)(a), 2573(1)(a), and 3012(2) require that the superintendent of schools notify the teacher in writing at least 60 days prior to the expiration of the probationary period that a recommendation for appointment on tenure will not be made. Notice must also be provided that the board of education will examine the denial of tenure appointment at a board meeting at least 30 days prior to the board meeting when that recommendation will be considered (Education Law 3031). A single written statement can contain both of these notices or they may be provided separately. Some negotiated agreements establish longer notice. An administrator should keep a chart of required observations and notices and a time frame for each.

6-15. What are the legal guidelines for disciplining a staff member?

The guidelines for discipline of a tenured staff member are rigid and formal. They have evolved through Education Law (Education Law 3020-a), decisions and regulations of the Commissioner of Education, and the decisions of the Public Employment Relations Board (PERB). A teacher who has received tenure has earned the right to keep his or her job free from discipline or dismissal except for just cause to be proven by school officials in a due process hearing under Education Law 3020-a. The legal guidelines are complicated and involve a great deal of time and paperwork. In most cases, the guidance of a labor relations specialist, personnel administrator, or attorney for the school district is recommended before proceeding. A hearing officer in a 3020-a proceeding will consider efforts to correct the teacher's behavior, including remediation, peer intervention, teacher improvement plans, ratings on the summative evaluation system (APPR), and/or an employee assistance program (Education Law 3020-a(4)(a) (see also question 6-9).

6-16. What steps should be taken when dealing with staff regarding inappropriate behavior?

Before inappropriate behavior can be dealt with, it must be determined that such behavior actually occurred, and the circumstances and severity of the behavior must be established. The burden of proof lies with the administration concerning claims of inappropriate behavior. When investigating such claims, care should be taken to ensure that proper procedures are followed concerning confidentiality, access to information, ethical considerations relative to questioning others and acquiring information, and due process.

Basic instances of minor inappropriate behavior usually are dealt with through a conference with the teacher. In more serious instances, a written memo should be provided to the teacher as a summary of the meeting. This should include the basic topics of conversation between the supervisor and the teacher, details of the inappropriate behavior, and future expectations. The memo may or may not be placed in the file of the teacher depending on the severity of the inappropriate behavior, recidivism of the behavior, and the general reaction of the teacher to the request for behavioral improvement.

Discipline should be considered progressive in nature. Memos may include previous documented evidence of inappropriate behavior that may be used to build a case for discipline (see question 6-21).

6-17. What steps should be taken concerning a teacher with a

problem outside of the classroom that affects classroom performance?

Dealing with such problems has an unpredictable quality. A determination must be made relative to the degree in which the behavior is illegal, or negatively affects the health, safety, and welfare of students or the educational process. See question 6-16 for steps to follow. Additionally, most boards of education have a policy regarding the ethical behavior or moral character of its faculty. Lastly, Part 83 of the Commissioner's Regulations identifies potential ethical violations by a certificated employee that are required to be reported, by the superintendent of schools, to the Commissioner of Education.

In all of the above, an administrator would be wise to consult with district human resource personnel, the school superintendent, school attorney, and/or labor relations specialists before attempting to pass judgment on an individual's "outside" activities.

6-18. If a teacher is continually absent, at what point can you require a doctor's note to explain the situation? How should an administrator broach the topic with the teacher?

This situation is often specified in the collective bargaining agreement between the teachers' association and the superintendent of schools and determined by the severity of the issue at hand. As the cause may be some form of illness or disability, this is a complicated situation that requires sensitivity. With the advent of HIPAA (Health Insurance Portability and Accountability Act), doctor's notes may not contain information regarding the specific illness or injury of the employee. Instead, the notes may only contain a general statement that the employee is under his/her care and that the employee is not able to return to work until a specified date. Caution is advised when dealing with issues related to disability. Stress, in addition to mental and physical illness, may be a factor in teacher absence. School districts are required to provide employee assistance programs (EAPs) to assist employees with a myriad of problems. A referral to an EAP program for legitimate issues related to teacher absenteeism is sometimes warranted.

It is also worth noting that an administrator should never allow an employee to return to work after being out for an extended period of time without a release from his/her doctor. If an employee is allowed to return to work earlier than the note provided by the physician says is allowed, the district may be liable should the employee become ill while at the school. Always follow the physician's timeline for return. If the employee wants to return earlier, make him/her get an updated note from the physician before allowing the employee to begin work again. See also question 6-13, 6-19, and 6-21.

6-19. How should an administrator deal with employees who continually ask to leave early and have a pattern of using most or all of their sick time every year?

Employees who often ask to leave early naturally incur scrutiny. Principals are advised to seek reasons for such patterns of behavior to determine their legitimacy. In some cases extenuating circumstances exist that may lead to accommodations from the district or the teacher. However, care should be taken so as not to build a precedent or changed expectations for teachers that hinder the safe and smooth operation of the school, violate the collective bargaining agreement, or defy common sense. The administrator must remember that all staff may expect a similar concession in like circumstances.

Cases of continual absenteeism that suggest illness must be handled carefully as they often are very personal matters that influence work effectiveness and relationships. The situation could have physical, psychological, or other causes. The key to success is to be vigilant with regard to such matters. When open and trusted avenues of communication exist between the administrator and teacher, such matters can be privately discussed with sensitivity. The administrator can determine options available based on the information from such discussions. Sometimes these situations are simple to address, but other times they may require the assistance of the director of personnel, superintendent, or the school attorney.

In the most severe cases the district may institute legal proceedings. The board of education can require any employee to submit to a medical examination, including a psychiatric examination, to determine an employee's physical or mental capacity to perform his or her duties in order to safeguard the health of children attending the public schools (Education Law 913). Further, these findings must be reported to the board of education and may be used for the performance evaluation of the employee, for determining the need for a disability retirement, or for possible disciplinary action.

These situations should be examined and addressed on a case-by-case basis.

6-20. What is a procedure for addressing suspected alcohol or drug abuse by an employee?

Such instances are serious and require the assistance of a seasoned personnel administrator or labor relations specialist. They may result in discipline of the employee and/or may be the sign of a disability. See also questions 6-16, 6-17, 6-18 and 6-19.

6-21. How are counseling memos used, and are they part of the teacher discipline process?

The term "counseling" implies a written communication that provides guidance, direction, recommendations, and expectations in an encouraging manner. In a formal sense, a counseling memo is not considered discipline. Discipline requires a formal action, often by a board of education, that triggers a legal process with due process rights for a teacher. Such proceedings may result in a reprimand as a penalty under Education Law 3020-a. The 3020-a statute places the burden of proof on the school district. A district may place a counseling letter (also commonly known as a "Holt" memo or letter) critical of a tenured teacher's performance in the teacher's personnel file. This type of counseling memo is not considered a reprimand.

A counseling memo or multiple memos assist in establishing a pattern of responses that may be helpful when proceeding to formal disciplinary action. The law requires that a progressive discipline model be used. This means that a hearing officer in a 3020-a proceeding will look to see if the disciplinary measures being sought seem to have a steady increase in severity of response each time a similar issue has arisen. For example, if a teacher has poor classroom management, a hearing officer will most likely not agree to terminate the individual if the district has not demonstrated attempts to re-train and had some smaller levels of discipline before seeking such a drastic outcome.

It is important for an administrator to check the local contract and consult with a labor relations specialist or the school's attorney about provisions that relate to counseling or disciplinary procedures.

6-22. Does a teacher have a right to union representation when a teacher is being counseled?

The right to union representation depends on the content of the collective bargaining agreement between the teachers' association and the superintendent of schools and the severity of the issue. Generally speaking, if the issue could result in the formal discipline of the teacher, or as specified in the collective bargaining agreement, the teacher is permitted representation by the union. On issues that do not seem as though they could rise to the level of future disciplinary actions, the teacher is not legally entitled to representation; however, practice, culture, or history within the district may make representation advisable as a practical matter.

It would be prudent to seek the guidance of a labor relations specialist, personnel administrator, or school attorney before proceeding.

6-23. When is it necessary to notify the union president regarding a concern about one of their members?

Practices within districts vary. However, the superintendent should always be aware of any communications with unions in the district. Often these communications have historical and cultural protocols that must be understood and followed for the communication to be effective. Notification is important whenever discipline of the member is a goal or when an administrator believes that he/she may get support or questions from the union. Often a union will assist in the investigation or counseling of one of its members when the union believes the member has erred. The union representative's role is to assure that the member is properly treated during the related investigation. No professional union wants to reinforce the inappropriate behavior of one of its members. However, the union has a legal duty to represent members and ensure that their rights are secured.

6-24. If an administrator keeps a journal with background information regarding communications with teachers, parents, or students, is the journal a document of public information?

Often school districts have policies approved by the board of education with regard to access to school district records. This is an area that changes constantly. It is wise to consult with the school attorney before any assumptions are made.

Communications about students may become part of a student's record. Student records are not public records. Statutes such as FERPA (also known as the "Buckley Amendment"), HIPAA (health records), and IDEA determine the release of student information. Requests include those by parents for such information or requests made by a court through a subpoena. See questions 1-37 and 3-17 for more information.

Communications with teachers could be part of a personnel record and thus subject to rules related to the release of personnel records. Personnel records are not public records. See also question 6-30.

6-25. If an administrator keeps a journal with background information regarding communications with teachers, parents, or students, is the journal a document that can be used in litigation?

If litigation arises from an incident with a teacher, parent, or student, a journal of the events probably will be subject to disclosure in that process if the journal reflects contemporaneous notes of what happened. Do not presume privacy with the journal if it describes a situation that is part of litigation.

6-26. What steps should be taken if there is a concern regarding a staff member who is shared with another district or who is a BOCES employee such as a substitute teacher or a special service provider?

All concerns or complaints should be directed to the supervisor of that employee. Details of any findings or investigation into the matter should be provided with a specific suggested remedy. The ultimate decision about action rests with the service agency/supervisor of the person in question. The relationship between the service agency and your school district best operates in a spirit of cooperation and mutual respect.

6-27. Are there state standards for teacher dress in schools?

No. A school district may not unilaterally impose a dress code on its faculty. The imposition of a specific dress code for faculty is a mandatory subject of collective bargaining (*Catskill CSD*, 18 PERB ¶ 4612 (1985)). However, the attire of a teacher must not be deemed a barrier to his/her ability to conduct professional responsibilities with authority and in an orderly manner.

6-28. How should an administrator handle a parent(s) who has a complaint against a teacher? How should an administrator handle a teacher who has a complaint against a parent(s)?

Complaints are best dealt with directly and professionally. The complaint should be articulated to the party who has the greatest ability to provide remedy. Reasons for the complaint, and the history of the situation that led to the complaint, should be discussed. Other pertinent information that will clarify issues and provide insight into the problem or symptom that preceded the complaint should be added.

Unresolved complaints are often appealed to a higher authority. Appeals may move through a number of levels. Often the largest obstacle to resolving complaints is a lack of understanding of the complaint and the remedy sought by the participants.

See question 3-30 that addresses an established chain of command or process to resolve problems.

6-29. Can a teacher's child who is not a student in the class be in the classroom when a teacher is teaching a class?

This is not a good practice. It has insurance implications and is generally considered inappropriate. The duty of the teacher while teaching a class is to focus attention on the education of the class. Supervision of his/her child presents an organizational dilemma. One should apply the following test. If other teachers in the building used this practice, would it in any way interfere with the educational process or supervision of the children they are hired to educate?

6-30. What rights does a school district have to monitor technology use?

A district has a right to monitor the use of its equipment and computer networks. A district must consider to what extent and under what conditions, such as investigating illegal use of the networks or another business-related purpose, that monitoring will take place. The district must consider what notice will be given to personnel and how it will be communicated in order to avoid any misunderstandings about the purpose and use of monitoring. The acceptable use policy (see questions 4-28 and 6-31) should include these considerations and balance them with any right to privacy for an individual. It is important to train all staff so they understand that every aspect of computer use in schools is district property. Staff should also know that all correspondence, including emails, is subject to the Freedom of Information Law (FOIL).

Recently, many issues have arisen regarding social networking and its use by teachers to communicate with students. The district reserves the right to dictate how and when social networking may be used as a classroom tool. However, the district is limited in its rights to control what teachers do from their own computers and electronic devices. It is important to assist staff in knowing that they are doing so at their own risk, and the district will assume no liability should issues related to this practice arise. This is an area where the local teachers' union and the district often agree and work together to share the dangers of such a practice.

6-31. Does an employee have the right to use the Internet or the district's network for personal use?

The acceptable computer use policy should include what privileges the employee has with regard to appropriate use of the Internet and email through the district's computer network. The policy should clarify if email and Internet use is only for business purposes or limited personal use under conditions specified by the district. The policy should also link the email use to other human relations policies such as the district policy concerning harassment. The district needs to inform employees that use of the district networks is not private since the networks are property of the district. Specific questions in this area should be referred to the school's attorney. See question 4-28 for more information about acceptable use policies.

6-32. When a faculty member or prominent community member dies, how should the administrator handle requests to go to the funeral during the school day?

This depends on the history, frequency, and relative importance of each situation. The instructional day must be maintained; however, there are occasions when instructional focus in such a situation is difficult to maintain. Any decisions for the release of staff in numbers that are clearly not ordinary should be discussed and approved by the superintendent, as precedent, contract administration, and other conditions may apply.

It is important to have planning in place in case of the death of a faculty or staff member. These plans are often developed by the building's crisis team and should include the availability of counseling support for staff/students during these tragic events.

6-33. What is the law regarding staff reduction as it relates to seniority?

If a position is abolished, the teacher with the least seniority in that tenure area in that school district must be the individual dismissed. This is also true if a position is to be involuntarily reduced from full-time to part-time. Districts are not required to keep seniority lists but most do to ensure that the least senior teacher is known in case of a need to reduce staff.

It is important to know what counts as service toward seniority. Only full-time teaching is counted toward seniority credit. If an individual is in a long-term substitute capacity for a semester or more and subsequently receives a probationary appointment with no interruption between the two, the time prior to the probationary appointment must also count in the calculation of service credit toward seniority. Conversely, any time a teacher is out on any type of unpaid leave (parental, medical, etc.), the days they are out are not counted toward seniority credit.

It is important to work with district office personnel when attempting to determine issues related to seniority as there are many additional components to the law that must be followed.

See also Education Law 2510 and Commissioner's decision No. 16,158 for more information about preferred eligibility lists, recall rights, and length of service in a system versus length of service within a tenure area.

6-34. What is collective bargaining?

Collective bargaining is the process by which terms and conditions of employment are defined. The Taylor Law (Sections 200–214, New York State Civil Service Law, Article 14) regulates the employee bargaining process and the rights and obligations of unions and school districts with regard to terms and conditions of employment.

The responsibilities, obligations, and rights of employees and employers are written into a binding agreement. Items that are often written into the collective bargaining agreement include: recognition of which employee groupings are covered by the agreement; length of the agreement; the mechanism used to negotiate subsequent agreements;

enumeration of retirement benefits and retirement incentives; personal day use and accumulation; sick day use and accumulation; termination and disciplinary clauses; seniority; payroll dates; grievance procedures; length of school day; mileage reimbursement; salary credit for completion of in-service training; graduate hour remuneration; summer school and other forms of compensation; extra duty pay schedules; salary schedules; longevity steps; sabbatical leave benefits; sick leave; bereavement leave; jury duty; military leave; workers' compensation; childbearing and/or child-rearing leave; other extended leaves; staff evaluations; personal file rules; work year; length of lunch periods; faculty meetings; discipline and reprimand procedures; job postings; job transfers; job terminations; staff reduction; and substituting for absent colleagues.

6-35. What steps should a principal take when a superintendent and staff are at odds on an issue?

The principal reports to the superintendent. However, a collegial relationship should always exist between them. Guidance should be sought and provided by each and to each other. The principal should let the superintendent know what the staff is thinking. Often a better understanding of the issues or concerns at hand can be examined with an exchange of information and views. This is a challenging situation that requires effective communication so that there is support of the superintendent, and the staff knows that their concerns are being fairly considered.

Section 6B
Professional Development

6-36. How can faculty meetings be effectively used for staff development?

Commit "housekeeping" communications to memos and/or verbally through key communicators within the building such as grade-level or department chairpersons. Create an agenda for each faculty meeting that reflects topics of interest and educational value, with specific outcomes of targeted staff development connected with the professional development plan (PDP) for each district. Ensure that the program is meaningful, important to the attendees, and motivational. Be sure to establish a mechanism for follow-up and improvement of new knowledge and skills.

6-37. How can time be created during the school day for staff development?

Current innovative practices include the use of significant portions of faculty meetings for targeted staff development rather than housekeeping tasks or items of less importance. The use of team or grade-level common time can often create staff development opportunities directed at specific goals germane to specific groupings of teachers. Before-and-after-school exchanges of instructional information, strategies, best practices and relevant student performance data are often successful in helping teachers focus on emerging or unfulfilled goals. Discussions with faculty members and leaders can result in additional ideas that may work well. The attributes of a successful staff development initiative are that the participants perceive the effort as relevant, valuable, and enjoyable.

Some districts use shortened instructional sessions, consistent with the state requirements for minimum daily sessions and minimum hours of weekly instruction, or parts of superintendent's conference days, consistent with the state requirements for staff development on conference days. For more information, see https://stateaid.nysed.gov/attendance/attendance_memo.htm.

6-38. What are the regulations for a teacher/mentor program?

Section 100.2(dd)(2) of Commissioner's Regulations requires

schools, they also must participate in a mentored program in their first year of employment unless they have successfully completed two years of teaching prior to such service. The State Education Department recommends:

> Principals take on such vital roles as participating in the design of the program, selecting mentors, supporting the program with other teachers and parents, assisting in coordination of scheduling the mentoring, and in evaluating the impact of the program. http://www.highered.nysed.gov/tcert/faqmentoring.html.

The PDP mentoring program must describe the procedure for selecting mentors, the role of mentors, the preparation of mentors, types of mentoring activities, and time allotted for mentoring. Aspects of the mentoring program such as pay for mentor training, time allocated for mentoring activities, and time allocated for activities occurring beyond the hours of a regular teacher workday are subject to collective bargaining.

The PDP mentoring program requirement is separate and distinct from the New York State Mentor Teacher Internship Program (MTIP) that has been subject to annual funding.

6-39. What is the professional development requirement for teachers and administrators in New York State?

When teachers first begin their careers, they usually have an initial certificate. During the time of initial certification, a teacher must complete a master's degree, have at least one year of a mentored experience, and complete at least three years of teaching. Upon completion of all New York State Education Department requirements, a teacher may apply for a professional certificate.

Those who hold a professional classroom certificate or a level III teaching assistant certificate are now required to complete 100 hours of Continuing Teacher and Leader Education (CTLE) credits every five years and will be responsible for tracking and submitting those hours to the New York State Education Department for renewal of their professional certifications. (Credits should be reported through the TEACH account). CTLE credits can only be obtained by attending approved CTLE professional development courses offered by an approved CTLE provider. Most schools have become, or will become, CTLE providers but not all professional development provided by a school will qualify as a CTLE credit. All districts are required to have a professional development plan that includes the opportunities available to teachers that will enable them to meet this requirement. It should be noted that SAANYS is an approved provider of CTLE.

More information regarding the Continuing Teacher and Leader Education requirement for teachers can be found at http://www.highered.nysed.gov/tcert/resteachers/ctle.html.

Principals who hold a professional certificate must also complete 175 hours of professional development every five years. For both teachers and principals, the district must submit a record of these hours to the State Education Department yearly.

6-40. What is a teacher induction program? How may it be implemented?

The purpose of a teacher induction program is to familiarize teachers new to a school or school district with the policies, procedures, practices, expectations, and protocols necessary to be an effective and efficient professional. An induction program includes mentoring, but is more than simply a mentoring program. An induction program is progressive and conducted over several years. It includes teachers new to the profession and supports their transition to teaching. It also includes veteran teachers new to a district and supports their transition to the culture and expectations of a new district. Such programs often include periodic meetings for the dissemination of information. Additional goals are to enhance the abilities and skills of teachers, support an acceptable level of instructional expertise in the classroom, and develop contributing members of the instructional team. Good induction programs enable districts to attract and retain the very best teachers.

Districts need to commit to developing an induction program, provide resources to implement one, and engage an outstanding teacher to lead the program. It is always helpful to consult with a district that has established a successful teacher induction program when planning a program.

Section 7
Special Education and Section 504

7-1. What is IDEA?

The Individuals with Disabilities Education Act (IDEA) was originally enacted by Congress in 1975 to ensure that children with disabilities have the opportunity to receive a free appropriate public education, just like other children, in the least restrictive environment. The law has been revised many times over the years.

The most recent amendments were passed by Congress in December 2004, with final regulations published in August 2006 (part B, for school-aged children) and in September 2011 (part C, for babies and toddlers).

The federal register hosts copies of both the part B IDEA regulations, which apply to children and youths ages 3-21, and the part C IDEA regulations, which apply to children from birth through age 2. For more information, see http://www.p12.nysed.gov/specialed/idea/.

7-2. What is Section 504 of the Vocational Rehabilitation Act of 1973?

Section 504 of the Vocational Rehabilitation Act of 1973 is a federal law that protects individuals from discrimination on the basis of their disability. The purpose of this legislation is to prohibit discrimination against individuals with disabilities by any organization that receives federal funds. It guarantees their rights to equal opportunity in all programs and activities. Subpart D of Section 504 applies to preschool, elementary, and secondary education. Section 504 requires that schools identify students as eligible for services if the student has, has had, or is regarded as having a physical or mental impairment that substantially limits one or more major life activities. Major life activities are defined as "functions such as caring for one's self, performing manual tasks, walking, seeing, hearing, speaking, breathing, learning, and working" (see 34 Code of Federal Regulations Part 104.3). Schools must make sure that educational programs are accessible for students. A school administrator should also ensure that his/her district has the required grievance procedures in place to address complaints about discrimination. For more information, see http://www.ed.gov/about/offices/list/ocr/504faq.html#interrelationship.

7-3. What is the Americans with Disabilities Act (ADA)?

The Americans with Disabilities Act of 1990 is a federal law that prohibits discrimination on the basis of a disability. As defined by this act, a person with a disability is one who:

- has a physical or mental impairment that substantially limits one or more major life activities;
- has a record of such impairment;
- is regarded as having such an impairment.

ADA has specific provisions for employers and government services that include schools and public accommodations. ADA was amended in 2008 to clarify and reiterate who is covered by the civil rights protections of the law. The ADA Amendments Act of 2008 changes the term "disability" to more broadly encompass impairments that substantially limit a major life activity. The amended language also states that mitigating measures, including assistive devices, auxiliary aids, accommodations, and medical therapies and supplies (other than eyeglasses and contact lenses), have no bearing in determining whether a disability qualifies under the law. Changes also clarify coverage of impairments that are episodic or in remission that substantially limit a major life activity when active, such as epilepsy or post-traumatic stress disorder. A final rule revising the regulations took effect on October 11, 2016 to incorporate the requirements of the ADA Amendments Act that made a number of significant changes to the meaning and interpretation of the ADA definition of "disability." The objective of this revision was to ensure that the definition would be broadly construed and applied without extensive analysis.

See questions 2-21 and 2-22 for more information about a school's responsibilities for accessibility and the webpage http://www.usdoj.gov/crt/ada/adahom1.htm.

7-4. Are all schools required to have an evacuation plan for special education students?

The New York State Education Department recommends that school emergency plans include procedures for students with disabilities who need assistance in an emergency situation. If the student's unique needs require a plan that would be different from a plan for general education students, a notation should be made in the management section of the IEP stating the need for the plan and where the plan can be located. The plan should not be a part of the IEP, since it may need to be amended and, if included as a part of the IEP, changes would require a meeting of the CSE. See also questions 2-20 and 2-21 for related information.

7-5. What are the federal regulations regarding accessibility?

See questions 2-20, 2-21, and 7-3 for more information.

7-6. How does New York State Special Education Law differ from federal law?

Federal law and regulations require states to meet minimum federal special education requirements. States may exceed these standards as long as the federal requirements are met. In some cases, New York State laws and regulations are more prescriptive than federal law and regulations and give more rights to students with disabilities than does the federal law. In such instances, state law must be followed. State law and regulations are amended in order to conform to IDEA requirements (see http://www.p12.nysed.gov/specialed/idea/nys-laws-and-regulations-that-differ-from-federal-requirements-june-2016.html).

7-7. What is free appropriate public education (FAPE)?

The New York State Education Department uses the definition of Free Appropriate Public Education contained in federal regulations (34 CFR 300.17). "FAPE" means special education and related services that are

> provided at public expense, under public supervision and direction and without charge; meet the standards of the SED (New York State Education Department)...; include preschool, elementary school, or secondary school education in the state [New York State] involved; and are provided in conformity with an Individualized Education Program (IEP)...(34 CFR 300.17).

A student with a disability is entitled to a free appropriate public education. An appropriate education will provide a program for a student with a disability that is tailored to meet the student's individual needs according to the student's IEP or Section 504 accommodation plan (see question 7-3). FAPE ensures that the student receives an educational benefit from that instruction (see 34 Code of Federal Regulations, Parts 300.13 and 104.33).

A working definition of FAPE is consistently found in numerous decisions by state review officers and is based on the U.S. Supreme Court case *Board of Education of Hendrick Hudson Central School v. Rowley*, 458 U.S. 176 (1982). A district meets its burden of offering to provide a free appropriate public education to a student by demonstrating that the district complied with the procedural requirements set forth in IDEA and that the IEP developed for the student through IDEA procedures is reasonably calculated to enable the student to receive educational benefits (*Application of the Board of Education of the Arlington Central School District*, Appeal No. 03-100 (2003), at http://www.sro.nysed. gov/).

Any questions relating to a free and appropriate education for a particular student should be discussed with an attorney who has experience with Special Education Law.

7-8.   What is least restrictive environment (LRE)?

"Least restrictive environment" means that placement of students with disabilities in special classes, separate schools, or other removal from the regular educational environment should occur only when the nature or severity of the disability is such that even with the use of supplementary aids and services, education cannot be satisfactorily achieved. The placement of an individual student with a disability in the least restrictive environment shall:

- provide the special education services needed by the student;
- provide for an education of the student to the maximum extent appropriate to the needs of the student with other students who do not have disabilities; and
- be as close as possible to the student's home and the school that the student would have attended if not disabled, unless the IEP requires some other arrangement (Section 200.1 (cc) of Commissioner's Regulations).

The NYSED office has issued a field advisory to maximize participation of students with disabilities in general education programs and to ensure that students with disabilities are being provided with opportunities to receive high-quality instruction in the LRE. Such opportunities include actions each school district should take to conduct an in-depth review of its data and to assess the quality of its inclusive programs for students with disabilities. For more information, see http://www.p12.nysed.gov/specialed/publications/2015-memos/least-restrictive-environment-district-responsibilities.html.

7-9. What is an individualized educational program (IEP)?

An individualized educational program (IEP) is a written document that outlines the specialized educational program for a student with a disability. The New York State Education Department states:

> An IEP is a written statement for a student with a disability that is developed, reviewed, and revised by a Committee on Special Education (CSE), Subcommittee on Special Education or Committee on Preschool Special Education (CPSE). The IEP is the tool that ensures a student with a disability has access to the general education curriculum and is provided the appropriate learning opportunities, accommodations, adaptations, specialized services and supports needed for the student to progress towards achieving the learning standards and to meet his or her unique needs related to the disability. Each student with a disability must have an IEP in effect by the beginning of each school year. Federal and state laws and regulations specify the information that must be documented in each student's IEP. In New York State (NYS), IEPs developed for the 2011-12 school year and thereafter, must be on a form prescribed by the Commissioner of Education. For more information, see: http://www.p12.nysed.gov/specialed/formsnotices/IEP/home.html and http://www.p12.nysed.gov/specialed/publications/iepguidance/intro.htm.

7-10. What is a 504 plan?

A 504 plan is generally used when a disability seems temporary and is medically based. The student must qualify according to Section 504 of the Rehabilitation Act of 1973 (see questions 7-2 and 7-38). Eligible students must be provided a free appropriate education that meets the individual needs of the student (see question 7-7). Section 504 requires that eligible students have an accommodation plan. This plan differs from an IEP in that the Rehabilitation Act does not specify the specific components of the plan, other than that it must be a written document. Although a 504 plan is not as specific as an IEP, the plan focuses on the accommodations and modifications that are necessary for the student to receive a free appropriate education. The nature of the student's disability will dictate the specific contents of the plan.

7-11. What is the role of the Committee on Special Education?

The Committee on Special Education is responsible for:

- the identification, evaluation, review, and recommendations for educational placement and programs for each district resident school-aged student who has been identified as having a disability or thought to have a disability (Sections 200.3 and 200.4 of Commissioner's Regulations);
- an annual report to the board of education regarding the status of facilities, services, and programs for district students with disabilities (Education Law 4402 (1)(b)(3) (f));
- the maintenance of a master list of the district's school-aged students with disabilities who are served by the district's CSE (Section 200.2 (a) of Commissioner's Regulations).

7-12. Who are the members of the Committee on Special Education?

According to Section 200.3 (a) of the Commissioner's Regulations, the membership of the Committee on Special Education must include, but is not limited to:

- the parents or guardian of the student;
- one general education teacher of the student if the student is or may be participating in the regular education environment;
- one special education teacher of the student;
- a school psychologist;
- a representative of the school district qualified to provide or supervise special education and knowledgeable about the general education curriculum and the availability of resources of the school district; an individual who meets these qualifications may also be the same individual

appointed as the special education teacher or the
special education provider of the student, or the school
psychologist. The representative of the school district shall
serve as the chairperson of the committee;

- an individual who can interpret instructional implications
  of the evaluation results. This individual may also be the
  individual appointed as the regular education teacher, the
  special education teacher or special education provider,
  the school psychologist, or the representative of the school
  district;
- other persons having knowledge or special expertise
  regarding the student, including related services personnel
  as the school district or the parent(s) determine; and
- if appropriate, the student;
- a school physician, if specifically requested in writing by the
  parent of the student or by a member of the school at least
  72 hours prior to the meeting;
- an additional parent member of a student with a disability
  residing in the school district or a neighboring school
  district, provided that the additional parent member may
  be the parent of a student who has been declassified within
  a period not to exceed five years or the parent of a student
  who has graduated within a period not to exceed five years,
  if specifically requested in writing by the parent of the
  student, the student or by a member of the committee at
  least 72 hours prior to the meeting.

7-13. What is a Subcommittee on Special Education?

A board of education may appoint subcommittees on special
education according to Commissioner's Regulation 200.3 (c).

A subcommittee does not have as much authority as a full
committee. It may not recommend a full-time special education class for
the first time, agree to a special class in another school, or recommend a
more restrictive placement such as private school, or home or hospital
instruction.

Annual reviews are not as comprehensive as initial meetings or
triennials, and are primarily used to review progress and make minor
changes. As a result, the membership requirements are fewer. The
team includes the chairperson, parent, special education and regular

education teachers of the student, and the student if appropriate. Multiple requirements, including district representative and the individual responsible for interpreting any new evaluation material, are often fulfilled by one person.

If parents believe that a substantially different or more intensive program is required, arrangements should be made for a comprehensive and thorough reevaluation and submit the new information to the CSE committee for review.

7-14. Who can make a referral to the Committee on Special Education?

Commissioner's Regulation 200.4 (a) states:

A student suspected of having a disability shall be referred in writing to the chairperson of the district's Committee on Special Education or to the building administrator of the school which the student attends or is eligible to attend for an individual evaluation and determination of eligibility for special education programs and services. The school district must initiate a referral and promptly request parental consent to evaluate the student to determine if the student needs special education services and programs or if a student has not made adequate progress after an appropriate period of time when provided instruction as described in section 100.2(ii) of this Title. Referrals for an initial evaluation may be made by:

- a student's parent;
- a designee of the school district in which the student resides, or the public school district the student legally attends or is eligible to attend;
- the commissioner or designee of a public agency with responsibility for the education of the student; and/or
- a designee of an education program affiliated with a child care institution with Committee on Special Education responsibility pursuant to section 4002(3) of the Education Law.

A request for referral for an initial evaluation of a student may be made by:

- a professional staff member of the school district in which the student resides, or the public or private school the student legally attends or is eligible to attend;

- a licensed physician;
- a judicial officer;
- a professional staff member of a public agency with responsibility for welfare, health, or education of children; or
- a student who is 18 years of age or older, or an emancipated minor, who is eligible to attend the public schools of the district.

For more information, see Section 200.4 procedures for referral, evaluation, individualized education program (IEP) development, placement, and review at http://www.p12.nysed.gov/specialed/lawsregs/documents/regulations-part-200-oct-2016.pdf.

7-15. What steps must be taken prior to a referral?

A referral to the Committee on Special Education must describe all intervention programs, services, and instructional methodologies that have been provided in the general education setting or explain why they were not attempted. The fact that the referral must include the educational efforts prior to a referral means that these steps must take place and the school should have documentation to indicate the level of effectiveness of the efforts (see Section 200.4 (a)(2)(ii) of Commissioner's Regulations).

> A school district's process to determine if a student responds to scientific, research-based instruction shall include the application of information about the student's response to intervention to make educational decisions about changes in goals, instruction and/or services and the decision to make a referral for special education programs and or services.
> [8NYCRR §100.2(ii) (1) (v)]

> If a student has not made adequate progress in attaining grade-level standards after an appropriate period of time when provided with instruction utilized in a Response to Intervention (RtI) framework, the school district must make a referral and promptly request parental consent to evaluate the student to determine if the student needs special education services and programs. (http://www.p12.nysed.gov/specialed/RTI/guidance/application.htm)

7-16. What is the building administrator's responsibility when a CSE referral is received?

The building administrator, upon receipt of a referral to the Committee on Special Education, should note the date that it was received and forward it immediately to the chairperson of the Committee on Special Education.

The building administrator, upon receipt of a referral or copy of a referral, may request a meeting with the parent or guardian and the student, if appropriate, to determine whether the student would benefit from additional general education support services as an alternative to special education, including the provision of support services, speech and language services, academic intervention services, and any other services designed to address the learning needs of the student and maintain a student's placement in general education with the provision of appropriate educational and support services. (Section 200.4 (a)(9) of Commissioner's Regulations).

If a professional staff member requested the referral, that person shall also attend this meeting. At this meeting the parent and the building administrator may agree in writing that, with the provision of additional general education support services, the referral is unwarranted. If that is the case, the referral would be withdrawn. The building administrator shall provide a copy of the written agreement to the chairperson of the Committee on Special Education, the professional staff person who requested the referral, the parent, and the student, if appropriate. The agreement shall contain a description of the additional general education support services to be provided, instructional strategies to be used, and student-centered data to be collected as well as the proposed duration of such program. A copy of the agreement shall also be placed in the student's cumulative education record.

The meeting shall be conducted within 10 school days of the building administrator's receipt of the referral (see Section 200.4 (a)(9) of Commissioner's Regulations).

7-17. What is the responsibility of the district for students who are parentally placed in a nonpublic school in regard to CSE?

If a student is parentally placed in a nonpublic school and is suspected of having a disability, the district of location is responsible to conduct the CSE meeting to determine a student's eligibility for special education and, if determined eligible for special education, to recommend the special education services the student will receive and document such recommendations on an individualized education services program (IESP). The school district of location is responsible for providing the special education services. However, consistent with the manner in which services are provided to other students in their school district, the school district of location could negotiate in its contract with the receiving school district that such district would also provide special education services to parentally placed students with disabilities.

Under the provisions of section 3602-c, students with disabilities placed by their parents in nonpublic schools are entitled to receive special education services in accordance with an IESP from the public school district in which the nonpublic school is located while they receive general education from the nonpublic school where their parents enrolled them. The district of location is responsible for conducting the evaluation to determine a student's eligibility for special education. The district of location is also the district that must obtain the informed written consent of the parent to conduct the initial evaluation or reevaluation.

The definition of "services" in Section 3602-c (1)(a) of the Education Law is limited to services provided in programs operated during the course of the regular school year. It does not apply to services provided in summer programs. For more information, see Students with Disabilities Parentally Placed in Nonpublic Elementary or Secondary Schools at http://www.p12.nysed.gov/specialed/publications/policy/nonpublic907.htm.

7-18. What are the timelines for a district after the receipt of the referral to the Committee on Special Education?

Within 60 school days of the receipt of consent to evaluate a student not previously identified as having a disability, or within 60 school days of the referral for review of the student with a disability, the district shall arrange for appropriate special programs and services. However, if the recommendation is for placement in an approved in-state or out-of-state private school, the district shall arrange for such programs and services within 30 school days of the recommendation of the committee.

There should be no delay in implementing a student's IEP,

including any case in which the payment source for providing or paying for special education to the student is being determined. The school district shall ensure that each student with a disability has an IEP in effect at the beginning of each school year (see Section 200.4 (e) of Commissioner's Regulations).

The 60-day time frame does not apply if a student enrolls in a school served by the school district after the relevant time frame has begun and prior to a determination by the student's previous school district as to whether the student is a student with a disability. This option applies only if the subsequent school district is making sufficient progress to ensure a prompt completion of the evaluation, and the parent and subsequent school district agree in writing to a specific time when the evaluation will be completed; or if the parent of a student repeatedly fails or refuses to produce the student for the evaluation (see Section 200.4 (b)(7) of Commissioner's Regulations).

7-19. What are the evaluations that the Committee on Special Education may use in determining if a student has a disability?

An individual evaluation to determine if a student has a disability must be at no cost to the parent, and the initial evaluation must include at least:

- a physical examination;
- an individual psychological evaluation, if deemed appropriate by the school psychologist;
- a social history;
- an observation of the student in the student's learning environment (including the general classroom setting) or, in the case of a student of less than school age or out of school, an environment appropriate for a student of that age, in order to document the student's academic performance and behavior in the areas of difficulty; and
- other appropriate assessments or evaluations, including a functional behavioral assessment for a student whose behavior impedes his or her learning or that of others, as necessary to ascertain the physical, mental, behavioral, and emotional factors that contribute to the suspected disabilities (see Section 200.4 (b) of Commissioner's Regulations).

7-20. Depending on the purpose of meeting such as for an initial referral, program review, or annual review, what are the recommended time allotments for a CSE meeting?

There are no federal or state requirements about length of time for CSE meetings. Meetings should be scheduled to allow enough time for the CSE to complete its work. Initial referral meetings generally require a longer time than subsequent meetings in order to allow the CSE to review all evaluations and consider input from the student's teacher and parents in determining if the student has a disability. Committees should plan at least one hour for an initial meeting and a half-hour for annuals and program reviews as a general rule.

7-21. What is the role of the parent member on the Committee on Special Education?

The parent member on the Committee on Special Education is an optional member of the CSE who is the parent of a student with a disability who resides in the district if specifically requested in writing by the parent of the student, the student, or a member of the committee at least 72 hours prior to the meeting. This individual helps parents understand and participate in the meeting by explaining procedures, asking questions, and clarifying information. The district should provide training for parents who serve in this role. Helpful training would include knowledge of the CSE process, knowledge about the district placement policies, and familiarity with local services.

7-22. Can there be a conflict of interest for the parent member of the Committee on Special Education?

The parent member of the CSE only attends per the written request. The parent member of the CSE provides support and information to the parent(s) of the student, and keeps all information confidential so there should be no conflict of interest.

One practice used by districts is to appoint more than one parent member to the CSE. This is helpful when scheduling CSE meetings and would provide an option should there be a perceived conflict of interest or one volunteer parent is not available.

7-23. What procedures must the Committee on Special Education follow when discussing a student?

The CSE must first review evaluation information to determine if the student is eligible for special education services. If the student is determined eligible, an IEP is developed. The following are sections that are discussed and developed for each student's IEP.

- IEP Identifying Information
- Present Levels of Performance and Individual Needs
- Measurable Postsecondary Goals/Transition Needs
- Measurable Annual Goals, Short-Term Objectives and Benchmarks
- Reporting Progress to Parents
- Recommended Special Education Programs and Services
- Coordinated Set of Transition Activities
- Participation in State and District-wide Assessments
- Participation with Students without Disabilities
- Transportation
- Placement Recommendation
- IEP Implementation
  (http://www.p12.nysed.gov/specialed/publications/
  iepguidance/develop.htm)

All discussions of the CSE are confidential, and the committee members must act in compliance with FERPA (see questions 1-37, 3-17, and 6-24 for related information). Commissioner's Regulations state that conversations involving school personnel and teaching methodology, lesson plans, and coordination of services are not to be included in a meeting unless they are referenced in the IEP (see Section 200.4 (d)(2)).

7-24. What is the continuum of services?

The continuum of services refers to the range of educational services that extend from the least restrictive to the most restrictive environment for a student with a disability as described in Section 200.6 of Commissioner's Regulations. The least restrictive point on the continuum begins in the general education classroom with modifications and accommodations that can be made by the classroom teacher or an instructional support team before classification (see questions 7-37 and 7-58). The next level of intervention is a referral to the Committee on Special Education or the 504 Committee to determine if the student has a disability. If the student is found to have a disability, the continuum includes services in the general education setting and extends through the levels of special education services. The range of services considered for the student to be educated to the maximum extent possible with nondisabled students includes:

- transitional support services;
- consultant teacher services: the total number of students assigned to one consultant teacher may not exceed 20; consultant services may be direct or indirect services;
- related services: the number of students receiving services at the same time may not exceed five;
- resource room services: the services must be at least three hours per week and cannot be more than 50 percent of each day; an instructional group may not exceed five; total number of students assigned is not to exceed 20 at the elementary level or 25 at the secondary level;
- integrated co-teaching services: the number of students with disabilities in a co-taught classroom may not exceed 12; staff assigned is to minimally include one special and one general educator;
- special class: a class consisting of students with disabilities who have been grouped together because of similarity of individual needs for purpose of receiving specially designed instruction in a self-contained setting, meaning that such students are receiving their primary instruction separately from their nondisabled peers.
- home/hospital instruction: these services require a minimum of five hours a week at the elementary level and 10 hours a week at the secondary level; and
- residential placement for in-state or out-of-state private schools.

For more information, refer to http://www.p12.nysed.gov/specialed/publications/policy/schoolagecontinuum.html.

7-25. What are consultant teacher services?

Consultant teacher services, according to Section 200.1 (m) of Commissioner's Regulations, are direct and/or indirect services provided to a special education student who attends general education classes, including career and technical education classes, and/or to the student's general education teachers.

- Direct consultant teacher services are specially designed instruction provided by a certified special education teacher, either individually or in a group, to aid a student with a disability in benefiting from the student's general education classes.
- Indirect consultant teacher services are supports provided by a certified special education teacher to the general education teachers of a student with a disability to assist them in modifying instructional methods, and adjusting the learning environment, to meet the student's needs.
- Each student with a disability requiring consultant teacher services shall receive direct and/or indirect services consistent with the student's IEP for a minimum of two hours each week. Each student with a disability requiring a resource room program shall receive not less than three hours of instruction per week in such program except that the Committee on Special Education may recommend that a student with a disability who also needs consultant teacher services in addition to resource room services may receive a combination of such services consistent with the student's IEP for not less than three hours per week.

7-26. What are integrated co-teaching services? Are the students considered to be in a general and/or special education class?

Integrated co-teaching services, as defined in regulation, means the provision of specially designed instruction and academic instruction provided to a group including both students with disabilities and nondisabled students. Integrated co-teaching services are provided in a student's general education class; students are intentionally grouped together on the basis of similarity of need for the purpose of receiving specially designed instruction in a general education class. Recommendation for integrated co-teaching services for a school-age student is documented in an IEP in the special education program under the heading of Recommended Special Education Programs and Services along with the recommended frequency, duration, location, and projected beginning date of the services. The maximum number of students with disabilities receiving integrated co-teaching services in a class shall be determined in accordance with the students' individual needs as recommended on their IEPs, provided that the number of students with disabilities in such classes shall not exceed 12, unless a variance is provided. School personnel assigned to each class shall minimally include a special education teacher and a general education teacher.

7-27 How is "integrated co-teaching" written in the IEP section "Participation with Students without Disabilities"?

A recommendation for integrated co-teaching services would not be documented in the Participation with Students without Disabilities section of the IEP. It would be listed under Recommended Special Education Programs and Services. The Participation with Students without Disabilities section is used to document the extent to which a student's disability precludes his/her participation with students without disabilities. Such documentation would include an explanation of the extent, if any, to which a student will not participate in regular class and/or extracurricular and nonacademic activities, and the extent to which the student will participate in specially designed physical education. Documentation would also include the Committee's recommendation, if any, that a student be exempt from the languages other than English (LOTE) requirement because the student's disability affects his/her ability to learn a language.

7-28. What are push-in and pull-out services?

These terms describe whether services to students with disabilities are located within the classroom or delivered outside the classroom. Push-in services are special education and/or related services that are delivered inside the general education classroom. Push-in services may involve collaboration between the general education and special education teachers. Pull-out services are special education and/or related services that are delivered outside the general education classroom and are typically supplemental instruction. Location of services on the IEP indicates if the services are pull-out or push-in.

7-29. What reports are required specific to special education students?

The student's progress toward IEP goals must be communicated to parents as identified in the student's IEP (see Section 200.4 (d)(2) (iii)(c)). The frequency of reporting must be at least as often as that for parents of nondisabled students. For more information, see http://www.p12.nysed.gov/specialed/publications/iepguidance/progress.htm.

In addition, each student with a disability is assessed yearly to determine annual progress and to identify the student's needs for the following year (see Section 200.4 (f)).

7-30. Does a parent have the right to remove a student from special education services?

Yes. 34 CFR section 300.300(b)(4) states that if the parent of a student with a disability revokes his/her consent in writing for the continued provision of special education and related services to the student, at any time subsequent to the initial provision of special education and related services, the school district:

- may not continue to provide special education and related services to the student, but must provide prior written notice to the parent before ceasing the provision of special education and related services;
- may not use due process procedures (i.e., mediation, resolution meeting, and/or an impartial due process hearing) in order to obtain agreement or a ruling that the services may be provided to the student without parental consent;
- will not be considered to be in violation of the requirement to make a free and appropriate public education (FAPE) available to the student because of the failure to provide the student with further special education and related services; and
- is not required to convene an individualized education program (IEP) meeting or develop an IEP for the student for the further provision of special education and related services.

The definition of consent in 34 CFR section 300.9 explains that if the parent revokes consent in writing for his/her child's receipt of special education and related services after the child is initially provided special education and related services, the school district is not required to amend the student's education records to remove any references to the student's receipt of special education and related services because of the revocation of consent.

7-31. What is inclusion?

Inclusive education means that children with and without disabilities participate and learn together in the same classes. The Individuals with Disabilities Education Act clearly states that all children with disabilities should be educated with nondisabled children their own age and have access to the general education curriculum. Under federal law, the presumption is that students with disabilities will attend the same schools they would have attended if they did not have disabilities and that removal or restriction from their regular schools and classrooms can only occur for reasons related to the student's disability when the student's individualized education program (IEP) cannot be satisfactorily implemented in that setting, even with the use of supplementary aids and services.

The SED defines high-quality inclusive settings as settings in which:

Instruction and configuration of classrooms and activities include both students with and without disabilities;

Students with disabilities are held to high expectations for student achievement;

Special education and general education teachers intentionally plan teaching lessons to promote the participation and progress of students with disabilities in learning and social activities;

Individualized accommodations, supports, and specially designed are provided to students with disabilities to participate and progress in regular education classes and activities; and

Evidence-based services and supports are used to foster the cognitive, communication, physical, behavioral, and social-emotional development of students with disabilities (http://www.regents.nysed.gov/common/regents/files/P12-Inclusion%20.pdf).

7-32. What rights does a parent have to demand that his/her child remain in a general education classroom?

Students with disabilities cannot be removed from general education classroom instruction unless the Committee on Special Education determines that they cannot be educated successfully in the general education environment even with the use of supplemental aids and services (see Section 200.1 (cc) of Commissioner's Regulations). If the parent disagrees with the decision of the CSE, the parent can request mediation or an impartial hearing to resolve the matter.

7-33. What is a language other than English (foreign language) exemption?

When a student's disability adversely affects the ability to learn a language other than English, the Committee on Special Education may exempt the student from the second language requirement. Only the CSE can grant the exemption, and the reason for the exemption must be documented on the student's IEP (see Section 100.2 (d)(1)(iii) of Commissioner's Regulations and also question 7-27).

7-34. What is an impartial hearing?

An impartial hearing is a formal proceeding in which disagreements between a parent and a school district are decided by an impartial hearing officer appointed by the board of education. A parent or a school district may initiate a hearing on issues relating to the identification, evaluation, and educational placement of a student with a disability, or the provision of a free appropriate public education to the child.

An impartial hearing officer must be certified by the Commissioner of Education to conduct impartial hearings. Impartial hearing officers are selected on a rotational basis from a list maintained by the school district. The list includes IHO names and statement of qualifications (see Commissioner's Regulations, Sections 200.5 (i) and 200.5 (j)).

However, before initiating an impartial hearing, parents are encouraged to discuss their concerns with appropriate staff at the school district to make sure that the school district understands the parental point of view. If it is not possible to resolve disagreements informally, mediation is a suggested method to work through differences in a timely way. Special education mediation is a voluntary process for working out disagreements about the recommendations of the CSE or CPSE. All school districts must offer mediation to parents. Discussions that occur during mediation are confidential. The New York State Education Department is responsible for the cost of the mediation process.

See *Special Education in New York State for Children Ages 3-21: A Parent's Guide* (New York State Education Department, May 2002) at http://www.p12.nysed.gov/specialed/publications/policy/parentsguide.pdf.

7-35. How are parents made aware of due process rights?

Parents are made aware of due process rights through the procedural safeguards notice. A school district must use the procedural safeguards notice prescribed by the Commissioner of Education.

The school district must ensure that the procedural safeguards notice is provided in the native language of the parent or other mode of communication used by the parent, unless it is clearly not feasible to do so. If the native language or other mode of communication of the parent is not a written language, the school district shall take steps to ensure that the notice is translated orally or by other means to the parent in his or her native language or other mode of communication; that the parent understands the content of the notice; and that there is written evidence that the requirements of this section have been met.

A copy of such notice must be given to the parents of a student with a disability, at a minimum of one time per year and also:

- upon initial referral or parental request for an evaluation;
- upon the first filing of a due process complaint notice to request mediation or an impartial hearing as described in subdivisions (h) and (j) of this section;
- upon request by a parent;
- upon a decision to impose a suspension or removal that constitutes a disciplinary change in placement pursuant to section 201.2(e) of this Title; and
- upon first receipt of a State complaint pursuant to Section 200.5(l) of this Part.
(Commissioner's Regulations 200.5 (f))

A school district may place a current copy of the procedural safeguards notice on its Internet website if such website exists.

A district must use a copy of the notice as prescribed by the Commissioner. See a copy of the notice at http://www.p12.nysed.gov/specialed/formsnotices/documents/PSGN-RevisedJune2016.pdf.

7-36. What is due process? How does it differ for general education and special education students?

Students have constitutionally protected property and liberty interests, and may not be deprived of property or liberty without notice of the reason why and an opportunity to admit, deny, or explain the conduct. *Goss v. Lopez*, 419 U.S. 565, established the guidelines for due process in student suspension cases as they relate to the due process clause of the Fourteenth Amendment. As a result, any disciplinary procedures must meet minimal standards of fairness and due process (*Appeals of McMahon and Mosely et al.*, 38 Ed Dept Rep 22, Decision No. 13,976).

The Commissioner has held that "minimal due process requires that an individual be afforded an opportunity to appear informally before the person or body authorized to impose discipline and to discuss the factual situation underlying the threatened disciplinary action" (*Appeal of Bussfield*, 34 Ed Dept Rep 383, Decision No. 13,352).

Due process is the same for special education students except for suspensions of 10 or more days in a school year (see questions 7-62 and 7-64).

Special Education in New York State for Children Ages 3-21: A Parent's Guide (New York State Education Department, 2002) has a section on due process rights for parents that is helpful for an administrator to read. See http://www.p12.nysed.gov/specialed/publications/policy/parentsguide.pdf.

7-37. What is the role of the principal in an impartial hearing?

An impartial hearing officer who is certified by the Commissioner of Education conducts the hearing. The principal needs to work closely with the CSE chairperson and the attorney for the school district to provide the records, background information, and witnesses that will be required for the hearing. The principal may be asked to provide testimony at the hearing. See also 7-34.

7-38. What is the principal's role in the creation and implementation of the individualized education plan or 504 plan?

Although the principal is not a mandated member of the CSE, the principal may participate in the meeting to develop an IEP. The principal is responsible for having procedures in place for the dissemination of the IEP (see question 7-39), and arranging for the special education program and services to begin. The principal should expect all involved teachers and service providers to comply with an IEP for a student. See also questions 6-8 and 7-39 as they relate to personnel evaluation and implementation of the IEP. School district personnel and principals should establish a clear understanding of the district's expectations for building administrator responsibilities regarding IEP implementation.

7-39. What are the legal requirements for a principal to disseminate IEPs to all appropriate staff?

Section 200.4 (e)(3) of Commissioner's Regulations states the district's requirements for dissemination of a student's IEP. Section 200.2 (b)(11)(iii) of Commissioner's Regulations states that the CSE chairperson must designate a professional employee of the district who has knowledge of the student's disability and education program to inform the teachers, staff, and service providers about the IEP according to regulations. The principal should clearly designate the person who has that responsibility in the school. The role of the designated person is to ensure that all staff members working with a student with a disability are informed of their responsibilities for the implementation of the student's IEP and are provided with access to the IEP, if they are designated. Section 200.2 (b)(11)(i) provides that, in lieu of providing a paper or electronic copy of the IEP, the student's teachers, related service providers and other service providers shall have access to a copy of a student's IEP electronically; and that if the policy provides that the IEP is to be accessed electronically, the policy must ensure that the individuals responsible for the implementation of the IEP are notified and trained on how to access the IEP electronically.

The special education teacher assigned to the student should meet with each staff member who will work with the student. At this time, the special education teacher can communicate the mutual responsibilities for implementation and explain the confidentiality requirements of the student's IEP.

Supplementary personnel who assist providers with implementation of the IEP must review the IEP and have access to it. Staff members' signatures provide the principal with verification that the requirement to review the IEP has been met. Access can also be verified through most electronic IEP systems, which can provide information regarding who has accessed what students' IEPs and when the principal will review and monitor to ensure staff are reviewing IEPs as necessary.

7-40. What is the responsibility of a teacher who has a student with an IEP or 504 plan?

A teacher's responsibility is to become familiar with the IEP or 504 plan and to implement the plan. Prior to the student's entry in the classroom, a teacher should meet with the student's special education teacher to discuss the student's strengths and weaknesses, go over the IEP or 504 plan, and become familiar with the student's classroom modifications and accommodations. Ongoing communication between the classroom teacher and the special education provider(s) regarding the student's needs and progress is an important factor in student success. The progress of students who are instructed in the general education setting is a shared responsibility. Special educators are excellent sources for effective strategies and techniques. In co-taught classrooms, the special educator and the general educator work hand in hand to support all students.

7-41. Are teachers required to follow the IEP?

Yes, all staff members working with a student with a disability are required to follow the IEP (see Section 200.4 (e)(3) of Commissioner's Regulations).

7-42. What is the liability of the principal and the teacher if the IEP is not followed?

Professionals should follow Commissioner's Regulations for implementing the IEP. The principal should ensure that procedures are in place for implementing the IEP, including documentation to show that requirements have been followed for communication to staff members about the IEP. A good faith effort, clearly documented, by all parties to follow the procedures and implement the IEP should minimize any considerations about liability. See also questions 7-38 and 7-39.

If the principal is aware that the teacher is not following the IEP, the principal should meet with the teacher and formally review the teacher's responsibilities. Failure to implement the IEP can be a serious cause for concern by the parents, who have trusted the school district to adhere to the recommendations of the CSE and provide their child a free appropriate public education (FAPE).

Finally, if the principal or teacher believes that the IEP should be reviewed, a referral is sent to the Committee on Special Education to discuss the current program. This is the appropriate process for focusing on the school's interest in the success of the student, and it ensures that the professional educators are following required procedures.

7-43. What are the requirements for a principal regarding confidentiality of information for special education students?

A principal is responsible for the preservation of the confidentiality of personally identifiable information and records pertaining to students with disabilities. The board of education must establish administrative practices and procedures to ensure the confidentiality of such information and records according to Section 200.2 (b)(6) of Commissioner's Regulations. See Sections 200.5 (e)(1) and 200.5 (e)(2) of Commissioner's Regulations and also questions 1-37, 3-17, 6-24, and 7-23.

All teachers who are responsible for the implementation of a student's IEP should have access (paper or electronic) and should have been informed of their responsibility for implementation, according to Section 200.4(e)(3) of Commissioner's Regulations. See also question 7-39.

Additionally, Section 99.31 of the Family Educational Rights and Privacy Act (FERPA) indicates that prior consent is not required to disclose information if the disclosure is to other school officials, including teachers, who have been determined to have legitimate educational interests in the student. For example, two teachers could communicate via email regarding the IEP; however, it becomes their responsibility as well as the responsibility of the institution to preserve the confidentiality of the student information in accordance with district policy, procedures, and practices, including the sharing and maintenance of electronic information.

7-44. What are the diploma options for students with disabilities?

No IEP diploma can be awarded (see Commissioner's Regulation 100.9 (g)).

Under the new "4+1" pathway assessment option, students must take and pass four required Regents exams or State Education Department-approved alternative assessments (one in each of the following subjects: English, math, science, and social studies) and a comparably rigorous assessment for the fifth required exam to graduate.

The fifth assessment required for graduation may include any one of the following assessments:

- Either an additional Regents assessment, or a [State

Education] Department-approved alternative, in a different course in social studies or English (humanities pathway); or

- One additional Regents Examination in a different course in mathematics or science or a [State Education] Department-approved alternative (STEM pathway); or

- A pathway assessment approved by the Commissioner in accordance with Section 100.2 (f)(2) of the Commissioner's Regulations (which could include a Biliteracy [LOTE] Pathway); or

- A CTE pathway assessment, approved by the Commissioner in accordance with section 100.2(mm), following successful completion of a CTE program approved pursuant to Section 100.5(d)(6) of the Commissioner's Regulations (CTE pathway); or

- An arts pathway assessment approved by the Commissioner in accordance with Section 100.2(mm)(arts pathway). (http://www.p12.nysed.gov/ciai/multiple-pathways/docs/multiple-pathways-4+1-field-memo.pdf)

See options for Regents and local diplomas at http://www.p12.nysed.gov/ciai/gradreq/Documents/CurrentDiplomaCredentialSummary.pdf.

More information related to graduation requirements for students with disabilities is at http://www.p12.nysed.gov/specialed/gradrequirements/home.html.

7-45. What is the Career Development Occupational Studies (CDOS) graduation pathway option?

The NYS CDOS Commencement Credential is a credential recognized by the NYS Board of Regents that certifies a student has the standards-based knowledge and skills necessary for entry-level employment. The requirements to earn the credential were developed consistent with research and the guiding principles established by the Board of Regents. The requirements are rigorous in that the student must receive instruction that supports the achievement of the CDOS learning standards through access to career and technical education (CTE) course work and have opportunities to engage in school-supervised, work-based learning experiences in school and/or in the community. In addition, students must participate in career planning and preparation and have an employability profile demonstrating readiness for entry-level employment.

Under the "4+CDOS" pathway option, a student may graduate with a high school diploma if the student meets the graduation course and credit requirements established in Section 100.5 of the Regulations of the Commissioner of Education; passes four required Regents exams or State Education Department-approved alternative assessments (one in each of the following subjects: English, mathematics, science, and social studies); and meets the requirements to earn the New York State (NYS) CDOS Commencement Credential.

There are two options available for students to earn the CDOS credential:

- Complete a career plan; demonstrate attainment of the commencement-level career development and occupational studies (CDOS) learning standards in the areas of career exploration and development, integrated learning, and universal foundation skills; satisfactorily complete the equivalent of 2 units of study (216 hours) in career and technical education course work and work-based learning (including at least 54 hours of work-based learning); and have at least 1 completed employability profile; OR
- Students meet criteria for a national work readiness credential. For more information, see http://www.p12. nysed.gov/ciai/multiple-pathways/memos/cdos-graduation-pathway-option.html.pdf.

In addition, the Commissioner's Regulations were revised to expand the opportunity to all students to earn the NYS CDOS Commencement Credential. Previously, only students with disabilities could exit school with the NYS CDOS commencement credential as a supplement to a regular high school diploma. Students who are unable to earn a regular diploma may graduate with the NYS CDOS commencement credential as their only exiting credential.

"Students exiting high school with only the CDOS Commencement Credential would be considered a 'high school completer.' These students would not be included in either the 'dropout' or 'graduation' counts (http://www.p12.nysed.gov/specialed/gradrequirements/CDOS-QA-eligibilty.htm)."

There is no cap on the percentage or number of students with disabilities who can receive the CDOS Commencement Credential where the credential is not a supplement to a regular diploma. However, when a district awards the credential to more than 20 percent of the students with disabilities in the cohort, where such credential is not a supplement to a regular high school diploma, NYSED may, at its discretion, determine that the reason for the numbers of students receiving the CDOS Commencement Credential as their sole credential is that the district failed to provide students with disabilities with appropriate access to participate and progress in the general education curriculum necessary to earn a regular high school diploma. The amount of funds to be redirected would be determined on a case-by-case basis, depending on the findings of the state (See http://www.p12.nysed.gov/specialed/gradrequirements/CDOS-QA-instruction.htm).

7-46. What is the New York State Skills and Achievement Commencement Credential?

Students with severe disabilities who are assessed using the NYS Alternate Assessment (NYSAA) are eligible for the Skills and Achievement Commencement Credential. See also 7-44. All students with severe disabilities who attend school for not less than 12 years, excluding kindergarten, exit with this credential, which must be accompanied by documentation of the student's skills and strengths and levels of independence in academic, career development, and foundation skills needed for post-school living, learning, and working. The credential would not be considered a regular high school diploma in accordance with state standards or for federal accountability purposes. See Commissioner's Regulation 100.5(b)(7)(iii).

7-47. What is the Superintendent Determination of Graduation with a Local Diploma?

This option is available to students with disabilities with a current individualized education program (IEP) only. It does not apply to students with Section 504 accommodation plans or students who have been declassified from special education. The superintendent may only consider an eligible student for a local diploma through the superintendent's determination option upon written request from the student's parent(s) or guardian(s). Such requests must be submitted in writing to the student's school principal or CSE chairperson. A written request received by the school principal, CSE chairperson, or any other employee of the school, must be forwarded to the superintendent immediately upon its receipt. Upon receipt of the request the superintendent, in consultation with the school principal, must review, document, and provide a written certification that there is evidence that the student has otherwise met the standard for graduation with a local high school diploma. The superintendent must sign the form prescribed by the Commissioner certifying that the student did or did not met the requirements for a local diploma and notify the student, parent, and NYSED. For more information see Information Related to Graduation Requirements for Students with Disabilities. See http://www.p12.nysed.gov/specialed/publications/2017-memos/superintendent-determination-of-graduation-with-a-local-diploma-updated.htm.

7-48. What are the mandatory testing accommodations for a classified student?

There are no mandatory testing accommodations for a student with a disability (Section 200.4 (d)(2)(vi) of Commissioner's Regulations). The Committee on Special Education must consider each student's individual needs and provide a statement of them in the IEP. These accommodations must be used consistently throughout the student's educational program for district-wide and New York State assessments, according to SED policies. Information about accommodations for state assessments is available at the Office of State Assessment (http://www.p12.nysed.gov/assessment/accommodations/) and in the publication, Testing Accommodations for Students with Disabilities, which can be found at http://www.p12.nysed.gov/specialed/publications/documents/testingaccommodations-guide-february-2018.pdf.

Many students with disabilities require testing accommodations in order to equitably participate in state and local assessments. Such accommodations provide students with the ability to demonstrate their skills and knowledge without being limited or unfairly restricted due to the effects of a disability. The Committee on Special Education (CSE) or Section 504 Multidisciplinary Team (504 MDT) must identify and document in the student's IEP or 504 plan respectively the individual testing accommodations recommended for the student's participation in state and local assessments. Testing accommodations must be recommended, as appropriate, for all students with disabilities, including students with disabilities taking the New York State Alternate Assessment (NYSAA).

In order to make appropriate recommendations for testing accommodations, CSE/504 MDT members, including parents and students, should have knowledge about:

- the purpose of tests administered, what they measure and how the results are used;
- the need and rationale for testing accommodations, where appropriate; and
- the types of testing accommodations available and how they are administered.

Students with disabilities whose individualized education programs (IEPs) or Section 504 accommodations plans (504 plans) document that tests be read aloud (by way of human reader or technology) must be provided this testing accommodation in accordance with the specifications in the IEP/504 plan. In previous years, only directions were to be read to students on the grades 3-8 ELA assessments; no other portion of the test was to be read aloud regardless of the circumstances. Additionally, this testing accommodation will be provided to students upon declassification with documentation indicating the accommodation will continue. For more information, see the field memo from SED entitled Changes in Allowable Testing Accommodations on the Grades 3-8 New York State English Language Arts Assessments. See http://www.p12.nysed.gov/specialed/publications/documents/changes-in-allowable-testing-accommodations-grade-3-8-ela.pdf.

7-49. What is the New York State Alternate Assessment (NYSAA)?

State and federal laws require that all students at specified grade levels participate in state assessments. Students with severe disabilities as defined in Section 100.1 of Commissioner's Regulations are also required to participate. The Committee on Special Education determines if a student with a disability is eligible to take the New York State Alternate Assessment.

English Language Arts, Math, and Science

NYSAA is the state testing program that measures attainment of the state's learning standards in the areas of English language arts

(ELA), mathematics, and science for all students with severe disabilities in grades 3-8 and high school. Students must be assessed once a year beginning in the school year they become 9 years old through the school year they become 14 (grade equivalents 3-8). The secondary level NYSAA is administered during the school year they become 17-18 years of age (high school).

Beginning with the 2017-2018 school year, NYSAA-eligible students will be assessed using the Dynamic Learning Maps (DLM) computer- based assessments for English language arts, math, and science. DLM is a computer-delivered adaptive assessment measuring a student's achievement of the ELA and mathematics Common Core Learning Standards at a reduced level of depth, breadth, and complexity. This assessment provides the opportunity to customize the assessment to the individual abilities and needs of the student. It is designed to measure a wide range of proficiencies of students, is quicker and easier to administer and score, and provides useful information to teachers to inform future instruction for the student.

Social Studies

Beginning with the 2017-2018 school year, the NYSAA program will no longer include a social studies component. "The goal of the elimination of the social studies is to require the least amount of testing necessary to provide accurate information about student achievement and to minimize the instructional time to administer the NYSAA program to students." (See http://www.p12.nysed.gov/assessment/nysaa/2016-17/nysaasocialstudies-science.pdf).

The CSE decision of eligibility for NYSAA is based on the following criteria:

1. The student must have a severe cognitive disability, significant deficits in communication/language, or significant deficits in adaptive behavior; **and**

2. The student must require a highly specialized educational program that facilitates the acquisition, application, and transfer of skills across natural environments (home, school, community, and/or workplace); **and**

3. The student must require educational support systems, such as assistive technology, personal care services, health medical services, or behavioral intervention.

There currently is an application that districts must submit if they are to exceed the one percent cap for accountability for students taking the New York State alternate assessment. For more information, see http://www.p12.nysed.gov/irs/nysaa/.

7-50. What is assistive technology for students with disabilities and how is need determined?

"Assistive technology device" means any item, piece of equipment, or product system, whether acquired commercially off the shelf, modified, or customized, that is used to increase, maintain, or improve the functional capabilities of a student with a disability. Assistive technology devices can range from "low technology" items like pencil grips, markers, or paper stabilizers to "high technology" items such as voice synthesizers, Braille readers, or voice-activated computers.

"Assistive technology service" means any service that directly assists a student with a disability in the selection, acquisition, or use of an assistive technology device.

Effective consideration of assistive technology for a student with a disability should include a team discussion that is focused on the student's individual needs. Assistive technology must be documented appropriately in a student's individualized education program (IEP). The IEP must describe any assistive technology devices and/or services needed for the student to benefit from education, including whether the use of a school-purchased assistive technology device is required in the student's home or in other settings. Documenting the specific assistive technology support is required by the student in the IEP, even if the device is generally available in the student's classroom.

When a student needs an assistive technology device or service, the Committee needs to consider what instruction the student might require to use the assistive technology device as well as any supports and services the student and/or the student's teachers may need related to the use of the device.

For more information, see http://www.p12.nysed.gov/specialed/publications/2016-memos/assistive-technology-webinar.html.

7-51. What is the Blueprint for Improved Results for Students with Disabilities?

The Blueprint for Improved Results for Students with Disabilities clarifies expectations for administrators, policy makers, and practitioners to improve instruction and outcomes and prepare students with disabilities for postsecondary readiness and success. Schools should use these principles to review their programs and practices that identify areas where improvements are needed. See http://www.p12.nysed.gov/specialed/publications/2015-memos/blueprint-for-improved-results-for-students-with-disabilities.html.

7-52. What is adapted (or adaptive) physical education?

Adapted (or adaptive) physical education is a specially designed program of developmental activities, sports, and games that are matched to the capabilities of students with disabilities who are not able to successfully or safely participate in a general physical education program (Section 200.1 (b) of Commissioner's Regulations). Adapted physical education is required when a student with disabilities cannot meaningfully participate in a regular physical education program with appropriate modifications. The following link provides some additional information: http://www.p12.nysed.gov/ciai/pe/documents/qa.pdf.

Physical education is required for all students in grades K-12, as specified in Section 135.4 of the Regulations of the Commissioner of Education. If a student with a disability is not participating in a regular physical education program, the IEP developed for that student must indicate the extent to which the student will participate in specially designed instruction in physical education, including adapted physical education.

A student must have adaptive or adapted physical education on either the IEP or in a Section 504 accommodation plan for the student.

7-53. Does the IEP need to be followed if a student with disabilities is involved in extracurricular activities, athletics, or programs that are before or after school?

Yes. School districts must have a written policy that provides for the adoption and implementation of procedures to ensure that students with disabilities can participate in extracurricular activities according to Section 200.2 (b) (1) of the Commissioner's Regulations.

Districts are not mandated to ensure that students with disabilities are able to participate in all of the extracurricular activities that the parent or student chooses. The administrator should review the following decision by a state review officer that addresses meaningful access to activities for students and the use of federal funds from IDEA for transportation to extracurricular activities not on a student's IEP

(Application of the Board of Education of the East Syracuse-Minoa CSD, Appeal No. 92-11 [1992] at https://www.sro.nysed.gov/decision/1992/92-011).

Section 3208-a of the Education Law states that school districts can make an individual determination regarding the physical ability of a student with a disability to participate in an extracurricular athletic activity. If the district denies the student the right to participate in the athletic activity, the student may appeal the district's decision in a court proceeding. If the court mandates participation, then the school district is absolved from any liability for an injury sustained by the student that can be attributed to the physical impairment that caused the district to deny the student's right to participate. The school district is not responsible for the cost of any special or preventative equipment or measures that are required to protect the student, unless stated in the IEP.

7-54. If a student is assigned an aide, is the aide required to be present during extracurricular activities and athletics?

It is required if this accommodation is stated in the IEP. The provision of the aide would be necessary if the student could not participate in the activity without the assistance of the aide.

7-55. Under what circumstances is a special education student entitled to an aide or teaching assistant?

A teacher aide performs noninstructional duties such as supervising students, physical care tasks, behavior and management needs, and the technical preparation of programs. The assignment of a one-to-one aide is one of the most intensive services that the CSE can consider. Primary purposes of a one-to-one aide are to provide management support and physical assistance for students with severe disabilities. One-to-one aides should be considered only after less intensive measures have been utilized without success. Determination of the need for a one-to-one aide is made on an individual basis and reviewed annually.

A teaching assistant works under the general supervision of a teacher and provides instructional services such as working with students on special instructional projects and assisting with instructional work. The teaching assistant is generally assigned to a student who, because of the student's disability, requires significant modifications in the grade-level curriculum.

Section 200.4 (d)(3) of the Regulations of the Commissioner of Education, relating to the assignment of an individual aide to a student with a disability, has a requirement that both Committees on Special Education (CSE) and Committees on Preschool Special Education (CPSE) make certain considerations prior to determining that a student needs a one-to-one aide.

These considerations must include:

- the management needs of the student who would require a significant degree of individualized attention and intervention;
- the skills and goals the student would need to achieve that will reduce or eliminate the need for the one-to-one aide;
- the specific support that the one-to-one aide would provide for the student (e.g., assistance with personal hygiene or behaviors that impede learning);
- other supports, accommodations, and/or services that could support the student to meet these needs (e.g., behavioral intervention plan, environmental accommodations or modifications, instructional materials in alternate formats, assistive technology devices, peer-to-peer supports);
- the extent (e.g., portions of the school day) or the circumstances in which (e.g., for transitions from class to class) the student would need the assistance of a one-to-one aide;
- staff ratios in the setting where the student will attend school;
- the extent to which assignment of a one-to-one aide might enable the student to be educated with nondisabled students and, to the maximum extent appropriate, in the least restrictive environment;
- any potential harmful effect on the student or on the quality of services that he or she needs that might result from the assignment of a one-to-one aide; and
- the training and support provided to the one-to-one aide to help him or her understand the student's disability-related needs, learn effective strategies for addressing the student's needs, and acquire the necessary skills to support the implementation of the student's individualized education program (IEP).

Section 200.4 (d)(3) also clarifies that the assignment of shared one-to-one aides at the discretion of the school to meet the individualized needs of students whose IEPs include the recommendation for one-to-one aides is not prohibited or limited. The duties of a teacher aide or a teaching assistant providing individualized support to a student with a disability must be consistent with the duties prescribed in 8 NYCRR 80-5.6.

See http://www.p12.nysed.gov/specialed/publications/policy/schoolagecontinuum-revNov13.htm for more guidance in determining the appropriate roles for teaching assistants and teacher aides. The administrator should also check local bargaining agreements for any specific duties.

7-56. What are the different responsibilities for a teaching assistant and a teacher aide assigned to a student?

The teacher aide's primary responsibility is to assist teachers with nonteaching duties (Education Law 3009 (2) (a), Commissioner's Regulations Section 80-5.6). Such duties may include:

- Assisting with physical care tasks and health-related activities as appropriate;
- Assisting students with behavioral/management needs;
- Assisting with the correction of papers and tests;
- Assisting with the preparation of materials for classroom activities; and
- Assisting with proctoring and other tasks related to the administration of exams.

The teaching assistant's primary responsibility is providing instructional services to students. This instruction must take place under the general supervision of a certified teacher (Education Law 3009 (2b), Commissioner's Regulations Section 80-5.6). Teaching assistants, unlike teacher aides, are considered members of a teaching staff and, if serving in a tenure track position, must be given a probationary appointment in the special subject tenure area of the teaching assistant (Part 30.8 of the Commissioner's Regulations). See, for example, *Appeal of Banschback and Dowler*, 38 Ed Dept Rep, Decision No. 14,078. The duties of a teaching assistant may include:

- Working with individual or small groups of students;

- Assisting the teacher in the preparation of lesson plans;
- Presenting segments of the lesson plan as directed by the teacher; and
- Communicating with parents.

See also question 7-55.

7-57. What is the difference between the Committee on Special Education (CSE) and the building-level response to intervention (RtI) or child study team?

The Committee on Special Education is composed of mandated members and must follow state regulations and guidelines in the evaluation and identification of students with disabilities (see question 7-14).

The response to intervention team or child study team is a building- level team. It is composed of representatives from general and special education as well as individuals from other disciplines that include individuals with classroom and student support experience. The guidelines for RtI team members and procedures are developed at the local level. Instructional support and/or child study teams function in the general education environment. The RtI team is part of a prereferral system that uses a collaborative approach and instructional strategies to avoid inappropriate referrals and classification of students in special education programs. For more information on prereferral strategies, it may also be helpful to review response to intervention guidelines at http://www.nysrti.org.

7-58. What are the primary roles of a response to intervention team or child study team and the Committee on Special Education?

A primary function of the RtI or child study team is to assist students who are experiencing academic and behavioral difficulties that affect learning in the general education program. The team also provides support for the teacher to meet the needs of the student. The team reviews data about the student and considers approaches that the teacher could try in the classroom to assist the student. The team may design a support plan that provides instructional strategies and general education services targeted to assist the student in the regular education classroom. This plan is shared with the student's parents.

The Committee on Special Education's role is the evaluation and identification of, and program planning for, students with disabilities. See question 7-11 for additional information.

In making a determination of eligibility for special education, the CSE must determine that underachievement of the student is not due to lack of appropriate instruction in reading (including the five essential components), mathematics, or limited English proficiency. The data from RtI can help document that the reason for a student's poor performance or underachievement is not due to lack of appropriate instruction or limited English proficiency. Along with other individual evaluation information, RtI data can yield important descriptive information about how children learn and why they may be having difficulties.

7-59. Can a nonclassified student participate in any special education programs?

No. Special education means specially designed individualized or group instruction or special services and programs designed to meet the unique needs of students with disabilities (Section 200.1 (ww) of Commissioner's Regulations).

7-60. How does a district develop a consistent discipline policy given the discipline requirements associated with special education students?

The development of a code of conduct is the process for a district to construct a consistent discipline policy for all students. The code of conduct must include provisions to ensure that disciplinary procedures comply with state and federal laws for students with disabilities (see question 1-1.). Students with disabilities should be expected to adhere to the same discipline rules and policies that nondisabled students do. A difference is that there must be an awareness of a student's disability and the number and the type of suspensions that are given to the student. For more information, see http://www.p12.nysed.gov/specialed/lawsregs/part201.htm; and http://www.p12.nysed.gov/specialed/publications/topicalbriefs/FBA.htm.

7-61. How should a principal address a situation that involves a classified student whose behavior interferes with the learning of others?

The principal should contact the Committee on Special Education and request a program review. The purpose of this review is to examine the student's special education program and services to determine if there are other types of support that might more effectively contribute to student success. The principal or CSE should request a functional behavior assessment to determine the cause of the behavior, followed by the development and implementation of a behavior intervention plan. Section 200.4 (d)(3)(i) of Commissioner's Regulations notes that the CSE shall, when a student's behavior impedes the learning of others, "consider strategies, including positive behavioral interventions, and supports, and other strategies to address that behavior."

7-62. What is the proper procedure to follow for a classified student who is suspended?

The principal should follow the same procedures that are followed for the suspension of a general education student. If the suspension is for a short term, less than five days, with no previous suspensions that would total more than 10 days, the Commissioner has held that there is no obligation to determine if there is a nexus between the student's alleged misbehavior and the disability (*Appeal of a Student with a Disability*, 34 Ed Dept Rep 634, Decision No. 13,435). See also question 7-64.

If a hearing to suspend for more than five days is held according to Education Law 3214 (3)(g), several steps must be taken. There must be guilt established for the charges. The manifest determination team must determine if the charges are related to the disability (see question 7-63). The manifestation team shall review all relevant information in the student's file including the student's IEP, any teacher observations, and any relevant information provided by the parents to determine if:

1. the conduct in question was caused by or had a direct and substantial relationship to the student's disability; or
2. the conduct in question was the direct result of the school district's failure to implement the IEP

In some districts, it is a helpful practice to send copies of all disciplinary referrals involving identified students to the CSE chairperson. Depending on district practices, the CSE chair or another designated teacher or administrator should track the days of suspension, monitor behavior problems, and convene a meeting if a change of placement, program, or further evaluation is contemplated. A functional behavioral assessment should be considered in order to determine whether a behavior intervention plan is indicated.

The suspension of a student with a disability may pose some unusual questions and it may be helpful to consult with the school's attorney.

7-63. What is a manifestation determination meeting?

A manifestation determination is a decision of whether there is a relationship between the student's disability and the behavior subject to the disciplinary action.

Commissioner's Regulation 201.4 indicates that the manifestation team must be comprised of a representative of the school district knowledgeable about the student and the interpretation of information about child behavior, the parent or person in parental relation to the student and relevant members of the CSE as determined by the parent or person in parental relation and the school district. The CSE no longer has the responsibility to make a manifestation determination. The regulation requires that "the Manifestation Team shall review all relevant information in the student's file, including the student's IEP, any teacher observations, and any relevant information provided by the parents to determine if:

1. the conduct in question was caused by or had a direct and substantial relationship to the student's disability; or
2. the conduct in question was the direct result of the school district's failure to implement the IEP."

Such a determination must be made immediately, if possible, but no later than 10 school days after an authorized school authority makes a decision to either place the student in an interim alternative educational setting (IAES) or impose a suspension that constitutes a disciplinary change of placement. Districts must provide parents written notification prior to any manifestation determination meeting.

If the manifestation team decides that the behavior is related to the student's disability, no further disciplinary action can take place. If the behavior involved weapons, illegal drugs or controlled substances, or serious bodily injury, the student can be placed in the interim alternative education setting. See also question 7-62 and Education Law 3214 (3)(g).

If the behavior is a manifestation of the student's disability, the CSE must conduct a functional behavioral assessment (FBA) and implement a behavioral intervention plan (BIP) for the student, or review and modify, as necessary, an already existing BIP. In addition, no further disciplinary action may be taken, except placement in an IAES, unless the district and parent agree to a change of placement as part of the modification of the student's IEP. For more information, see http://www.p12.nysed.gov/specialed/publications/topicalbriefs/FBA.htm.

7-64. Can a student with a disability be suspended for more than 10 days?

A suspension of more than 10 days for a student with a disability constitutes a disciplinary change in placement, which requires a parental consent. A disciplinary change in placement occurs when:

- The suspension is more than 10 consecutive school days; or
- For a period of 10 consecutive days or less if the student is subjected to a series of suspensions or removals that constitute a pattern because they cumulate to more than 10 school days in a school year. The school district determines on a case-by-case basis whether a pattern of removals constitutes a change of placement. This determination is subject to review through due process and judicial proceedings (Section 201.2 (e) of Commissioner's Regulations).

Please see questions 1-6 and 7-62 which relate to suspension procedures for more than five days.

7-65. Under what circumstances may a student with a disability be placed in an interim alternative education setting (IAES)?

A student with a disability can be placed in an interim alternative education setting, without parental consent, for no longer than 45 days for each instance where:

- The student possesses a weapon at a school function or at school;
- The student uses, possesses, sells, or solicits the sale of a controlled substance or illegal drugs at school or a school function;

- The district can demonstrate through substantial evidence, that by keeping the student in the current setting, there is the likelihood of injury to the student or others; or
- The student has inflicted serious bodily injury as defined by Section 201.l (m) of Commissioner's Regulations.

This placement must be done through procedures according to Education Law 3214 and Commissioner's Regulation 201.7 (e) or by an impartial hearing officer in an expedited due process hearing according to Commissioner's Regulation 201.8.

A student with a disability can be placed for the above reasons even if the behavior is a manifestation of the student's disability (Commissioner's Regulations 201.9 (c)(3), 201.8(f)).

The CSE determines the IAES for a student with a disability.

7-66. How does a principal meet IEP mandates for students who are assigned in-school suspension or alternative education settings?

A student with a disability who is placed in an alternative education setting must continue to receive the same level of services that the student received prior to the placement, including all of the program services and modifications outlined in the student's IEP. This level of service must enable the student to progress in the general education curriculum and toward meeting the IEP goals. The student must also be provided with services and modifications to address the behavior to ensure that it does not recur (Sections 201.10 (d) (e), and 201.2 (k) of Commissioner's Regulations).

The district may contract with the local BOCES to provide the services, or contract with certified individuals if the interim alternative setting does not provide the needed services.

7-67. What are the regulations regarding extracurricular activities for special education students attending school at an alternate site?

The student with a disability is entitled to participate in all extracurricular activities offered by the home district. A district must have a written policy and procedures to ensure that students with disabilities have the opportunity, to the maximum extent appropriate to the needs of the student, to participate in all district programs. The programs include extracurricular activities that are available to all other students in the district's public schools (Section 200.2 (b)(1) of the Commissioner's Regulations). If this is an interim alternative education setting due to a disciplinary change in placement, the student could be subject to the conditions set forth as a result of the disciplinary hearing. See question 7-53 for more information and reference to a state review officer's decision that involved a student with disabilities in a BOCES-sponsored program who participated on another school district's athletic team.

7-68. If a student with a disability misbehaves on the bus, what steps may be taken?

The student should be dealt with the same manner as a nondisabled student. See also questions 7-69 and 8-2.

It is a helpful practice to send copies of all disciplinary referrals involving identified students to the CSE chair so that the student's behavior can be monitored and, if needed, a functional behavior assessment can be requested. Based on the functional behavioral assessment, a behavior intervention plan may be implemented to address the behavior.

7-69. How should an administrator handle a bus suspension?

A bus suspension for a student with a disability should be handled in the same manner that it would be handled for a nondisabled student. A suspension from transportation does not require full formal hearing as with a school suspension, but it does require minimal due process that provides an opportunity to meet informally to discuss the facts relating to the misbehavior (*Appeal of Hale*, 30 EDUC. Dept Rep 26, Decision No. 12,381). See question 7-36 for more information about minimal due process. An administrator should reference district policy regarding the procedures and responsibilities of the school or district designee in the case of a suspension from transportation.

The Commissioner has also ruled that a board of education may use a suspension of less than 10 days to remove a child with a disability from school transportation if the child poses a threat to student safety. He noted that there is not a significant change in educational placement for an isolated short-term suspension to initiate the due process protections of IDEA (*Appeal of Cellini*, 30 Ed Dept Rep 473).

Section 8
Transportation

8-1. Where can a principal get a good general overview of bus safety?

These sites on the New York State Education webpage offer resources for administrators:

http://www.p12.nysed.gov/schoolbus/district.html
http://www.p12.nysed.gov/schoolbus/

8-2. What rights does the principal have to suspend students from riding school transportation? What are the considerations if the student is receiving special education services?

The Commissioner of Education has ruled that a board of education must be free to regulate the conduct of students being transported by the district in order to ensure the safety of other students. Commissioner's decision No. 14,837 adds, "A pupil's entitlement to transportation is not the equivalent of the right to attend upon instruction and petitioner's son is not entitled to the protection of Education Law 3214(3) with regard to the suspension of transportation services."

Suspension of bus privileges may take place without a formal hearing. However, a student or the student's parent must be given the opportunity to discuss the facts of the matter relative to the potential disciplinary action with the individual who is authorized to administer discipline in the case. A meeting of student, principal, and parent should take place prior to this suspension. The administrator should consider all disciplinary options with transportation and their impact on the student's ability to get to school.

Procedures for suspending students from school transportation should be clearly defined in a district's code of conduct. The length of the suspension should be determined by each district's code of conduct. Education Law 2801 (1) includes school bus in the definition of school property, and a district is required to enforce its code of conduct on buses, even if the district contracts with an outside vendor for its transportation (*Appeal of M.H.*, 43 Ed Dept Rep 210, Decision No. 14,973).

In Commissioner's decision No. 14,952, a student was suspended for several months. The Commissioner did not grant interim relief or overturn the suspension after the fact. The Commissioner has also ruled that a board of education may use a suspension of less than 10 days to remove a child with a handicapping condition from school transportation if the child poses a threat to student safety (*Appeal of Cellini*, 30 Ed Dept Rep 473). See also questions 7-68 and 7-69.

A bus driver may not unilaterally suspend a student's transportation privileges by ordering him to leave the bus. See *Appeal of Pennett*, 40 Ed Dept Rep 227, Decision No. 14,466.

8-3.   What are the rules regarding the use of cameras on school buses? May schools use video recordings from a camera when disciplining students?

Video cameras are allowed on school buses even to the extent that they are eligible for transportation aid.

The Commissioner has allowed the use of videotapes from security cameras in a student disciplinary matter. See *Appeal of Sole*, 34 Ed Dept Rep 270, Decision No. 13,305.

The U.S. Department of Education has published the following information about the use of security cameras and video from the cameras.

> Schools are increasingly using security cameras as a tool to monitor and improve student safety. Images of students captured on security videotapes that are maintained by the school's law enforcement unit are not considered education records under FERPA. Accordingly, these videotapes may be shared with parents of students whose images are on the video and with outside law enforcement authorities, as appropriate. Schools that do not have a designated law enforcement unit might consider designating an employee to serve as the "law enforcement unit" in order to maintain the security camera and determine the appropriate circumstances in which the school would disclose recorded images. (Balancing Student Privacy and School Safety: A Guide to the Family Educational Act for Elementary and Secondary Schools. See https://www2.ed.gov/policy/gen/guid/fpco/brochures/elsec.html.

8-4.   What steps should the school principal take if there are student complaints against a school bus driver?

If the complaint is a result of discipline imposed or threatened by the bus driver, the student and his or her parent or guardian should have the opportunity to meet informally with the principal to discuss the facts underlying the disciplinary action. The principal needs to meet with the driver to hear the driver's version of the event. It may be helpful to have all parties present for the meeting.

If the complaints relate to other matters, the principals need to follow an established process that allows all parties to give their concerns or points of view in order to identify any problems and to determine a fair course of action. See also question 3-30 that addresses a district's chain of command or process for addressing complaints and question 6-28 that relates to complaints against teachers.

8-5.   How does a school principal deal with bus drivers who are not employees of the district?

All concerns or complaints should be directed to the supervisor of that person. Details of any matter involving the driver of a contract company should be provided to the employer. The company and the supervisor of the drivers are responsible for any action. However, the relationship between the district and the company is based upon the contract between the district and the company. The principal should not hesitate to contact the administrator who is responsible for that contract in order to clarify understandings and agreements about the way in which the company will address concerns.

8-6.   If a school district has student transportation contracted with an outside company, what right does an administrator have to handle student discipline issues that occur on a bus?

The administrator should be aware that the bus company works for the district. The policies and procedures of the district should be part of the contract and, therefore, would continue to be followed. The principal's role should not change in a contracted arrangement for transportation. The principal continues to have authority and responsibility for behavior of students on a bus.

Education Law 2801 (1) includes school bus in the definition of school property, and a district is required to enforce its code of conduct on buses, even if the district contracts with an outside vendor for its transportation (*Appeal of M.H.*, 43 Ed Dept Rep 210, Decision No. 14,973). See question 8-2.

8-7. What guidelines must be followed when a district uses a charter bus?

A district should have established procedures to follow when a charter bus will be used. The New York State Education Department notes:

> Several recent charter bus accidents involving fatalities have caused many school districts to examine their procedures for charter bus trips. If requested by the school district, the Division of Program Regulation of the Department of Motor Vehicles will provide factual information regarding the compliance and qualification status of the motor carrier and the bus driver. The information will assist districts in its choice of a motor carrier and help avoid:
>
> • booking charter trips with bus companies that were not in compliance with Article 19A of the Vehicle and Traffic Law or were currently under suspension;
> • assigning a driver with a less than clean driving record to the district's charter trip; and
> • assigning a nonqualified or unreported driver to the district's charter trip (http://www.p12.nysed.gov schoolbus/TransDirector/htm/FieldTripGuidelines.htm)

There are also suggested guidelines for districts at this website that districts should use in screening motor carriers and drivers to be used for charter trips.

The district should have a person designated to ensure compliance with district guidelines. It is helpful to work with the district insurance carrier, the business office, and the transportation department to develop a set of procedures to follow in selecting a charter company.

8-8. What role does a principal have when a charter bus is being used for a student group?

The principal should ensure that a request to use a charter bus is considered according to the guidelines of the district for use of charter buses (see question 8-7 for more information). In addition, the principal should make sure that there is funding to support the request. There should be administrative procedures in place that require the advisor to review safety precautions, including evacuation procedures and behavior expectations for students who are riding the bus.

8-9. Must students wear seat belts on school buses? Can a school administrator require a student to wear a seat belt?

Students are not mandated to wear seat belts that are on school buses. However, students must receive instruction on the use of seat belts at least three times each year according to Section 156.3 (g) of Commissioner's Regulations, including effective fastening and release of the safety belts, proper placement on students, times when the seat belts should be fastened and released, and appropriate placement of the safety belts when they are not in use. The state requires that all buses manufactured after July 1, 1987 be equipped with seat belts. It is a local school district decision to mandate seat belt use by students (see http://safeny.ny.gov/sbus-ndx.htm#faq).

The National Highway Traffic Safety Administration (NHTSA) notes that school buses are one of the safest forms of transportation on roads. They also report from several studies that lap belts did not improve occupant protection from severe frontal impacts and that seat belts "would not have prevented most of the serious injuries and fatalities from occurring in school bus crashes." The NHTSA notes that today's large school buses are designed with a system of "compartmentalization" that uses a "protective envelope consisting of strong, closely-spaced seats that have energy-absorbing seat backs."

The NHTSA adds that lap and/or lap/shoulder belts are necessary for occupant protection in small school buses of 10,000 pounds or less. (See https://www.nhtsa.gov/road-safety/school-buses.)

One of the difficulties in mandating seat belt usage is the capacity of school districts to provide the resources to enforce such a mandate.

8-10. What right do parents have for their children to have their transportation pickup point in front of their residence?

Bus pickup locations are the responsibility of a board of education. A board of education may use its discretion when designating pickup and drop-off points as long as the board uses reasonable care in exercising such discretion. A board of education must balance considerations of pupil safety and convenience, routing efficiency, and costs when determining pickup points. The Commissioner has ruled that the law does not require a district to transport a student directly to and from home. See *Appeal of Y. W.*, 50 Ed Dept Rep, Decision No. 16,092 and Education Law 3635 (1) (d).

Commissioner's decision No. 16,092 also notes that,

> dead-end streets, loop streets, and cul-de-sacs should be avoided by buses whenever possible. Forcing a bus driver to back up or maneuver the bus through a restricted space significantly increases the chance of an accident and exposes children in the area to greater risk. Bus routes for typical students should not go into dead ends in cul-de-sacs unless there is no alternative (New York State Education Department, Pupil Transportation Safety Guidance Manual Section IV.B.17).

SED summarizes:

- School districts are not required to provide door-to-door transportation for any child, not even those in kindergarten. Pickup points can be established, for efficiency and economy reasons.
- Some school districts have adopted local policies of picking up all young children at their homes, but the law does not require such service.
- The distance between a pupil's home and a pickup point cannot exceed the distance used by the district for determining eligibility for transportation.
- The Commissioner of Education has held that parents are legally responsible for the safety of the children while walking between home and a pickup point (http://www.p12.nysed gov/schoolbus/Parents/htm/Child_Safety_Zones.htm).

There should be a district policy to review and to process requests for transportation and consideration of pickup points that are based on medical needs and doctor's notes.

8-11. Do parents have a right to request that their children be transported to and from a location that is different than their residence?

A parent may request that children be transported to and from a location other than the student's residence. Some schools, especially with elementary ages, permit students to be transported to and from another residence for child care and supervision with the written permission of parents according to a regular schedule of days approved in advance by the district. Note that the Commissioner has ruled that "there is no statutory or regulatory requirement that a board of education must transport a student to different places on different days of the week" (*Appeal of Van der Jaqt*, 33 Ed Dept Rep 517, Decision No. 13,134).

Education Law 3635 (1) (e) holds that districts may decide to offer transportation between schools and child care locations within the district for students in grades K-8. The district may limit the transportation to child care locations within the student's attendance zone with the exception of child care locations licensed according to Social Services Law 390. In that exception, transportation must be provided district-wide. The law does not give discretion to transport students outside of the district to child care locations, and the policy of transporting must be applied equitably to all students. The Commissioner has also stated that financial or emotional hardship is not a legal basis for providing transportation to a child care location outside a district. In that case, the Commissioner noted that a CSE must consider a referral for the purposes of deciding classification and any related services, including transportation. See the *Appeal of a Student Suspected of Having a Disability*, 38 Ed Dept Rep 507, Decision No. 14,081.

The administrator should ensure that there is a district policy for transporting students that includes provisions to address such requests.

8-12. When custody is split between two parents, do they have a right that their child be transported to each parent on different days?

The Commissioner has ruled that "there is no statutory or regulatory requirement that a board of education must transport a student to different places on different days of the week" (*Appeal of Van der Jaqt*, 33 Ed Dept Rep 517, Decision No. 13,134). In that case, there was no documentation of a court order that described the custodial arrangement for the student. Therefore, if an administrator receives a court order that divides residency between parents in a district, the administrator should review the court order with the school's attorney before making a final decision. See also question 8-11 since a district may have a policy to provide transportation for students to different locations for child care purposes.

8-13. Is it necessary for someone to be at home when a bus drops
off a K-8 student at the end of a school day? How can you confirm someone is at home?

The law does not require that a district provide transportation directly to and from home for a student. The Commissioner's decision No. 16,827 has clarified:

Boards of education have discretion to require students to walk to pickup points from which transportation will be provided (*Appeal of Girsdansky*, 46 Ed Dept Rep 105, Decision No. 15,455). Where a student's home is on a dangerous road or at a remote location, the parents are not free from the obligation to assist the student in reaching the pickup point. It is the responsibility of the parent, not the district, to see that the child safely reaches the pickup point (*Appeal of Brizell*, 48 Ed Dept Rep 128, Decision No. 15,814; *Appeal of Weinschenk*, 47 id. 518, Decision No. 15,770).

The New York State Education Department also states:
Parents are responsible for assisting children to get to the [bus] stop and home from the stop. The district is not required to provide a protected corridor from students' homes to the bus stop any more than it is to provide that service for students who do not ride buses and must travel from home to school. (http:/ www.p12.nysed.gov/schoolbus/Parents/htm/school_bus_stops html)

It is always better to plan carefully in advance for an unexpected situation or emergency. Districts can communicate to parents their responsibility for making sure that someone is present when a student arrives home. Districts can also communicate the importance of having a family emergency safety plan for a student to follow in the event no one is home, or that the student arrives home early. It is important for an administrator to ensure that there is adequate and current contact information for each student at school, including more than one contact person in the event that a parent is not available.

See also questions 8-10 and 8-11.

8-14. What is the role of the principal in the state-required

emergency bus drills?

School bus drills must be conducted at least three times during the school year. The first must occur during the first seven days of school, the second between November 1 and December 31, and the third between March 1 and April 30. A record of this practice should be kept at each school building. The superintendent has to certify that instruction and drills have taken place for all pupils. See Commissioner's Regulation 156.3.

8-15. What rights does a district have to determine the transportation needs for sports trips, field trips, religious education, and late bus runs?

Transportation for interscholastic athletics, field trips and late bus runs may be part of a budget approved by community residents or part of a contingent budget adopted by a board of education. The administrator should work with the business office to ensure both a clear understanding of what expenses are covered by the budget and transportation guidelines that are equitable for students (see Education Law 2023 (1)). A decision by the appellate division of the New York State Supreme Court upheld the right of school districts to determine whether to fund these activities in a contingent budget and to what extent they should be funded (*Matter of Polmanteer v. Bobo*, et al.). See also *Appeal of Polmanteer* et al., 44 Ed Dept Rep 221, Decision No. 15,155.

The Commissioner has ruled that a school district is not authorized to provide transportation to and from religious education classes (*Appeal of Santicola*, 37 Ed Dept Rep 79, Decision No. 13,809). In that case, the Commissioner ruled that the district was correct in ending transportation from the site of religious education back to the elementary school at the end of religious class according to Education Law 3635 (1) (e). However, the Commissioner pointed out that he did not rule on transportation to the site for religious education since there had not been a challenge to it through the appeal process. An administrator should review the questions about any such circumstance with the attorney for the district.

8-16. In case of a bus accident, what procedures should be followed regarding the status of students involved? What is the role of the principal?

The training for bus drivers in New York State includes the procedures to follow in the event of an accident. The administrator should review these procedures with the transportation director before the school year begins. Guidelines for responses to school bus accidents should be included in the building-level emergency response plan (see question 2-9) and the school crisis plan.

The role of the principal is one of support if such an accident occurs. If an accident occurs, the transportation director should notify the principal, who will work with the transportation director following the established district response guidelines, in order to determine the extent of the accident, to contact parents, to visit the scene if necessary, and to ensure that medical treatment is provided each student. The bus driver and the transportation director are responsible for the necessary paperwork that must be submitted to the New York State Department of Transportation.

8-17. What are the definitions of a "school bus monitor" and a "school bus attendant"?

Section 156.3 of Commissioner's Regulations defines "school bus monitor" as one who assists "children to safely embark and disembark from a school bus … [assists] the school bus driver with maintaining proper student behavior on such school bus."

Section 156.3 of Commissioner's Regulations defines "school bus attendant" as one who serves "pupils with a disabling condition on a school bus."

8-18. What responsibilities does the LEA (local education agency) have associated with the McKinney-Vento Homeless Assistance Act and student transportation? What role can the principal play in the process?

The McKinney-Vento Homeless Assistance Act requires that states ensure homeless students access to free, appropriate public education equal to their nonhomeless peers. States are required to provide programming and remove barriers to such access, including enrollment and attendance; transportation is an essential part of this process.

> The National Center for Homeless Education explains: According to the McKinney-Vento Act, LEAs are required to implement a coordinated system to ensure that

transportation services are provided promptly, including those that allow the parent/guardian of each homeless student (or, in the case of an unaccompanied homeless youth, the youth) to exercise the student's option to attend either the school of origin or the local attendance area school [42 U.S.C. § 11432(e) (3) (E) (i) (III)]. Further, because the Act requires homeless students to be provided immediate school enrollment, defined as attending classes and participating fully in school activities [42 U.S.C. §11434a(1)], LEAs must arrange transportation without delay. (https://nche.ed.gov/downloads/briefs/transportation.pdf)

A field memo from the New York State Education Department dated September 7, 2016 outlined updates for district superintendents to the McKinney-Vento Act based on the Every Student Succeeds Act (see http://www.p12.nysed.gov/accountability/homeless/docs/MVESSAFMEMO.pdf). Regarding transportation, the memo stated that students experiencing homelessness are still able to select a district of attendance and that transportation and enrollment must begin immediately. The memo explained that students in a homeless situation are still entitled to remain enrolled in their school of origin for the duration of their homelessness and through the remainder of the school year when the student finds permanent housing. Families who submit an appeal regarding district of attendance are eligible for continued school services and transportation for the length of the appeal, until a formal decision is rendered.

The National Center for Homeless Education recommends using discretion and sensitivity when providing transportation for students in transition. The building principal may help to minimize stigma and support homeless students through small, yet important, steps such as reaching out to families by phone or in person, even though a district's liaison may already have made contact. The principal can work with the transportation department to ensure a smooth pickup and drop-off at the building for the student each day and can help to make sure the student arrives in time for and receives free breakfast each morning. The principal should also advocate for the student if the student wants to become involved in activities outside the school day, such as extracurricular activities or additional academic support, ensuring that the student has access to transportation to participate in these programs.

Table of Acronyms

ADA	Americans with Disabilities Act
AED	Automated External Defibrillator
AIS	Academic Intervention Services
AMO	Annual Measurable Objective
APPR	Annual Professional Performance Review
AYP	Adequate Yearly Progress
BETAC	Bilingual/ESL Technical Assistance Center
BIP	Behavioral Intervention Plan
BOCES	Board of Cooperative Educational Services
CCSO	Council of Chief State School Officers
CPSE	Committee on Preschool Special Education
CSE	Committee on Special Education
CST	Child Study Team
CTE	Career and Technical Education
DCEP	District Comprehensive Educational Plan
DINI	District in Need of Improvement
EAI	Epinephrine Auto-Injector
ECP	Exposure Control Plan
ELL	English Language Learner
EMSC	SED's Office of Elementary, Middle, Secondary and Continuing Education
ENL	English as a New Language
ERSS	Educationally Related Support Services
ESEA	Elementary and Secondary Education Act
ESL	English as a Second Language
ESOL	English for Speakers of Other Languages
ESSA	Every Student Succeeds Act
FAPE	Free Appropriate Public Education
FBE	Functional Behavior Assessment
FERPA	Family Educational Rights and Privacy Act
FOIL	Freedom of Information Law
FTE	Full-time Equivalent

HIPAA	Health Insurance Portability and Accountability Act
HOUSSE	High Objective Uniform State Standard of Evaluation
HQ	Highly Qualified
HQT	Highly Qualified Teacher
ICS	Incident Command System
IDEA	Individuals with Disabilities Education Act
IEP	Individualized Education Program
IHIP	Individualized Home Instruction Plan
IHO	Impartial Hearing Officer
IST	Instructional Support Team
JMT	Joint Management Team
LEA	Local Education Agency
LEP	Limited English Proficiency
LRE	Least Restrictive Environment
NCAA	National Collegiate Athletic Association
NCLB	No Child Left Behind Act of 2001
NOAA	National Oceanic and Atmospheric Administration
NSF	National Science Foundation
NYSAA	New York State Alternate Assessment
NYSAAA	New York State Athletic Administrators Association
NYSAIS	New York State Association of Independent Schools
NYSCHSAA	New York State Catholic High Schools Athletic Association
NYSED	New York State Education Department
NYSFSSAA	New York State Federation of Secondary School Athletic Associations
NYSPHSAA	New York State Public High School Athletic Association
OCE	SED's Office of Cultural Education
OHE	SED's Office of Higher Education

OMS	SED's Office of Operations and Management Services
OP	SED's Office of the Professions
OSHA	Occupational Safety and Health Administration
PDP	Professional Development Plan
PESHA	Public Employee Safety and Health Administration
RIC	Regional Information Center
RtI	Response to Intervention
SAVE	Safe Schools Against Violence in Education Act
SEA	State Educational Agency
SED	State Education Department
SES	Supplemental Educational Services
SETRC	Special Education Training and Resource Center
SINI	Schools in Need of Improvement
SRO	School Resource Officer
STAC	System to Track and Account for Children
STAR	New York State School Tax Relief Program
SUNY	State University of New York
SURR	Schools Under Registration Review
SWD	Students with Disabilities
USDOE	U.S. Department of Education
VADIR	Uniform Violent and Disruptive Incident Reporting
VESID	SED's Office of Vocational and Educational Services for Individuals with Disabilities
VLS	Virtual Learning System

Appendix

The following websites provide information that relates to the questions and answers in this book.

New York State Education Department Websites

Academic Intervention Services (AIS) Guidelines:
http://www.p12.nysed.gov/part100/pages/AISQAweb.pdf

Annual Professional Performance Review:
https://www.engageny.org/resource/appr-3012-d

Assessment Information:
https://www.engageny.org/common-core-curriculum-assessments

Attendance Laws and Regulations:
http://www.p12.nysed.gov/sss/lawsregs/

Attendance of Students and Conference Days, Length of School Days, Extraordinary Conditions and Exams:
https://stateaid.nysed.gov/attendance/attendance_memo.htm

Certification (Teachers):
http://www.highered.nysed.gov/tcert/

Chemical Storage Guidelines:
http://www.emsc.nysed.gov/ciai/mst/pub/chemstorguid.html

Common Core Learning Standards:
http://www.p12.nysed.gov/ciai/common_core_standards/

Confidentiality Guidelines for Social Work:
http://www.op.nysed.gov/prof/sw/swconfidential.htm

Education for Homeless Children:
http://www.p12.nysed.gov/accountability/homeless/

EngageNY:
http://engageny.org/

Epi-pens in Schools:
http://www.op.nysed.gov/prof/nurse/nurse-epipen.htm

ESSA:
http://www.p12.nysed.gov/accountability/essa.html

FERPA:
http://www.oms.nysed.gov/medicaid/resources/hippa_ferpa/home.html

Fingerprinting (Who Must Be Fingerprinted):
http://www.highered.nysed.gov/tsei/ospra/

HIPAA in the School Setting:
http://www.oms.nysed.gov/medicaid/resources/hippa_ferpa/home.html

Homepage:
http://www.nysed.gov/

IDEA:
http://www.p12.nysed.gov/specialed/idea/

Learning Standards:
http://www.p12.nysed.gov/ciai/standards.html

Medication Administration in Schools:
https://www.schoolhealthny.com/cms/lib/NY01832015/Centricity/
Domain/85/MedicationManagement-DEC2017.pdf

Medication Administration to Students During School-sponsored Events by Parent/Guardian Designee:
http://www.p12.nysed.gov/sss/schoolhealth/schoolhealthservices/
fieldtrips.pdf

Medication Storage in Schools:
http://www.p12.nysed.gov/sss/schoolhealth/schoolhealthservices/
MedicationAdministration.pdf

Military Recruiters and Access to Student Information:
http://www2.ed.gov/policy/gen/guid/fpco/hottopics/ht-10-09-02a.html

Office of Counsel (for Commissioner's Decisions).
http://www.counsel.nysed.gov/

Office of Facilities Planning: Health, Safety and Emergencies:
http://www.emsc.nysed.gov/facplan/HealthSafety.htm

Office of P-12 Education:
http://www.p12.nysed.gov/

Part 100 Regulations:
http://www.p12.nysed.gov/part100/

Part 100 – Hot Topics:
http://www.p12.nysed.gov/part100/pages/topics.html

Part 200 and 201 Regulations – Special Education in NYS:
http://www.p12.nysed.gov/specialed/lawsregs/part200.htm

Residency Guidance:
http://www.p12.nysed.gov/sss/pps/residency/

Response to Intervention Guidance:
http://www.p12.nysed.gov/specialed/RTI/guidance/cover.htm

School Leadership Certification:
http://www.highered.nysed.gov/tcert/certificate/typesofcerts.html

Teacher Mentoring Questions and Answers:
http://www.highered.nysed.gov/tcert/faqmentoring.html

Testing Drinking Water in Schools:
http://www.p12.nysed.gov/facplan/
LeadTestinginSchoolDrinkingWater.html

Professional Organizations

American Academy of Allergy, Asthma and Immunology:
http://www.aaaai.org/conditions-and-treatments

American Association of School Administrators:
http://www.aasa.org/

Association of Supervision and Curriculum Development:
http://www.ascd.org/

Education Commission of the States (ECS):
http://www.ecs.org/

Learning First Alliance:
http://www.learningfirst.org

National Association of Secondary School Principals:
https://www.nassp.org

National Association of Student Councils:
https://www.nasc.us

National Association of Elementary School Principals:
http://www.naesp.org/

National Association of School Resource Officers:
http://www.nasro.org

National Federation of State High School Associations:
http://nfhs.org/

National Pediculosis Association (for head lice):
http://www.headlice.org/

New York State Association of Independent Schools Athletic Association:
http://nysphsaa.org/About-NYSPHSAA/General-Information/
Membership-Affiliates

New York State Athletic Administrators Association:
http://nysaaa.org/

New York State Federation of Secondary School Athletic Associations:
http://nysphsaa.org/About-NYSPHSAA/General-Information/
Membership-Affiliates

New York State Public High School Athletic Association:
http://nysphsaa.org/

New York State United Teachers:
http://www.nysut.org/

Phi Delta Kappa International:
http://www.pdkintl.org/

Public Schools Athletic League
http://www.psal.org/

School Administrators Association of New York State (SAANYS):
http://www.saanys.org

Federal and State Agencies

Americans with Disabilities Act (ADA) Homepage:
http://www.usdoj.gov/crt/ada/adahom1.htm

Centers for Disease Control and Prevention:
http://www.cdc.gov/

Department of Agriculture (School Meals):
https://www.fns.usda.gov/school-meals/child-nutrition-programs

EPA Tools for Schools: Indoor Air Quality Action Kit:
http://www.epa.gov/iaq/schools/actionkit.html

National Weather Service's Guide to Developing a Severe Weather Emergency Plan for Schools:
https://www.weather.gov/media/grr/brochures/swep.pdf

New York State Department of Health:
http://www.health.ny.gov

New York State Division of Criminal Justice Services (sex offender registry information):
http://www.criminaljustice.ny.gov/nsor/

New York State Field Trip Attendance System:
https://www.troopers.ny.gov/Schools_and_Communities/Field_Trip/System_Description//

Section 504 of the Rehabilitation Act of 1973 (FAQ):
http://www.ed.gov/about/offices/list/ocr/504faq.html

Index

Please note that chapter and question numbers follow each subject.

• T •